Michael Codella retired from the Police Department in 2003 as a Detective Sergeant and is now a professional fight trainer and Brazilian Jiu Jitsu instructor.

Bruce Bennett's writing has appeared in the *Wall Street Journal* and the *New York Sun*; he has also performed and recorded music with the A-Bones, Yo La Tengo and Andre Williams. A former twenty-year resident of the Lower East Side, these days he lives and works in Brooklyn.

Alphaville

New York, 1988:
Welcome to Heroin City

MICHAEL CODELLA and **BRUCE BENNETT**

PAN BOOKS

First published 2010 by St Martin's Press, New York

First published in Great Britain 2011 by Sidgwick & Jackson
This edition published 2011 by Pan Books
an imprint of Pan Macmillan, a division of Macmillan Publishers Limited
Pan Macmillan, 20 New Wharf Road, London N1 9RR
Basingstoke and Oxford
Associated companies throughout the world
www.panmacmillan.com

ISBN 978-0-330-53363-8

9 8 7 6 5 4 3 2 1

A CIP catalogue record for this book is available from
the British Library.

Printed in the UK by CPI Mackays, Chatham ME5 8TD

Maps by ML Design

**To Rita, Marco, Bianca, and Santino,
for their love and inspiration**

Courage can't see around corners but goes around them anyway.

—Mignon McLaughlin

It is a man's own mind, not his enemy or foe, that lures him to evil ways.

—Buddha

Note to the Reader

Alphaville is a work of nonfiction. While some court transcripts and affidavits have been used to prepare the manuscript, the characters and events described in *Alphaville* are based on the recollections of the authors. Various names, nicknames, times, dates, and identifying personal characteristics have been changed, and some characters created from composites of several people.

Acknowledgments

If we managed to list the names of everyone to whom we owed thanks for helping us make *Alphaville* a reality, this book would have to be two volumes. Abridged, unabridged, excerpted, or otherwise, our friend, agent, and secret weapon Shawn Coyne's name must top the list. It was Shawn's instinct and enthusiasm that put us together under the nurturing umbrella of Genre Management. His eagerness and imagination brought our book to life, and his insight guided our work. Many thanks to editor Pete Wolverton, along with Liz Byrne and Anne Bensson and their team at Thomas Dunne Books. Like all the best creative professionals, Pete dealt in possibilities, not criticisms, and his contributions were indispensable. Thanks also to Mark Korman for schooling both a twenty-year NYPD veteran and a former Lower East Side bike messenger on some finer points of law outside our combined experience. Kirby Kim and Richie Kern at William Morris Endeavor have earned our gratitude and then some.

Looking back, Mike would like to express his appreciation to all those he worked with in law enforcement, particularly his former partner, who made every tour an adventure and not just an existence. Looking forward, Mike thanks Marco, Bianca, and Santino, his three beautiful children, who enrich his heart and his life every day. Most important, he thanks his lovely wife, Rita, who has taught him the true meaning of love and compassion. Mike would also like to thank his parents, Mimi and Mike Codella, for a lifetime of loving direction, and his sister, Linda, for her endless generosity. The blessing of his mother-in-law, Tillie Muniz, and father-in-law Tony Muniz's kindness has been and remains essential. Mike's lifelong friend Nick Cappadora proved once again that he's in for the long haul by reading and rereading early pages and drafts. Thanks and more are due to everyone at the Codella Academy, especially Mark Conroy and Gerry Fajardo, who kept the team in fighting shape during book-mandated absences. Respect and gratitude to Renzo Gracie for the opportunity to pass along his family's art. Thanks also to Chad Millman, without whom this book might never have been written.

Additionally, Bruce wishes to acknowledge his gratitude to Anna Thorngate, whose generosity, patience, acute intelligence, and wit made the rough stretches faster and smoother. Thanks also to his parents, Elizabeth and Robert Bennett. Much of *Alphaville* was researched and edited alongside Miriam Linna, Billy Miller, Mark Natale, Lars Espensen, and, occasionally, Ira Kaplan—bandmates and treasured friends of more than two decades. Their companionship lent much to a parallel creative enterprise partially conducted in minivans, airplanes, and hotel rooms in Spain, France, Canada, New Orleans, Japan, and Hoboken. More than anything, Bruce wishes to thank his old friends who generously (and anonymously) shared their war stories and recollections from the Lower East Side days, and those who, though gone, contributed in memory and spirit as much as those still close by—in the long run, possibly more.

From A to D

Battling the late eighties' Avenue D heroin trade as a cop on the Lower East Side of Manhattan fulfilled a need for barely controlled, boiling-over excitement that had gnawed at me for as long as I could remember. Alphabet City grabbed me by the throat and wouldn't let go, and that was just fine. The neighborhood was a darkly primal and seductive forty-square-block stretch of city built on roots going back generations and a history that justified the shape it was in when I got there. Those roots—the lines of cause and effect, coincidence, fact, and rumor—crisscrossed, intersected, and doubled back through the streets, floors, and stairwells I worked, the lives of the people I helped and I hurt, and the faces, places, and events that brought me there.

My story's the same as everyone's—it points back at a past I know and a past I'm still piecing together. What's maybe different about me is that I knew my whole life that I was the son of a cop and only found out later that I was also the grandson of a former wiseguy. I grew up in a neighborhood shared equally by cops and gangsters, and went to work on a police force where keeping your job and successfully enforcing the law were often opposites. Once I got to Alphaville, a daily fight with a gang of smack dealers nicknamed "the Forty Thieves" and a guy named Davey Blue Eyes who put them and kept them in business earned me the nickname "Rambo," plenty of attention from NYPD Internal Affairs, and a price on my head set by Davey and the bad guys I took down.

When I was young, wild, and wearing a badge and a gun in my Alphaville days, I didn't spend a lot of time marveling at how I managed to keep breathing. There wasn't any time, or any point, in doing a lot of reflection. Once I'd been off the job for a decade or so, I started to think differently. Out of the line of fire, it's only natural to pat yourself down for bullet holes, look back, and take stock of the close calls, the good choices, and the dumb luck that put me where I am now—alive and with family and friends so close and so real that those crazy years in the rearview mirror can almost seem like fiction.

Taking a journey from Canarsie to Coney Island to the Lower East Side brought me to a full boil. I needed the heat, I needed that action, and I needed to use it to square those two sides within me—the past I knew and the past I didn't, the cop side and the crook side that, in a way, we all share and show in the things we choose to do and choose not to do. Not many people have the chance to find out what they're really capable of at the same time as they accept who they are and where they came from. I did, and I had the time of my life doing it.

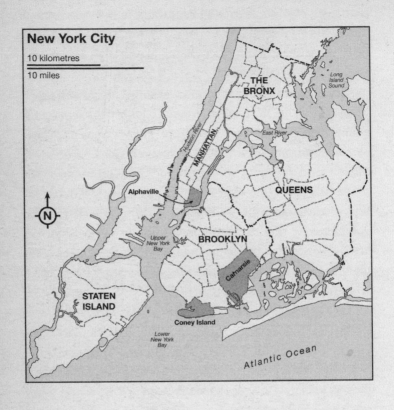

New York City

10 kilometres

10 miles

THE BRONX

Long Island Sound

Hudson River

MANHATTAN

East River

Alphaville

QUEENS

Upper New York Bay

BROOKLYN

Carnarsie

Coney Island

Lower New York Bay

N

STATEN ISLAND

Atlantic Ocean

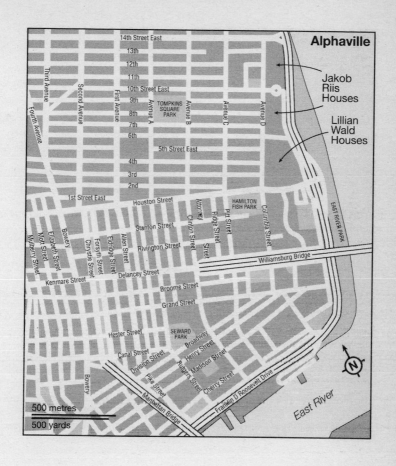

Alphaville

Jakob Riis Houses

Lillian Wald Houses

14th Street East
13th
12th
11th
10th Street East
9th
8th
7th
6th
5th Street East
4th
3rd
2nd
1st Street East

Third Avenue
Fourth Avenue
Second Avenue
First Avenue
Avenue A
Avenue B
Avenue C
Avenue D

TOMPKINS SQUARE PARK

Houston Street
Attorney Street
HAMILTON FISH PARK
Columbia Street
EAST RIVER PARK
Stanton Street
Clinton Street
Ridge Street
Pitt Street
Rivington Street

Bowery
Eldridge Street
Allen Street
Elizabeth Street
Mott Street
Mulberry Street
Forsyth Street
Chrystie Street

Kenmare Street
Delancey Street

Williamsburg Bridge

Broome Street

Grand Street

Hester Street
SEWARD PARK
Canal Street
Broadway
Henry Street
Division Street
Rutgers Street
Madison Street
Cherry Street
Bowery
Pike Street
Manhattan Bridge
Franklin D Roosevelt Drive

N

East River

500 metres

500 yards

A

Avenue D

Early summer, 1988. Sticky black bubbles on a new piece of macadam silently pop and drool oil as my partner Gio and I cruise up the avenue in R(adio) M(otor) P(atrol) 9864 for the umpteenth time today. We're housing cops in our first year assigned to Operation 8, a plainclothes task force combating the drug trade in PSA 4. Our beat is a stretch of public housing that Justice Department statisticians and local junkies both agree is the retail heroin capital of the world. The Feds used your tax dollars to buy the car, fill the tank, and pay our overtime while we sit in it. RMP 9864 has power everything, FM stereo, climate control, the works. But we drive with the windows down and the radio off—taking in as much of the sights, sounds, smells, and faces as our senses can handle.

Most people glaze over when they look at a block's worth of inner city hothouse humanity. New York's civilian population contains eight million experts at averting their eyes in order to avoid trouble. But with a badge, a gun, and a license to butt in, a New York plainclothes cop never thinks twice about looking the people they pass right in the eye. We're connoisseurs of the flash of recognition that precedes those civilian darted looks away.

We size up everybody—the steerers calling brands, the dealers making hand-to-hands, and the junkies crawling in feeling bad, hoping to walk out feeling nothing. We audition every face, every swinging arm, every sweating neck, every open eye that we pass. Who is waiting on someone? Who looks like they're hiding something? Who's new? Who's missing? Who can we toss for dope and a collar or hit up for some information?

There's a sun up there somewhere beyond the rooftops but the sky looks like spoiled milk and the gummy yellow haze won't betray a bright spot. I'm Brooklyn born and raised, we both are, and like the rest of the natives, I've learned that Mother Nature in New York can be as weird as any other local old broad talking to her shopping bags in a darkened movie theater or trying to convince her social worker that the people beaming gamma rays into her head are real. Heat lightning cackles above the Brooklyn skyline and her message is clear: "You may have it paved over, but it's still a swamp." Other places in the world, the summer months ebb and flow, the temperature rising up with the sun and going back down again after dusk. Here it's like somebody turns the broiler on in June and finally remembers to shut it off again in September.

The heat and the wet air smear sounds, smells, shapes, and colors. An anonymous clavero goes to town on a salsa track sputtering from a passing car stereo. For a moment the beat accompanies a steerer hawking bags of "Mr. T, Mr. T" for a corner smack dealer. His chant turns to "Five-O, Five-O. Yo, Rambo on the block," as he catches sight of our car and my face. The salsa track briefly jams with the crackle on our dash police radio, then a snatch of distorted thudding dance music from somewhere else and a shrieking seagull come inland from the harbor to trash pick the Dumpsters behind the projects. The mix of sweat and cologne my partner and I generate are no match for the sour garbage stink, garlic, cigarette smoke, sweet-scented disinfectant Hispanic supers use in their building hallways, and rotten-egg East River tidal funk wafting in the windows with the sounds.

Neighborhood girls calmly strut down the sidewalk so naturally flushed, sweat-shined, and breathless from the heat that it looks like they just got done fucking. But I'm not thinking about them. I'm not really thinking about anything. There's a trancelike slow rhythm to a day tour in weather like this. You save your focus. Likely as not you're going to need it for something later. The only thing going on in my head besides auto piloting the RMP and wordlessly registering and cataloging the world through the windshield, is a back-burner notion I can't shake about a big-time dealer I've only recently heard about called Davey. Since learning the name Davey Blue Eyes a few weeks ago, I'm like a kid with a new swear word. But much as I love to shock the mopes I try it out on, it's just too fucking hot to pull up on a dealing crew, peel myself off the seat, and collect more barely hidden surprised expressions by dropping Davey Blue Eyes's nickname with the sellers and users on the D.

Nearing Fourteenth Street I swing out to the right a little, cut left, and do a tight U-turn. It's too hot for the tires to even bother squealing. That same hydrant trickles water mid-block on Sixth Street, but a different junkie drinks from it than the last time we passed. A Third and D dealer crew heavy I tossed less than a week ago makes a show of not recognizing us and curses in Spanish at the strung-out guy at the hydrant. The skell doesn't react. He's chemically unable to.

It's ninety-two degrees and 98 percent humidity, according

to Pete Franklin on the Fan before I turned it off. This guy must not have heard—he's shaking and scratching in a thick wool sweater so oily and frayed it could make a sheep move upwind. Junkies this far gone create their own shitty climate. The hot days are always the worst on them. The smack this guy shoots burns through his body faster in summer than it does in winter. Out in the street he'll boot up, bark out vomit, and feel the high fade fast, leaving him jumpy and starved for more. The weather and his habit speed up the score-shoot-repeat cycle of his life like the conveyor belt on I Love Lucy.

Up ahead, then alongside, then looking back in the rearview, two muscular Hispanic dudes walk together. One has a Puerto Rican Bart Simpson T-shirt on. Maybe they're headed for a bodega for a cold soda or a little seven-ounce can of Bud. I think I know one of them from the Third Street dealing crew. Not a player nor a customer—maybe a neighbor of one of the main dealers who answer to Davey Blue Eyes, by all accounts the heaviest guy on the D.

As I turn onto Fifth Street a white guy walks down the street with an aluminum baseball bat, silver with black tape on the handle. My mouth goes dry. Hold the phone. Time to focus.

"Drive back around," my partner says.

Instead of looping around the block I do another U-ey, relaxing my hands as the steering wheel spins back into position and we head back up Avenue D.

"Ted Williams . . . ," I murmur.

"Yeah," Gio says. A half block later we see that the first pitch is already thrown. Just off the avenue on Sixth Street the guy with the Puerto Rican Bart shirt convulses on the sidewalk. His head bends sharply away from his neck and his scalp gushes blood into the gutter. The silver bat flashes over the white guy's head, he exhales hard and brings it down on the other Hispanic guy's face with everything he's got. Blood lazily sprays into the muggy air like he's beheaded the dude with a Samurai sword.

White Guy hits again, fast, then again, faster—like chopping down a tree. Either his fourth or fifth swing catches Hispanic Guy number two sharp across the temple. The guy's eye pops out as if he had an eject button on the side of his head. The eye's not just out, it's torn completely loose. I've never seen anything like it. I bounce the RMP up onto the curb as the eye rolls to a stop in the street. All I can think of is the time a kid lost a fingertip in shop class in Canarsie and the teacher kept yelling "save the piece" before getting sick on the floor.

"Police, get down! Get down!" Gio yells. We're out with guns drawn in a heartbeat maybe ten yards from White Guy with the bat.

"Drop the bat, get on the ground!" Gio's got no cover.

"Do it!" I add coming around the car alongside him. "On the ground now. Right now!"

White Guy stops hitting but doesn't start following instructions. Fuck. I hate this part. Once you pull your gun the game is rarely automatically over. It's not rock, paper, scissors. Gun beats bat? If you train a barrel on a bad guy and he says "Fuck you!" what then? Shoot, threaten, reason, beg, what? We're moving closer to him carefully but fast. I don't want to pull the trigger.

"Get down!" Gio says again. Even if he won't drop the bat, if we get the guy on the ground that's as good as disarming him. If he had anything hairier than the bat on him, we'd probably have found out by now. The bat drops a few inches as White

Guy's shoulders slump. He's spent. His mind is having a hard time processing what he just did. Good, at least he's not crazy. Gio holsters his gun a second before I put mine away, too. We go for a tackle.

Planting my left foot, I spring up and kick out with my right. My leg hooks the guy, pulling him off balance. Gio slams into him as hard as he can. I swing my other leg around and manage to catch the guy in the side of the head with my foot as he tumbles to the sidewalk, then fall on top of him, using his rib cage as a nice, flexy landing pad. He isn't going to want to laugh, cough, or sneeze for a few days. Somehow Gio's still standing up. He drops down and cuffs the guy hard. We both grab him, letting him know that he's helpless. I toss him fast: keys, wallet, condom—bingo—a few bags of dope. He's not up to talking right now but we'll make time to discuss those last items later. We shove him into the back of the RMP. A crowd lazily gathers. Nearly everyone points at the eye.

Gio grabs the radio through the driver-side window. "RMP nine-eight six-four, have EMS respond to Sixth and D, two victims in serious condition."

Dispatch comes back. "What do you have at Sixth and D, K?"

"Two victims assaulted with a baseball bat. One lost an eye. The eye is on scene. Have EMS respond." Gio looks at the mope in the backseat. "What are you, fuckin' Babe Ruth?" he asks as he lets go of the handset.

Gio stays near the car and keeps looking at the guy. He's beaten and cuffed but that doesn't mean he won't try to rabbit on us. My shirt sticks to my back with sweat and the front's bloody from the takedown, probably from the guy he hit. I move out into the street to keep anyone from parking or step-

ping on the eye and wait for EMS. Two uniform city cops from the Ninth Precinct pull up to help secure the scene.

"Hey," one of the uniforms says after looking at the eyeball in the street, "I got my eye on you."

"Eye caramba," the other uniform says, looking at the Bart shirt. "Eye yi yi."

I don't say anything and just stare at the first uniform cop to shut him the fuck up. Both uniforms get the picture and slither away.

EMS arrives a short time later. One tech is a burly guy who looks after the first bat victim. The other is a tall, skinny, big-cheekbone brunette that could've been a runway model a few years earlier. She takes in the scene expressionlessly, goes around back, gets an organ box and kneels on the blacktop. She unconsciously bites her tongue while carefully picking the eye up between her rubber gloved fingers and gently setting it in the box. It's strangely sexy. She has a tattoo on her forearm. It's still a few years before that becomes common.

"You can save it?" I ask her.

"Nah. Usually they dangle on the cheek by the nerves when they get knocked out," she says to me as she gets up. The uniforms try to think of something clever. "You'd wrap it in gauze against his head and transport, but like this . . . ? No chance. Do you know how much violent force it takes to actually clear the head like this?"

I shrug and nod, pointing to where her partner works like a dervish on Puerto Rican Bart. Scalp wounds bleed like crazy and the tech looks like he's been serving sloppy joes with his hands. "He took a few practice swings on him," I reply. She kneels to help and everyone, including her partner, automatically checks out her ass.

On the way back to our Housing Precinct Command, Gio looks at me crooked for a second.

"What the fuck was that?" he asks.

"What was what?" I know what he's saying, and we both like to break balls.

"The thing. With the foot?" Some cops love guns and collect them and know all the names of the different ammunition loads and accessories and stuff. That's not my thing. I collect beat-down moves. One week I'm training in kickboxing, the next maybe in Hawaiian Kempo. There's plenty of opportunities to try out the stuff I learn while on the clock. I've been boxing since I was a kid and eventually I will discover Gracie Jiu-Jitsu, a Brazilian grappling style that suits me well. But my first years in plainclothes I'm still sort of a pilgrim wanderer when it comes to working with my hands.

"So, you studying ballet this week?" Gio asks. "You looked like West Side Story or some shit."

"Tap," I say.

At the Command, I sit across a desk from White Guy and fill out his online booking report. I know all about the revolving door that keeps the same faces passing before my eyes from the D to the command to the Tombs and back out again, but this guy is for sure not walking around unsupervised for at least half a decade. Both of the guys he hit would be lucky to live past the weekend and Patrick Aloysius Mahoney as White Guy's known to his parole officer has priors like Calvin Murphy has kids. He's been pretty chill from the moment we dropped him so I loosen his cuffs and Gio brings him a drink of water. A little blood trickles from one hand where he's been cut by the cuffs. Where Patrick is going he's gonna need both his hands in working order. If a perp hasn't been an asshole, I try to make the re-

maining time I spend with them as painless as I can. Anyway, I wanted to talk to him about those bags of dope while we had some privacy.

"So Patrick, you want to call anyone?" I say.

"No," he kind of moans. "There isn't anyone." He's starting to drown in the reality of the situation. He's hunched forward and breathing shallowly. The rib shot has done a number on him.

"You sure? Family, friend, you don't wanna let anyone know you're going to jail?" I say.

"No," he sighs. "Fuck it. Those guys, those two guys Hector and Tingo, they were my best friends." He pauses. "I've known them since like forever."

"Feel like telling me what happened?" I say. He's talking it out. Fine with me.

"They were messing with my girl."

"Both? You caught them?"

"Both, yeah. No, she told me. We were in bed this morning and she tells me. She was into it. We're having problems. A lot of fights and shit . . ." Patrick looks at the floor and is back in bed with a freshly broken heart for a second.

"I went out and I got high and when I saw them walking down the street, I went after them."

"Yeah, you sure did. Where'd you get the bat?"

He looks across the table at me. "It's mine. I went home and got it from my closet, came back and started hitting on them." He starts to cry. "They were my best friends," he sobs. "I know them like my whole life." I wonder if he realizes how much of their blood he is wearing. He looks at his wrist. It's swelling fast. Turns out later he swung the bat so hard the impact broke a bone in his hand.

"So, a little C or D sometimes?" I ask him gently, matter-of-fact—like we're trading eyeglass prescriptions.

"Yeah," he says. "I like coke but a little dope like helps me chill. I'm not like a dope addict, though. Just snort once in a while."

"Right. So where did you go? For the dope." I hold up the bags we found on him. I haven't decided whether to voucher them or hang on to them and keep them and use them as sugar for our informants. "Third Street?"

"Yeah, Third Street. Mostly that spot."

"'Body Bag,' right? Yo, I seen you, bro." I have. It clicks in for sure now.

"Yo, you seen me?" Even though it's the least of his problems, it weirds the guy out that a cop knows a spot location, the name of a brand, and remembers him.

"Yeah. Yeah, I seen you. That's Eddie's spot. You know Eddie, right?"

Patrick nods. "You're friends with those guys, right? Eddie, Macatumba, they your boys, right?" He nods and smiles again. Then the $25,000 question.

"What about Davey Blue Eyes, bro? You ever see him?" I try to be nonchalant but, just like everyone else on the D who I ask about Davey, his expression transforms between my second and third syllable. He looks at me cold. "What?" I ask. "Eddie talks about him, maybe?"

"No."

"No? 'No,' you never seen him or 'no,' Eddie never mentioned him or what?"

Patrick Aloysius Mahoney leans forward and looks at me, clear-eyed and self-possessed and focused for the first and only time while we're together. "No, I don't even wanna say that dude's name," he says. "*You see* Beetlejuice? *You say the name three times and he fucking pops up and you're fucked, right? That's how it is with that guy. You already said it twice. I never seen that guy and I know for sure I never want to. That's all I heard and all I know and all I'm gonna fucking tell you, yo. Hey* papi," *he turns to Gio, nerve ebbing again.* "Can I get another glass of water or some juice or something? Fucking so hot . . ."

One

"Make-a sure you behave-a yourself!" After my mother's father Giovanni—"Papa"—passed away in the late seventies, I never heard those words spoken with a gravy-thick Italian accent again. Up till then it was as reliable as clockwork. Headed out the door to school, mass, to play ball, or fuck around I always got the same reminder. When you're a kid and an adult you trust tells you to be good what you usually hear is "have fun" or "don't get caught."

Papa was a Sicilian-American of the Old World school. He always dressed like he was going to a formal sit-down with equals, always unfussily attended to preparing food and made sure to have a glass of wine with every meal. He made the best eggplant parmigiana I've ever had in my life and the lasagna he set down next to the turkey at Thanksgiving (a given in any Italian home) would be gone before the bird lost a leg. To him the simple things were the finer things. The way Papa peeled an apple was its own lesson in Old World precision and grace. He used a paring knife to painstakingly shuck the peel in a single uninterrupted spiral as if he were making a watch.

When my grandmother died the day after Thanksgiving

1972 my mother's side of the family took turns putting up Papa. Actually, we fought over him. He was a great guy to have around the house. He took care of himself and let us take care of him in the right proportion. With Papa at my elbow I learned to make a grilled cheese sandwich, his favorite lunch, the right way—slowly, with just the right cheese, butter, bread, and frying pan temperature. It wasn't a lesson in haute cuisine, it was an initiation into the old ways of doing things for a member of the microwave-and-TV-dinner generation. Not a formula, but a feeling—a sense for how things should go that a kid could relate to. I knew to cut the crusts off and always anticipated and felt the same pride when Papa would pronounce the results perfect and take his first bite. My sister and I still joke about it—he wouldn't let her make his lunch. She rushed through it. Me, I was able to take it slow, savor the experience and get it done his way. I behaved myself. It was fun. We all loved him, and me, I worshipped him. I'd heard Papa's words of advice as I headed out the door for just over five years when he died in 1978.

Even during baseball and football season, if Papa was staying with us, I'd hang out with him as many afternoons as I could. After lunch he'd hike his trouser cuffs and settle into the big recliner in the living room like a bocce ball in a catcher's mitt and we'd watch *The Mike Douglas Show* together. Douglas was a toupee-and-leisure-suit guy who I guess must have had a singing career. His show was kind of an upscale Joe Franklin—John and Yoko would be on with Don Rickles. Alfred Hitchcock shared Mike's couch with James Brown. The top of each show was the same—Mike would come out on the brightly lit flower-power set and do a song (usually a standard that my grandpa knew) before going into a softball monologue of corny jokes. It was routine and schmaltzy and engaging and surprising enough that Papa loved it. So did my mom.

But one afternoon, Mike followed a Totie Fields fat joke with a crack about Italians and the Mafia. At the time *The Godfather* was breaking box office records across the country. For much of the sixties organizations like the Italian-American Civil Rights League, led by Joe Colombo, moonlighting from running the mob family that bore his name, lobbied Hollywood and Washington long and hard not to use "the M word" in scripts or legal proceedings. TV and movies in those days usually substituted more ominous sounding but less ethnically specific terms like "the Syndicate," "the Organization," or "the Outfit" in its place.

Paramount, the company that made *The Godfather*, broke ranks on a picture called *The Brotherhood* with Kirk Douglas a few years before. It bombed. Threatened with union hassles and boycotts the suits at Paramount agreed to bleach "Mafia" out of *The Godfather* script. Around the same time Nixon's attorney general John Mitchell caved and ordered "Mafia" banned and excised from federal legal documents and memos. None of this kept Joe Colombo from receiving three bullets in the head at an IACRL rally courtesy of a hitman hired by his "Syndicate" rival Crazy Joe Gallo. Sticks and stones . . .

The Godfather was such a sensation that the dam burst. Overnight a word that had been taboo in movies and television for generations was okay after all. Not with my grandfather. As the canned laughter hissed out of the TV speaker, he got up, muttered something in his Italian dialect I wasn't supposed to hear, changed the channel, and scowled word-lessly at the screen until supper. He never watched Mike Douglas again. My mother never watched it, either.

What I more or less understood at the time was that my grandpa Giovanni had arrived in New York from Sicily in the winter of 1900 aged eight years old with a paper suit-case in his hand. His sister had left the old country before he was born. They met face-to-face for the first time on the docks of the Lower East Side. Neither of them ever saw their parents again.

When they left, Sicily was still recovering from a civil war that saw thousands of their countrymen cut down. Their island was so remote and so barren of the coal and iron resources that leveraged northern Italy into the Indus-trial Revolution and the empire-building business that it was for all intents and purposes stuck in the Middle Ages. You couldn't build a factory or a battleship with an olive or tomato harvest. You also couldn't make a living in the fields and orchards in Sicily like you could doing just about any-thing on the other side of the Atlantic.

Thousands of years of invasions and occupations from It-aly in the north and just about every country around the Mediterranean had made Sicilians tough and tight. Sicilian immigrants arrived in the New World with a suspicion of official rules and established authority and a trust only in each other that had been earned over centuries at foreign sword point. The Sicilian struggle for independence and survival played out against one enemy or another for centu-ries and in any war the line between crook and freedom fighter is hard to draw. Sicilians had hundreds of years of chaos and conflict in which to hone secrecy, brutality, and revenge into an art. American English has dozens of words in common use culled from Gallic, Yiddish, northern Italian dialects, and other immigrant languages. There are only two imported from Sicily—"vendetta" and "Mafia."

By 1920, a million Italians (mostly Sicilians like my grandfather and his sister) had immigrated to the United States through New York Harbor. They were joined by about two million Jews driven from Eastern Europe from 1881 to 1924. Everyone was from somewhere else and the numbers grew larger every year. Legal and illegal opportunity knocked for new arrivals. The places to live were where other Italians had staked a neighborhood claim—Harlem uptown and inland from the waterfront on the Lower East Side at the downtown end of Manhattan. Gangsters and thieves lost their lunch over the same boat railings as everyone else headed to America to make some money. For these guys "yearning to breathe free" meant leaving home because they had to. Pioneers of American organized crime like Ignazio "Lupo the Wolf" Saietta and the Morello brothers left Corleone a step ahead of the gallows. Giuseppe "Joe" Masseria emigrated from Marsala to beat a murder rap.

Joe Masseria set up housekeeping in an apartment on Forsyth and Houston downtown and honed his god-given talent for harm as an enforcer in the Morellos' extortion, kidnapping, and counterfeiting rackets and as a soldier in a Sicilian Mafia versus Napolitano Camorra gang war that pitted lower Manhattan against Brooklyn. Unlike his "mustache Pete," first-generation gangster peers, Joe wanted more than just a piece of the transplanted homegrown rackets and local plunder. The era of nativist rule in New York's underworld was coming to a close. Irish crooks had moved on and up into the police and politics. In a relatively short time Joe capitalized on the contacts he made in and out of jail and went from a side business of burglaries and petty heists to running his own gambling and extortion rackets. Joe's timing was perfect. Shaking down store owners, running card games, fencing stolen goods, kidnapping the children of the wealthy, and other old school rackets could only have taken him and the rest of the new breed so far. But when Prohibition was enacted in 1920 it was as if the skies rained gasoline on what had been a bunch of little regional criminal barbecues.

Once Prohibition hit and he began running booze, Joe's operation grew big enough that he soon outstripped the Morellos completely. The nickname he'd picked out for himself years before finally stuck—"Joe the Boss." Any waiter that ever had to roll up the table cloth after the Boss finished a meal could explain his other nickname—"Joe the Glutton."

The Eighteenth Amendment was an ivory tower crusade led by a small group of people who equated drinking with unchecked immigration and the erosion of supposedly Anglo-Saxon family values. Nobody with half a brain thought it made any sense. Unless they were some kind of obsessed fanatic, cops, judges, bankers, and politicians all knew on some level that banning the sale and manufacture of alcohol was bullshit. Most politicians were too scared of moralist newspapers and public opinion to vote against banning liquor and no cop could bitch about it without looking like he was being soft on crime. And, for lawmakers and law enforcers willing to play ball with bootleggers, it maybe wasn't such a bad thing after all.

To Sicilian new arrivals in Papa's generation, banning the production and sale of alcohol was just more Protestant insanity. Catholics already had enough to worry about in this life and atone for in the next. If it's okay with the Pope, who was the U.S. Congress to say you can't take wine? Then, as now, the American dream was a tease for new arrivals and the have-nots. Big business offered most immigrants a spot on the bottom rung and an opportunity to stay there indefinitely. The legal booze industry and just about every other mainstream U.S. business at the time had a glass ceiling that new Americans like my grandfather could never penetrate. But the illegal booze racket was wide open. For Italians, Jews, Irish, African-Americans, or anyone else from anywhere else willing to risk prison or a one-way ride back to their birthplace in a ship's brig, it was the opportunity of a lifetime.

What I didn't learn until after he died was that my grandfather Giovanni seized that opportunity, took full advantage of the dawning underground economy, and went to work for Joe Masseria running bootleg booze and numbers. Papa was a good earner and the Boss became as fond of him in his way as Papa's own family eventually would. Joe would borrow a diamond stickpin Papa owned to wear in his tie at big sit-downs and the marathon meals and pinochle games he hosted to relax and talk shop. The Boss always wiped the pin clean of spilled food before he returned it. With Joe the Boss's blessing, Papa Giovanni went to Boston and ran numbers and liquor there until he got in a major jam with the local cops. Grandpa left Boston one night in a hurry, came back home to Little Italy, and married my grandmother.

My grandfather settled down and opened a café at 3 Catherine Street, a stone's throw away from what's now One Police Plaza. With a family of his own on the way, my grandfather was happy to run his business in the American style—an independent operator cultivating and maintaining necessary ties with the big shots. Big-talking tough guys like Joe the Boss made sure that the cops looked the other way while hardworking tough guys like Papa distilled and bottled unbonded hooch in the back of their storefronts and paid a percentage of what they made back to Joe in return. Joe the Boss still stopped by and still borrowed the stickpin when he wanted, but Joe was at war with his competition and with three kids at home and another on the way, Papa's wild days were ending.

Joe the Boss ran his business in the Old World way. Non-Sicilians weren't welcome on his payroll and pressures from competitors or anger from perceived insults were dealt with at gunpoint. Joe used a cadre of Sicilian natives handpicked from the Lower East Side tenements to stock his inner circle, his death squad, and his bodyguard.

In August 1922, Joe reached out to Rocco Valenti, one of his former employers', the Morellos, deadliest guns and arranged a sit-down at John's Restaurant on East 12 Street. Earlier that summer Joe the Boss had narrowly escaped an assassination attempt outside his apartment on Second Avenue around the corner from the future home of the Ninth Precinct on the Lower East Side. The hit had gone completely haywire. The shooters missed Joe with their bullets but nearly deafened him with close-quarter gunfire. When their getaway car accidentally ran into a labor protest, the hit squad gunned down, ran down, and pistol-whipped their way through the crowd to clear the street and escape. The newspapers howled for blood, the police chased their tails, but Valenti was Joe's prime suspect and he knew what to do about it.

After some pleasantries and half-hearted bridge building at John's, Joe excused himself and a trio of young turks on Joe's payroll flanking him at the table stood up and began shooting Joe's guest. They kept shooting as Valenti dragged himself out to the sidewalk and tried to escape one last time. The guns didn't stop until Valenti took a head shot on the running board of a taxi and a pair of bystanders, including an eight-year-old girl from the block, had been winged.

The assassin who did most of the shooting was also a neighborhood kid. He could've walked the few blocks home in under five minutes. Salvatore Lucania was born in Sicily in a sulfur mining town that made nearby Palermo look like Paris by comparison. His family headed for greener pastures in L'America but settled for a Lower East Side walkup apartment on East Tenth Street, a half block from Tompkins Square Park. Young Salvatore watched his father scrimp and save to put food on his family's table. The sweatshop and day-laborer work his father and their neighbors did was, Salvatore decided, "for crumbs." Outside of extorting pennies from straitlaced students for protection, school was for future crumbs. At fourteen, Lucania dropped out of P.S. 19 on East Fourteenth Street. For a while he bided his time working a five-dollar-a-day crumb job as a shipping clerk at a hat factory and hanging out in the back of the DeRobertis pastry shop around the corner from his house with two Jewish neighborhood kids—a little nebbish math whiz named Meyer who'd stood up to Lucania's shake downs at school, and another kid even wilder than Salvatore named Benny. Like a lot of teenagers their age they plotted to change the world to suit them. In a few years they did.

Lucania, Benny, and Meyer put in their time in the pool halls and back rooms of Little Italy and nearly anywhere in the city a dishonest buck could be had. By eighteen Salvatore had been arrested for armed robbery, gun possession, assault, grand larceny, and gambling charges. Benny was obsessed with broads. When he wasn't planning and pulling heists or balancing his illegal accounts, Meyer pored over glossy magazine pictures of South America and the Caribbean islands—dreaming big like the luftmensch he was. But Lucania was as much a visionary as fellow Lower East Sider Nikola Tesla or revolutionary as Emma Goldman in his way. His association with renegade financier Arnold Rothstein taught him to think in bigger numbers, always look to the next racket, and to dress the part he wanted to play in life. Lucania had his eyes on a future that neither his friends nor associates like Frank Costello, Vito Genovese, Dutch Schultz, and Lepke Buchalter could see their part in just yet.

After stretches in the reformatory and boot camp with the Five Points Gang and Al "Scarface" Capone, Lucania set out on his own, operating a racket nicknamed "the Broadway Mob" that reflected the diversification that Rothstein preached and the diversity of Lucania's own Lower East Side upbringing. Salvatore Lucania or Charlie "Lucky" Luciano as he began to be called (hell, Meyer's last name was originally Suchowljanski, not Lansky—and plenty of people called Benny Siegel, "Bugsy" behind his back) became a favorite of fellow Sicilian Joe the Boss. Joe admired Lucky's nerve and brains even if he couldn't understand his eagerness to consort with *fetuso* punks whose families came from northern Italy or Russia.

With Rothstein pointing the way, Charlie Lucky saw how the Rockefellers, Carnegies, Vanderbilts, Morgans, DuPonts, and other old money corporate big shots regulated the country's legitimate economy. Monopoly and vertical integration—manufacture, distribution, and collection under the same control—that was the way to make a real living in the land of the free. The Eighteenth Amendment to the United States Constitution and the Volstead Act that followed made the manufacture and sale of all alcoholic beverages a federal crime. But every man enjoyed a glass of beer, a friendly wager, and the company of a woman. Owning the supply lines and establishments that provided those services and cooperating with other owners from other parts of town and across the country to share the risk and rewards would reduce losses and increase profits. Under Lucky Luciano, American crime got organized.

Now twenty-three, Charlie Lucky set up a trucking company as a bootlegging front. His old friends Frank Costello and Vito Genovese ran the operation. They owned the east side docks and saw to it that the scotch from Scotland, rum from the islands, and whiskey from Canada were unloaded, stockpiled, sold, and delivered with as little hassle as possible. While clearing close to a half-million dollars a year tax-free servicing his territory, Luciano grew eager to expand and form alliances with other operators. It didn't matter one bit to him where they were from.

Lucky Luciano's genius was weaving the old—the Sicilian Cosa Nostra traditions of silence and loyalty, with the new—opening up the rackets to any and all earning possibilities and partnering with Jews, Irish, blacks, and anyone else, all in the name of profit. In Luciano's view Joe the Boss had taken big-time earning as far as he could. Joe's kind of backward thinking placed grudges and ancestry over money. Prohibition wasn't going to last forever. Any idiot could see that. Yet Joe Masseria and up-and-coming rival boss Salvatore Maranzano wasted a portion of the twenties' precious and obscenely profitable years in a bloody and costly turf war with each other. First off, that had to stop. Under the pretense of a leisurely meal and a card game Luciano arranged for two of Benny Siegel's guns to install four new holes in Joe's head at his favorite restaurant in Coney Island and Maranzano declared himself the winner.

But Maranzano was only a slight improvement on Joe the Glutton. A former candidate for the priesthood with an obsession with Roman history and customs, Maranzano resented Charlie Lucky, Frank Costello, and Vito Genovese's ties with non-Italian gangsters. Like Joe the Boss Maranzano respected Luciano's ambition and earning power, but saw his New World ways as a threat. For good reason. Eventually some more of Luciano's old neighborhood allies paid a call to Maranzano's plush offices in the Helmsley Building dressed as IRS auditors. Legend has it that they unknowingly passed the hitman Maranzano had hired to kill off Charlie Lucky in the hallway on the way in. Lucky's men lined everyone against the wall of Maranzano's office then shot and stabbed the boss and his retinue to death. Their gunshots were muffled by the plush shag carpeting and enormous Roman tapestries decorating his office.

Charlie Lucky didn't substitute ego for brains and install himself as "boss of bosses," the way his two predecessors had. Instead, he streamlined, unified, and stabilized a volatile group of gangs by cherry picking the things that worked for Joe Masseria and Salvatore Maranzano. The Sicilian code of silence—*omerta*—that both Joe and Salvatore swore by would remain. Shutting up paid off handsomely, no matter what you called it. Charlie Lucky learned that the hard way while being tortured at blowtorch and knife point on a Staten Island beach while still in Joe the Boss's employ. If the more sentimental bosses wanted to make it some kind of blood oath, that was just okay with him.

Some of Maranzano's Roman legion-style organization stayed in place, too. It was a new country and a new century with a new deal on the horizon. Ring kissing, ceremony, swearing allegiance, and symbolic acts of discipline had their place, but ultimately decisions would be made with one thing in mind only—making a buck. Though it was mostly bullshit to Lucky, the mustache Pete pomp helped morale and curbed unchecked individual ambition.

With Joe the Boss out of the picture, my grandfather's illegal business came under Lucky Luciano's control. By day Papa sold food and coffee. At night you could also get booze—Lucky's booze. Most days Luciano operated out of the back room of Celano's Garden, a restaurant on Kenmare Street. Celano's Garden was strategically located a few blocks from the curb exchange Luciano ran on the corner of Mulberry Street—an unofficial depot and marketplace where bootleg booze was bought and sold, loaded and unloaded from trucks, car trunks, wheelbarrows, and handcarts. Sitting in one place too long made Charlie Lucky nervous and he liked to move around the neighborhood. Papa's café became a regular destination in Charlie Lucky's rounds. A few times a month Luciano's limo would pull up and the uncrowned king of organized crime would come in and have espresso with my grandfather and bounce my uncle Paul on his knee.

When he got into a beef, my grandfather didn't call the cops. Like everyone else in New York making a living off the Eighteenth Amendment, he called Lucky Luciano. A neighborhood competitor approached Giovanni about selling him a few extra barrels during a periodic booze drought. When it came to buy them back from Papa, the guy welshed and refused to fork over the fair market price they'd agreed to when supplies opened up again. Charlie Lucky ruled in my grandfather's favor. When Giovanni's prized Cadillac, the same one he lent out for the Columbus Day parade and drove his wife, my mother, her sisters, and brother to the Jersey Shore was confiscated by the police during a liquor run, Luciano saw to it that it was stolen from NYPD headquarters and returned to my grandfather.

With repeal on the horizon, my grandfather began investing in the stock market, while Lucky Luciano took more of Arnold Rothstein's advice and solidified his narcotics connections. My grandfather lost nearly everything in the crash of 1929. After a long illness he went the straight and narrow for the rest of his life, working as a military contractor making parachutes. Lucky Luciano began forging the international dope network that would prime the pump for the heroin trade I fought in Alphabet City in the eighties. I had no way of knowing all this as Papa cursed out Mike Douglas. As far as I knew I was just the son of a cop.

Avenue D

They have names like School Boy, Macatumba, Londie, Cha-Cha, and Animal. They arrive in tricked-out Jeeps, Beamers, and Mertzs done up in gloss black, camo, or Day-Glo custom finish, with spoilers on top, speakers inside, and glowing neon underneath. They come and go at all hours—taking stock of their dope spots and their corner hand-to-hand guys, collecting cash, vanishing into the buildings to see an employee, a relative, or a girlfriend inside. They show off to each other while hanging out across the street from their spots clustered around Third Street and Avenue D holding a pitbull leash in one hand, and picking lint off flash designer clothes that would cost me a month's pay with the other. They have leases in the rat-and-roach-infested projects but own houses in Queens, apartments in Manhattan, and second homes in Puerto Rico and the Dominican Republic. They're barely midway through their twenties and making "way" money—mounds of cash so big you don't count the bills, you weigh them.

With millions of dollars in money and drugs changing hands every week, Avenue D should be like Dodge City—constant rip-offs, infighting, renegade big haul dope and money grabs, back-and-forth volleys of insults and gunfire.

But when these guys in the Third and D crew beef with each other or within other crews they settle it fast, so fast all I ever see is the aftermath—a body leaning against a stairwell that's painted with brains, a car left running on East Houston Street with the remains of two overambitious teenagers locked in the trunk, a lifeless rat-bitten face down in the bushes in East River Park, a family of four dead in their project apartment, kids seated in front of the TV each with a small caliber bullet in their head, Mom hacked to pieces in the bedroom, Dad tortured to death with a stun gun and a blowtorch in the shower. Arguments end bad, but they end. A sudden, swift execution, a body or a stack of bodies then back to business as usual.

Vaya con dinero. *Go with the money. The dealers coexist just peacefully enough to work the D profitably at all times. It's too clean for there not to be someone at the top ultimately calling the shots. A DEA agent I work with down the line will dub the Third and D crew "the Forty Thieves." They were thieves—they stole people's lives with dope and bullets. It's still months before I hear the name Davey Blue Eyes. But I know from where I grew up that there's more to this iceberg than I can see. Somebody is the top guy. The knock-around, mobbed-up guys I knew growing up were too young, mean, crazy, fucked up, or just plain dumb to keep things together by themselves, and so are Avenue D's Forty Thieves.*

It's just common sense. Somebody somewhere is enforcing the peace, keeping supplies going, sanctioning necessary killings and earning themselves a generous cut of the profits for doing it. Like the Lucchese family's boss Vic Amuso in my home neighborhood in Brooklyn or John Gotti over in Ozone Park, Queens, there has to be a guy or core group of guys that everybody on the D is scared of and beholden to enough that order prevails. Maintained from above. Or else. Just like when I was a kid.

Part of every dollar exchanged for every bag sold by the Third and D crew goes back up the supply line to whoever that somebody is running the big store. The supply line, the food chain, whatever you want to call it is plain enough to see at curbside but who was at the top is a mystery. All that Gio and I can do is what we've been doing since I arrived in Alphaville— bust anyone and everyone we see working the Avenue D dope machine, toss them, scare them, or buy them or both, get them talking and listen to them. By taking out the lower floors we hope we're weakening the pyramid. The big picture? It's still too wide a view to make out. Days and weeks of twenty-question sessions with everyone we bust are beginning to fill in the details a little.

We make every possible collar we can. We terrorize customers, hassle the dealing crews, even stake out a store on St. Mark's Place that sells the glassine dope bags these guys use—anything to make business hard to conduct and dealers looking to negotiate their way out of getting taken off the street for a day, a weekend, or ten years upstate. Always, in every side street, apartment, stoop, interrogation room, and RMP backseat conversation we have with everyone we bust, bribe, or bullshit, we ask for a name. Who's heavy? Who's your boss? Who's his boss? Who's the man?

A name I hear a lot early on after getting promoted to plainclothes Operation 8 is Sabu. I'm still getting a handle on who's who, who knows who, and who doesn't know shit. Everyone's working some angle and there are a lot of people on the D with the liar's golden touch for telling you what you want to hear. But the name keeps coming up. Sabu. I repeat it back to the people I cuff or let go and heads nod. "Sabu, he's for reals, yo . . . He got style . . ." There's a shrugged consensus that he's popular. Maybe more important or better connected than the other corner dealers and hand-to-hand guys?

We put Sabu under the microscope—full shifts watching him from an empty apartment, our own cars, rooftops, taking photos, keeping logs, the whole bit. When we get close we listen. Sabu looks and sounds the part—a gravelly voiced, pimped-out, dark-skinned Hispanic guy in his early thirties, always dressed in a bloodred ankle-length leather trench coat no matter what the weather, always strutting around the avenue checking in with other dealers and shooting the shit with the people he knows out front of the buildings. And he knows everybody. The junkies, the neighborhood kids, the small-time dealers, and girls from the block all say "hey." But no two people we bust can tell us exactly where he fits into the picture. Everybody's too focused on their own role. We decide to ask the man himself.

"Mira, no Rambo," Sabu croaks in a gravelly matinee villain tone. We pick him up and find dope and money when we toss him. Sitting in a chair rubbing his wrists at the Command, he looks like he's going to cry.

"Who's been saying this shit about me? I only have the one spot. I need to make some extra cash, you know? You see me. I'm outside all the time 'cause I gotta work my corner myself. I can't get nobody to work that doesn't rip my shit off! Why would I be on the street if I didn't have to?"

It turns out that the crime Sabu is guilty of is operating a small-time dope concern and impersonating a big-wheel dealer from a seventies blaxploitation flick. Wheedling with us he sounds like a Puerto Rican Orson Welles. Up close the *truth is pretty easy to see. And smell. The only shots Sabu calls are for rum at the bars along Houston Street. His breath reeks of booze 24-7 and he's on his way to death while on the list for a liver transplant before he's fifty. Sabu's second home isn't a beach house near Santa Domingo, it's a tool shed at the Pitt Street Pool—the man we were auditioning for super villain is moonlighting selling dope from his job as a custodian for the City Parks Department to pay gambling debts. The next time I see him he's in a green uniform skimming the pool at Pitt Street.*

Two

There were two kinds of people in Canarsie when I grew up there. The neighborhood was home to scores of city employees, especially NYPD and FDNY personnel, but it was also Lucchese country. Originally based in the Bronx, the Lucchese mob grew out of a racket that controlled the horse-and-wagon ice delivery trade in the teens. With the support of Charlie Lucky and under the leadership of Gaetano Reina, Gaetano Gagliano, and his underboss Gaetano Lucchese ("Tommy," "Tommy Gun," or "Three Fingers Brown" depending on which paper you read back in the day), the Bronx operation spread to Manhattan, Jersey, and Brooklyn. When Luciano created the Mafia "crime commission," the Luccheses became one of the fabled Five Families that ran American organized crime for most of the last century. After Gagliano stepped down and Lucchese took over in the fifties, Canarsie became one of the family's strongholds. The majority of the kids I went to school with, played sports with, and hung around with went home at night to households owned by cops or by wiseguys.

Growing up in a Brooklyn neighborhood that was half NYPD and half mob was like a real-life version of the Looney

Tunes cartoon with the wolf and the sheepdog. The episodes all began the same way—a big dog named Sam and a wolf named Ralph would walk through a meadow, each with a lunch pail in their hand.

"Morning, Sam."

"Morning, Ralph."

"How's the missus, Sam?"

"Good, Ralph. Yours?"

The wolf and the sheepdog go to a tree with a time clock on it and punch in. Their workday boils down to Ralph stealing sheep by any means he can figure out while Sam tries to keep him from getting any. The whistle blows, the sun sets and the two of them punch the clock and head home together, lunch pails once again on their hips. In Canarsie, you were either in a sheepdog family or a wolf family. Both sides literally lived next door to each other. In the cartoon the sheepdog usually won, but in real life the wolves made out a hell of a lot better than the dogs. The Canarsie Lucchese crew is all over *GoodFellas*. They masterminded the 1978 Lufthansa heist at JFK and collected an eight-million-dollar payday. Nobody ever made a movie about the housing police. All my father ever got was a weekly paycheck and, eventually, a pension and a letter from the mayor.

My father and his kid brother Nick, better known throughout Canarsie as "Chickie," grew up playing ball and hanging out with Vic Amuso. Chickie took a job with the Transit Authority, my father became a cop, and Vic began his career as an enforcer and foot soldier for the Colombo family and Crazy Joe Gallo. When Gallo was gunned down at Umberto's Clam House for ordering the Joe Colombo hit,

Vic jumped ship for the Luccheses. Vic made his bones in kickback schemes and narcotics, did time, got out, and went back to earning. The dope sold in Alphabet City in the eighties no longer came from Vic, but the Lucchese family was still profitable and Canarsie was still his.

Make a fist with your right hand and turn it toward you with the pinky finger at the top. If you picture that fist as Brooklyn, then Canarsie is the knuckle of your thumb pointing down. Long before they were packed off to the Midwest and Canada, the Algonquin Indians named a coastal wilderness on Jamaica Bay where they fished and hunted, "Canarsie" after their word for "fort." The Lower East Side was the last stop on the L line in Manhattan, and Canarsie was the end of the line in Brooklyn. And like the Lower East Side much of Canarsie was originally swamp and tidal marsh. The borders that kept the Algonquin safe until the Europeans came also tell the story of how the neighborhood resisted change once the creeks and marshes were filled in and successive generations of immigrants claimed the new land there for themselves.

Fresh Creek and the upscale homes of the Flatlands section of the old neighborhood form the eastern border. Like Paedegat Basin, a polluted moat separating Canarsie from Bergen Beach and Coney Island beyond, Fresh Creek permanently and definitively buffers the old neighborhood from the new developments at Starrett City, a huge cluster of residential towers looming over the cattails and oily, brackish water to the east. The neighborhood ends at Jamaica Bay. Walking back from the water's edge at Canarsie Pier you cross the Shore Parkway section of the Belt Parkway, then follow Rockaway Parkway past the Bay View

Houses and inland to the crossroads at Flatlands Avenue, which was the heart of Canarsie.

It was over Canarsie's northern border at Linden Boulevard that the Italians, Jews, and Irish arrived by wagon, truck, and eventually subway during the late nineteenth and early twentieth century. That same borderland yielded the neighborhood to families from neighboring Brownsville and across the marsh in East New York in the seventies and eighties. The Canarsie I grew up in bore little resemblance to the marsh and farmland it was fifty years before. New waves of immigration from the Caribbean and West Africa continue to transform the community I knew like the back of my fist into a place I barely recognize today. The children of the kids growing up there today likely won't recognize it themselves in a few decades. That's just the way things go.

Until Jamaica Bay got too filthy to eat from after World War I, Canarsie was home and livelihood for legitimate fishermen and a sanctuary for smugglers. When my father grew up there in the thirties and forties there were still working fruit and vegetable farms and open cook fires tended by off-the-boat Italians trying to get by the same way they had in the old country. But by the time my dad graduated from Franklin K. Lane High, and went into the service, most of the people he knew on the street were either in "the trades" as they used to say—carpenters, plumbers, plasterers, and the like—or they were city employees—sanitation workers like his father, ConEd employees, transit workers, fire fighters, and cops. Or they were mobsters.

My dad returned from his postwar stint in the submarine service onboard a diesel boat called the U.S.S. *Blenny,* a veteran of unrefereed fights with drunk Marines and the proud defender of a handful of official boxing titles in sanctioned bouts held on various naval bases throughout the States. After settling back home in Canarsie, he commuted seven days a week to a factory job in the garment district in Midtown Manhattan. Within a couple of years he was making the trip with his new bride, my mother, Emilia Privitera, a first-generation Sicilian-American who worked as a seamstress in the same shop. Pressing clothes in a fifty-pound steam iron every day gave him eighteen-inch biceps, but it wouldn't support a family, and my old man took a job at sanitation like his old man. My sister and then I arrived and one afternoon he went to the local high school and took the police department test. He passed and became a housing cop.

I never gave what my dad or anyone else's parents did for a living much thought until late into high school. Made-man families had barbecues and attended Little League games same as cop and fireman families and everyone else. Wiseguy or not, nobody talked about their business. Friends from my father's Housing PD Command in Brownsville would come over, but my dad wasn't much for war stories and neither were they. Except for the police radio squawk, they could've been any group of guys watching the Jets.

Once a partner of his gave me an old heavy bag to work out on when he got a new one.

"I bought this because of your dad, Mike," he told me. "A guy in the Farragut Houses got tough with us on a family dispute and your dad dropped him without even taking a swing. I never saw anybody knock a guy down with a single left jab like that." He pointed to a worn out part of the canvas bag, "I worked it hard, see? You want to hit as hard as your old man does, you're gonna have to work it hard, too."

Every once in a while I'd tag along with my father when he went to the Command to pick up his paycheck. Business was always booming there in the seventies. On weekends they'd handcuff the spillover from the holding cells to a metal bar in the precinct lobby. My dad was big and he was known. None of the guys chained together ever so much as swore when we went down the line with me in tow. Cop or wiseguy, sheepdog or wolf, that was what it was all about in Canarsie—respect.

My father's friends were a mixture of both sides and so were mine. The thing we all had in common was that we lived to raise hell. As far back as I can remember I've had a bone-deep craving for thrills and excitement—the real kind, the kind you get fighting, joking, and messing around. When I grew up that craving was often satisfied by doing takedowns and busts in the police. Kid or adult, I got a huge kick when things were close to out of hand. Not fucked up, just on the border. When you're a cop that's not picky about bending rules, chasing perps, and using your hands, you find other cops that see the job the same way, and when you grow up looking for that wild zone between safe and sorry, you fall in with other kids that do, too, no matter what kind of household they came from. Two of my closest friends growing up were the Flynn boys—Timmy and Tommy. Their father held court at a bar called the Nut on Flatlands Avenue. My dad's old baseball teammate Vic Amuso also hung out there.

For Timmy, Tommy, me, and the other kids I grew up with, Canarsie in the seventies had plenty to offer in the having-fun-and-not-getting-caught departments. In elementary school my neighbor Sal and I would sneak in the back door of Grabstein's Deli around the corner from my house and swipe hot knishes off the cooling racks just outside the kitchen. The only real risk we ran was burning our mouths on the hot potato filling inside. When we got older we'd climb the fences around the railyards at the end of the BMT 16 line (later the double L) where MTA janitors scrubbed huge graffiti murals and tags off the outside of subway cars. We'd break stuff and play chicken with oncoming trains, ignoring the blasts from their horns, hock loogies onto the shiny business side of the live third rail and watch our spit drip down, connect with the ground, and *zap!* go up in a crackling hail of smoke and sparks. When we heard a radio hiss or saw a flashlight beam heading our way we'd silently break into a sprint. Running across rail ties and tracks, doing the thirty-yard dash to the torn piece of fence you came through, physically wasn't much different than the stutter step we did in and out of old tires in football practice. It was fun. We didn't get caught.

As I got older, the games got hairier. And even more fun. Once we hit driving age, Timmy and Tommy Flynn, Mark Hedigan, Nicky Capp, Richie Gascon, and a few other guys, would head into Times Square in "the City" just about every weekend. We started out going there for the double features in the crumbling old opera house theaters. But the campy grindhouse gore and crime onscreen paled in comparison with the action in the audience and outside on "the Deuce."

The movies ran all night, and a lot of the crowd more or less lived there in the flickering dark halls whose walls and balconies hadn't seen a paint brush or a new sheet of wallpaper in decades. Junkies shot up, puked, pissed, passed out, and sometimes died in the seats. You never went in the

men's room of the Lyric or any of the other old derelict theaters. They were reserved for bums that looked like degenerate versions of Popeye the Sailor and hustlers in tight
jeans to do God knows what to each other for money or
drugs in the stalls. Times Square bars never checked IDs.
Every dark flagstone- or linoleum-floored dive was equipped
with a steam tray of inedible food, the stench of decades of
spilled beer, a junkie stripper on a makeshift backroom
stage, and a dozen guys scamming each other or ignoring
everything but the drink and the ghost in front of them.

It's hard to imagine now how lawless and crazy Times
Square and Forty-second Street were back in the late seventies and early eighties. It was anything goes—drugs, whores,
you name it. And all of it kicking back to Genovese family
boss, Matty the Horse Ianniello, and the Gambinos' porno
king, Robert DiBernardo. Compared to lid-on Canarsie, it
was like a degenerate's Disney World. At first it seemed like
there were no rules, and no matter what we did, we weren't
risking pissing off our cop or mobster fathers. My friends and
I prowled the bars and the lobby and halls of the old Remington Hotel, a $10.40 fleabag (ten bucks for the room, forty
cents tax), in search of trouble. If there wasn't a whore, pimp,
or john to hassle in the Remington, we'd scour the streets
looking for action. It never took very long to find it. One night
as we turned the corner from Forty-second Street onto Eighth
Avenue my friend Mark pointed at a pimp we'd seen dozens
of times in the Remington and on the sidewalk. He was a
flash guy with a shitty attitude even for an asshole in his line
of work.

We found out later his name on the street was Cat.

"Stop the car," Mark said. "Keep it running."

Before we knew it his door was open and he was out on the curb and had Cat by the belt of his leather coat. The rest of us poured out and surrounded them, then all of us were hitting the guy—open-handed but with a lot behind it. For a crazy second it looked like Mark started stabbing him, too. But what I thought was a knife turned out to be Cat's shirt collar torn loose in Mark's hand. Cat fought us off at first, but we had surprise, numbers, and outer borough teen balls on our side. The ambush, disorganized as it was, worked. We pulled nearly four hundred bucks in neatly faced twenties and fifties that stank of sweat and perfume from the pimp's coat pocket. He probably paid his girls in the tattered smaller bills. Cat the pimp swore that he was gonna kill us if he ever saw us again.

"I see your motherfucking guinea faces! I don't need to know nothing else!" We laughed and shoved him to the curb. One of his shoes came off and a heel lift fell out. We drove home and bought pizza with his perfumed money. A racket was born.

After that, rolling Times Square pimps like Cat was like our paper route. The cops didn't notice or didn't care. We did it fast, mean, and clean. Brakes, door, grab, beat, frisk, shove, laugh, and split with the smell of British Sterling and Jheri curl still in our nostrils. We figured those guys were mostly lone wolves, and got shook down too often by the cops to pack guns. We figured wrong. Late one Saturday night, we were packed into Richie Gascon's dad's Buick, driving down Forty-second Street looking for action. As Richie turned the corner onto Eighth Avenue we saw a group of pimps on the sidewalk. The local men of leisure had had enough of a bunch of laughing Brooklyn *cousines,* helping themselves to the fruits of their whores' labors, and they'd seen us first. Three of them pulled guns and fired point-blank at us as we passed. Cat was leading the pack.

"Fuuuuuuuck!!" You've never seen a Buick head for Brooklyn as fast as ours did after that first shot. The next day Richie Gascon told his parents he was too sick to his stomach to go to mass. He and I spent Sunday in a junkyard on Flatlands and Pennsylvania avenues looking for a replacement door and quarter panel to swap out for the ones that now had .38 slug holes in them.

As fucked up as that experience was, it still went into the win column. We didn't get caught, didn't get hurt, and it was fun. I didn't really care about the money—I don't think any of us did. We were addicted to the action. It felt like as long as I was having fun and getting away with something, I'd live forever. The only rules were the ones enforced in Canarsie. And those had to be learned the hard way.

The Flynn boys, they had juice. If they stayed smart their future was set. I had great times with the Flynns. They were up for anything, always had money, and usually drove a nice car. But as we got older they got sloppier. Every year I got a little clearer about how the world worked and what I could and couldn't get away with. But the Flynns seemed oblivious to effects of what they did. It's something that kids from all made families struggle with—mobbed up, rich, famous, politically wired up, whatever. Sometimes they seemed untouchable. Sometimes they just seemed stupid.

It was Friday night, I was seventeen and me and the Flynns and a few other friends were hanging out in front of a pizza place on Flatlands Avenue. We'd all walked past this joint a hundred times, but we never really hung out there. On this particular night we stopped and bullshitted in front of the place.

"Yeah, I'm telling you, I know you fucked that fat pig, I fuckin' saw you kissin' her," Timmy insisted, knowing Tommy couldn't take a joke.

"I wouldn't fuck that girl with your dick and Mike pushin'," Tommy replied making a face like he smelled something dead.

This kind of thing could go on for hours some nights. After us classing up the front of his place this way for about ten minutes, a high-waistbanded little Italian guy comes out.

"Get away from my store, goddamn it."

"One minute, pops," Timmy says without even looking at him. No one moves. Fuck him. The guy goes back inside and the macho teenage bullshit and arguments resume. We get louder and the little Italian guy comes out again—beet red. He's pissed—Sicilian pissed—and begins cursing in a mixture of two languages.

"*Putana diavolo,* get the fuck outta here now you sons of bitches." It was hard not to crack up.

"Go make yourself some nice fucking pies," somebody told him. That didn't seem like the right response, and anyway, it was his fucking store. I'd had enough. The fun was gone somehow. "Behave-a yourself," you know? Richie felt the same way, I guess. We left together so we wouldn't seem like total pussies to our friends.

The rest of the guys stayed put and continued doing what they did best, break balls. After I left Mr. Beet Red comes out again—this time swinging a baseball bat. Bat or no, one older guy against four pretty tough teenagers isn't much of a fight. My friends took the bat and punched and kicked the guy into the ground. They knew enough not to seriously hurt him, and outside of a few bruises and a lost bat, he was okay. But the guy's pride was destroyed, and wolf or sheep, pride was what 90 percent of the beefs in Canarsie were all about. It was only about nine at night and his pizza place was on the main drag. There were probably more people watching his beating in the neighborhood than tuned to the Mets that night.

It turned out that the pizza man was an old time capo who'd been around forever named Bruno Facciolo. He was one of the guys who escorted Tommy DeSimone to his death at the fake Cosa Nostra initiation reenacted in *GoodFellas*. Bruno's brother was a soldier in the Gambino family and the Facciolo brothers served as intermediaries between the Gambinos and the Luccheses. This guy was a double untouchable. We'd all heard of him, but none of us recognized him when he came out to the sidewalk with pants up to his armpits and pizza sauce on his shirt.

Bruno healed up fast and made inquiries even faster. Usually as teenagers you're pretty much off everyone's radar. But he got everyone's name. One of the bystanders could've ID'd the kids who beat him, but it's more likely that one of my friends sold everyone else out.

My buddy Mark held Bruno down. Mark was a tough kid. His father was a working stiff who died when Mark was young. No one in the neighborhood ever stepped up to mentor Mark into either of Canarsie's two main industries so Mark made do with a construction gig—the kind where you really had to show up and put in the work. Mark worked his way far enough up the ladder that he could borrow the company truck on weekends. He was on his way to work about five in the morning one Monday a few weeks after the pizza brawl, when two guys cut him off, got out of their car, and shot the truck's doors and hood and Mark's legs full of holes. The truck was a goner but Mark survived. He took painkillers and walked with a major hitch in his step to show for it for the rest of his life.

The Flynn boys didn't sweat it. They figured that if their father's juice wouldn't get them out of the jam, a word or two from their father's drinking buddy, Vic Amuso, would. Instead of an anonymous pullover at dawn, they received a personal invitation to have a sit-down and make things right. They didn't have to say a word in their own defense. As they came in the door of the meeting, both Timmy and Tommy got whacked on the head with a baseball bat. It was probably the one they hit Bruno with. Their father had to just stand there and watch. Tommy was beaten so brutally, he was in the hospital for weeks. They say Timmy has a plate in his head, but he would never talk about it. I didn't see either of them for the rest of that summer.

The last guy involved was the son of a connected guy, too. His dad probably had a little more juice or brains than the Flynns. Either he made good with cash, made his kid rat on the guys who beat Bruno down that night, or most likely both. Word was the kid's brand-new Corvette was torched in his family's garage, but no one I knew confirmed it.

Nothing happened to me. Not a talking to, not a dirty look, nothing. Leaving when I did helped. So did being from a sheepdog family. The wolfpack closed ranks to discipline their own. I wonder if those guys would've gone as far as they did if they'd been from cop households.

Maybe that brush with Canarsie "justice" taught me a

lesson about people and the laws and codes they create and uphold. You can only get away with so much. If you think that the world is yours to fuck with, you're wrong. Maybe it didn't. Either way I would eventually take the police exam and join the force with a few experiences under my belt that most of my Long Island and Rockland County native fellow officers hadn't had. I'd been shot at, I'd shaken down pimps, and I'd eaten steaks grilled by the head of one of the most powerful mob families in America, all before ever putting on a badge.

Avenue D

"Big Arthur wants his spots back." I'm standing on the roof of 50 Avenue D talking to Venus. Born and raised in the Wald Houses, one of the oldest high-rises in New York's public housing system, Venus has been earning her nickname since her early teens. She's a head turner for sure, what the locals called a jincha. Her long, dark hair and wholesome, Ivory girl looks earn her a loyal following of junkie buyers and she commands a weird sort of "no molestar" respect from the other corner dealers. She has just about every guy she knows wrapped around her finger.

She's also been doing and dealing smack for almost as long. I've known her for nearly a year now—since my first week assigned to plainclothes Operation 8. When I busted her then, she tried to swallow a bag of dope she was holding, and I had to improvise a variation on the Heimlich maneuver before she could choke it down. I collared her, but we became friends. It's hard not to like her—she isn't just incredible looking, she has a blunt kind of honesty about everything except her own dope habit that's endearing and comes in pretty handy sometimes. Like now. It's a few months after the Sabu fiasco and I still want a name. A real one. One that fits the organization and order enforced within the Third Street crew.

The goddess of love is a reliable informant. Her info is always on the level, and she never once asks for any of the things I'll trade with other snitches—money, dope, or some uninterrupted dealing time—in return. Venus always says she's going to clean up, move out to California with a boyfriend, leave the Lower East Side behind, and all that. I kid her about meeting a rich stockbroker and getting herself set up in a house with a pool in return. A few months from now she'll vanish from the scene. Some guys on the avenue will claim she OD'd. I kid myself and pretend she's out in L.A. in a little pink house on a hillside with a husband and a kid that looks like her.

Right now she's alive and beautiful, talking from the hip the way she does, her hair licking the wind at the start of her final summer in Alphaville.

"He's for sure gonna start some crap," Venus says, tugging a strand from her mouth. I've heard her curse out guys on the street in two languages worth of blue and it kills me how she censors herself when she gives us a tip-off.

"Big Arthur used to have a lot of spots and move a lot of stuff, like way before you guys. He's been upstate for a long time, but he's coming back like right soon. He's a nasty SOB, Rambo. Worse than his brother."

Shit. Michael Washington, Big Arthur's brother, is a first-class asshole and a neighborhood menace. Though barely out of his teens, Michael has already done enough time to culti-vate the classic prison yard bodybuilder look—arms the width of fire hydrants and a tight, swaggering walk. When I first meet him, the word on Michael is that he had gone into the stickup business to support a newfound dope habit. Driving down Avenue C one afternoon, Gio and I see Michael strutting along the sidewalk like Ric Flair, forcing people to step aside and put a foot in the gutter as he passes. We slow to a crawl, matching his pace. After about half a block, I punch the siren trigger on the steering wheel to jolt him. He doesn't even flinch. Is he fucking deaf? We pull over in front of him and get out. It's time to employ one of the most effective and adaptable tools in a cop's bag of tricks—the discon.

According to the NYPD Patrol Guide, article 240.20 of the penal code describes disorderly conduct—a C summons violation and a pink ticket like letting your dog go on the sidewalk or jumping a turnstile—as any situation in which a person "engages in fighting or in violent, tumultuous or threatening behavior," "makes unreasonable noise," "uses abusive or obscene language," or "makes an obscene gesture," "disturbs any lawful assembly," "obstructs vehicular or pedestrian traffic," "congregates with other persons and refuses to disperse," or "creates a hazardous or physically offensive act which serves no legitimate purpose."

In other words, issuing a disorderly conduct or discon summons was a perfect catchall allowing any cop to hassle, search, and lock up anyone annoying, threatening, or looking like they could use a search or a warrant check on the Command's computer. The law requires the unlucky but always deserving recipient of a discon to make a mandatory court appearance on a given date (announced at roll call each morning), something a majority of skells are too fucked up or arrogant to remember to do. Even if a search and warrant check doesn't turn up anything useful, issuing a discon ticket plants the seed for a future arrest for failure to appear in court.

We toss Michael but he's clean—no gun, no dope. It's an educational collar anyway. Once it's clear that we're arresting him, he cans the attitude and doesn't give us any fight. At least not on purpose.

"Fuck me," Gio says as he pulls at Michael's arms. He's gotten one side of his cuffs onto one of Michael's wrists, but the guy's arms are so pumped that Gio can't get them close together enough behind his back to attach the other cuff.

"Ow! Yo, you hurting my shoulder and shit!" Michael yells as I push his other arm. It eventually takes both of our sets of cuffs joined end to end to get his wrists fastened behind his back. By the time we get Michael cuffed and in the car, I feel like I moved a couch up a flight of stairs.

Within a month or so Michael's dope habit eclipses what little sense he has and the stickups we could never nail him for go from bold to ridiculous. He's finally arrested hours after going into his local bodega wearing a ski mask and carrying an Uzi. The guy behind the counter has probably seen Michael at the counter, minus the mask and the Uzi, for every day of Michael's entire life outside the pen. The guy hands over the contents of his register, waits for Michael to leave, calls 911, gives Michael Washington's name and points out where Michael lives with his mother to the officers that respond. The Uzi and the stolen cash are there on his bed and Michael works out in a prison yard for the next decade.

Three

Senior year of high school, two friends of mine, Zee and Lenny, approached me about a thing they were going to do as a favor to a wiseguy named Eddie Lino. Eddie was a coke dealer supplying Canarsie with his product. He was also a made member of John Gotti's Ozone Park crew, and a tough guy in his own right. Gotti and the Gambinos drank at Geffken's down the street from the Luccheses' hangout, the Nut, and things were getting a little tense. I didn't really care. Ever since the pizza guy thing, it was pretty clear to me that the Nut, Geffken's, Vic Amuso, and John Gotti were guys from Zee and Lenny's world, not mine.

I hadn't told anyone, but I finally followed my dad's suggestion and took the police exam. The department had long since evolved from a patronage gig where you got on the force because someone with juice sponsored you, to a civil service job like working for ConEd or sanitation where you took a test and sweated the results while waiting for a spot on the payroll to open up. Between World War I and World War II, the NYPD and other big city police forces started modernizing the same way the U.S. Army did. Cavalry horses gave way to tanks in the army, and precinct barracks and tall hats gave way to modern police methods and specialized assignments in the NYPD.

Soon after the New York City Housing Authority was created in 1934 to develop and maintain public housing projects all over the five boroughs, a small housing security patrol was chartered to go with the new developments, just like building maintenance and management. What nobody expected was that regular NYPD uniform cops would refuse to answer calls in the towering new public housing blocks. Citing regulations about entering domiciles with specific, dedicated street and avenue addresses (even the first generation of public housing developments were hard to identify by number and cross street), regular NYPD uniforms, what housing and transit police would come to refer to as "city cops" until the three branches merged in 1995, balked at doing their duty in densely populated clusters of middle- and low-income residential towers, where anyone above the second floor with a brick or bottle had the upper hand.

In 1952, the state of New York approved a proposal calling for the creation of an actual Housing Police Department. Initially the housing police was a security force with police powers—the right to detain, question, and arrest—along the lines of corrections or court officers. But as the NYCHA's holdings swelled to the equivalent of about one hundred and fifty World Trade Center-sized sites towering over more than twenty-five hundred acres of ground, the city and state kicked in for a bigger budget, and Albany made housing cops fully empowered police, whose beat was vertical as much as horizontal. By 1966, the year after my father was sworn in and began working the projects in Brooklyn, the

New York City Housing Authority Police was the fourth largest individual police force in the state, and the twenty-fourth largest in the country, with its own uniform rank-and-file, plainclothes squads, detectives, and specialized investigative bureaus—narcotics, burglary, homicide, and so on—all kept very busy by residents and visitors to the NYCHA's properties in each of the five boroughs.

After high school, I'd taken a long hard look at my prospects and my friends from the neighborhood's futures. Almost every kid that gets good at sports and receives encouragement from coaches that "get you," and a trophy with a gold guy doing whatever it is you do frozen in action on the top, thinks at least for a little while that they might make it professionally in their chosen sport. I was captain of my high school football team and played just about every minute of every game on both offense and defense. I'd boxed, winning often enough to inflate my ego, and holding my own sparring and competing at Gleason's gym. For a while I coasted on the encouragement of my coaches and little bits of coverage in the school and Canarsie papers. But like the majority of people with those dreams my bubble finally burst. I didn't have the size or talent to make it in the NFL. I loved boxing, but my instincts were better set for mixed martial arts. Eventually I became heavily involved with Gracie Jiu-Jitsu. But that kind of thing was still pretty rare and didn't pay in the eighties.

I gave college a try and then said no thanks. I loved to read, could keep all kinds of notes and ideas safely tucked in my head, but I couldn't stand writing anything down and doing homework. The nuns at Holy Family had seen to that. Not exactly a recipe for academic success. With high school behind me, my choices were pretty narrow. I wasn't from a wolf family and I was sick of that future wiseguy bullshit from friends who did have that card to play. For whatever reason the guys who were born to the mob career track were the hardest partiers and that wasn't my thing, either. I was never afraid to work—I'd been a waiter in a catering hall, worked at a Herman's sporting goods store, been a health club instructor, and done construction and other gigs of one kind or another my whole life, but those always just felt like stops along the way. But along the way to what? Well . . .

In those days the police exam was administered in person a few times a year by the New York City Department of Personnel. You waited for an announcement that the test was being given in your area, signed up, and then went off to take it in a big room full of other would-be cops like it was the SATs. My father wasn't exactly a chatterbox. We got on fine but it's not like we shared a lot of father-son heart-to-hearts. Looking back I have to admit that what advice he did give me was usually pretty good. From junior year of high school on whenever I changed jobs or grades came in, like clockwork he'd announce where and when a police test was being given and suggest that I go wherever that was and take it.

A few weeks before Lenny and Zee came to see me, I finally took my old man's advice, went to Canarsie High School one Saturday morning and sat down with about two thousand other applicants with pencils in hand. The written section was made up of a bunch of multiple choice questions mostly to test reading comprehension and memory. In an effort to weed out psychos along with illiterates, the

Department of Personnel included a lengthy psych portion with the test. Of the hundred or so questions about half of them seemed to be variations on the same two inquiries about your relationship with helpless animals and your mother.

Question 4: Have you ever hurt an animal?
No.

Question 7: Do you love your mother?
Yes.

Question 13: Would you ever kick a dog?
No.

Question 22: Does your mother's love matter to you?
Yes.

Question 32: Do you hit a pet when it misbehaves?
Yes. Wait, no! Shit, you almost caught me!

Question 37: Do you dream about your mother?
What a funny coincidence, I have a recurring dream in which Mom and I beat up small animals together.

The next part of the psych test asked us to draw a picture of a house. Guys that I knew from the neighborhood who were now in the academy or on the job told me to keep it simple and happy and to make it complete—a box with a triangle on it for a house and roof, a chimney, smoke, windows, smiling people outside, a tree, et cetera.

No gravestone with "Mom" written on it or a picture of a guy in the front yard kicking a dog and an arrow that says "me" pointing to it, I guess . . .

Along with the written evaluation, my fellow applicants and I were ushered into a gym in the police academy and put through a series of drills by some old-time cop who called everyone "Skippy"—wall-climbing, running, dragging a ninety-five-pound dummy a specific distance while a stopwatch ticked. I did fine.

Eventually you met with a police psychologist for an interview to see if there was maybe something not right enough about you to qualify you for police service that the questions and picture drawing hadn't revealed. I'd been tipped to what to expect from this, too. At the time there were two women doing most of the interviews. One was a dwarf, which rattled some guys so much right off the bat that they would clam up, stare, babble apologies, and blow it on their own. The other examiner was an unremarkable middle-aged civil servant who smoked through the entire exam. Either one could keep you in her office for as long as she liked while asking questions and taking notes.

"Should it be illegal to yell 'Fire!' in a crowded theater?" my examiner asked me after a few preliminaries and puffs.

"Isn't it?" I asked.

"I don't know, is it?" she replied.

"Yeah, it is." I was 99 percent sure on this.

"Should it be?"

"Yes."

"Why?"

"Because it's wrong to do that."

"Do what?"

"Yell 'fire' in a crowded theater." For a second I thought I may have said "theater in a crowded fire." I hadn't.

"Why?"

"Because someone might get hurt in the rush to get through the exit doors."

"How much do you drink?"

"I don't drink."

"You don't drink? Not at all?"

"No." I wasn't lying. I really didn't. The booze questioning was a tough issue for a lot of young would-be cops. I'm guessing that it still is. We went around like this for less than five minutes. I passed. Later I found out that some guys are in there for as much as half an hour and a surprising number don't pass the first time. Once I made plainclothes in Alphabet City, I'd learn a lot more about interrogations. In a potentially hostile interview the majority of people with something to hide will always offer too much information. Confession may be good for the soul but too much of the wrong kind will wash you out of a law enforcement career.

I had little to hide and not much to say and I guess that made me sane. The passing mark in sanity and the results of that supervised workout and the written testing were combined, I was ranked 10,463 against the rest of the people taking the test (not bad, actually) and placed on a list that any of the three divisions of the New York City Police Department—the city cops, housing police, and transit police—could pick from to fill spaces in their ranks. The test itself wasn't very hard. The difficult part was being between jobs and sweating the results.

Three hundred bucks for only one night's work was just what I needed. The job itself was a simple break-in at a closed-up longshoreman's bar in Red Hook, Brooklyn, that was used to store Joker Poker video games for some wannabe wiseguy who'd wound up on Eddie Lino's bad side. I was the quickest, so I would be the one to climb over a rusty old barbed wire fence, break in the back door, get in, and unlock the front door for my guys. Together we were supposed to move all the machines to the front as quickly as possible then load them onto a Penske truck that one of the boys backed up to the front.

"Hurry the fuck up!" Lenny had done break-ins before. He was nervous and knew that we were taking too long.

"What? I'm hurrying up, what the fuck!" Zee hissed back. We were each holding a side of a Joker Poker machine. Even though the metal edges were cutting through leather work gloves I wore and into my hands, I kept silent. We filled the truck with about twenty game machines and a half-dozen cigarette machines, Lenny and Zee piled into the cab, and I got in back. Whoever was driving did such a lousy job I didn't know whether to try to sit or stand. Just as I was about to tell them to pull over and let me drive, I heard a siren. My heart pounded and I started to sweat like Nixon. I had a momentary vision of my dad and his friends from the job setting fire to the police exam results in front of me. There was no way I would get on the force with a burglary bust on my record. Lights flashed and the sound of the siren passed and faded.

"It's not for us, they're not after us, we're cool," Lenny yelled from the front.

"Yeah, I know," I said. "That you behind the wheel up

there? Slow the fuck down. You drive like my ass."

We were supposed to meet up with Eddie at a parking lot in Marine Park. Along the way Lenny assured me for the thousandth time that Eddie was the real deal and that, yeah, I was going to get paid. I needed the money, and unlike the two would-be mobsters in front, I had no reason to do favors for made-guy coke dealers from Queens. By the time we arrived at the parking lot a fog and drizzle had descended over Brooklyn. We orbited the lot until Zee figured out where the entrance was, parked and killed the engine and lights. Some couples had parked away from the streetlights and were dry humping and making out. This sucked. Finally a big El Dorado coupe rumbled up and flashed its brights. It had to be Eddie.

"There he is. I told you he'd be here," Lenny whispered.

"Good," I whispered back. "I want to get the hell out of here, I'm tired of watching windows fogging up."

"Let me do the fucking talking, okay?" Lenny acted like this was his big score. "I know him pretty good." The three of us got out of the truck simultaneously. Eddie, a smirk and a two-hundred-dollar haircut in a suit, was already leaning on his Caddy smoking a cigarette.

"Hey kids," he said in a way that deserved a slap. I could already tell this was not going to go my way.

"Hi, Eddie," Lenny answered. Zee and I nodded.

"Do okay? You get 'em all?"

"We cleaned 'em out," Lenny replied. "Even got a few cigarette machines."

"Good. I'll need one of you guys to follow me over to Avenue P. The truck goes in a lot over there."

"Okay, I'll go," Lenny volunteered.

"All right then. See you two guys around," Eddie said, as he began to get into his car.

Wait a second.

"See ya around? What about my fuckin' three hundred bucks?" I asked. The smirk vanished. Lenny and Zee both stiffened.

"What the fuck's your problem?" Eddie demanded as his fingers let go of his car door handle.

"I ain't got no problem, I just want my three bills," I answered. Eddie faced me, shifted his weight, and waited for a moment before answering me.

"Three bills, huh? Is that it, three fucking bills?"

"That's it," I said, measuring the distance between us. Eddie was a heavyset guy close to six feet tall, over two hundred pounds, and probably about thirty or thirty-five years old, I guessed. I could tell by the way he moved his weight from foot to foot that he could handle himself.

"What the fuck's your name, kid?" he asked.

"Mike," I answered. As he walked toward me I turned to the side like Sugar Ray Leonard fighting Roberto Durán. If he was going to hit me, I didn't want to give him a big target. I didn't clench my fists but I was ready to bob and weave and roll with the punch if he went for me. For sure, I wouldn't get caught flat-footed. Eddie reached into his pocket, and whipped out a roll of hundreds big enough to choke a horse.

"Where you from, Mike?" he asked, as he counted out three bills.

"Canarsie," I answered.

"Figures," he said. He laughed, the smirk returned, and he lightly smacked the money into my hand and motioned for Lenny to get in the truck. As the Caddy and rental truck convoy headed out of the lot, Zee turned to me.

"What about my money?"

I just shook my head.

"He's your friend, go ask him for it."

Once many years after my family and I had long since turned our backs on the old neighborhood and I had moved on from Alphaville to a post with the DEA, I was in a diner on the fringes of Coney Island, near Stillwell Avenue and the Belt, sweating a bunch of bonus-round questions and sudden trips to the bathroom from a very uptight, very suspicious, and very dangerous heroin dealer. I was undercover and it was a preliminary meet: a setup for a setup to make a buy, then more buys, until we get enough on the guy and his crew to go up on a wiretap. First, however, I had to convince the dealer that I was just as bad a guy as he was and that I had the juice and money to back up all the bullshit I was telling him. My specialty when doing undercovers with the DEA was to pretend to be a wolf like the Canarsie wiseguys I knew growing up.

The contact was getting inquisitive and the food was getting cold. Eventually the dealer agreed to take me up the ladder to his supplier, but as we paid the check and left I wondered whether I should cut my losses. It felt like maybe I would never hear from the guy again or if I did I might be as sorry as a previous undercover someone in his crew had supposedly shot in the gut months earlier.

As we walked out to the sidewalk I spotted a familiar face from Canarsie in the parking lot. He was dressed in Armani and was getting out of a BMW that I couldn't afford in a thousand years. The only thing that had kept this particular guy from becoming a full-fledged mafioso was his half-Irish heritage and non-Italian last name. We had both played football for Canarsie High. He'd been big, mean, and dangerous on the field. From the look of him now, that hadn't changed. I heard he'd been jammed up in construction bid-rigging along with a lot of the Lucchese crew and was about to do some federal time.

I fought to not freeze up. My Canarsie pal knew I was a cop same as I knew what he did for a living. All he had to do to ruin my day and possibly get me shot was say, "Hey Mike, how's police business?" Morning, Sam. He locked eyes with me, walked to where I stood, flashed a disdainful look at my Colombian B-boy drug connection and wrapped me in a hug and a showy handshake and kiss that would've looked perfect in *The Godfather*. My lunch companion could tell this was a connected guy because of the look, the threads, the car, and the attitude. His narrowed eyes bugged out as we wordlessly greeted each other with such familiarity. In one gesture I became the real thing. Thanks, neighbor. Eight months later the dealer, a twelve-thug crew, and about a million dollars in heroin and crack were all locked up down on Foley Square in the Metropolitan Correctional Center.

Like the Lower East Side and every other New York neighborhood, Canarsie has two legacies. One is recorded history—the facts, dates, and stats, newspaper articles, police blotters, census records that track waves and cycles of immigration, growth, building, suburban exodus, decay, and a new population from somewhere else getting the ball rolling all over again. The other is the more ghostly remains—memories, stories, legends, and lessons that are all that remain of the individual lives, the fading faces and voices of the people who lived, worked, and died there.

For a while when I was a kid, the house next door to us was occupied by an off-the-boat Sicilian named Paulo and his family. Like my grandfather, Paulo had an old country ease and pride that showed in the way he did little things. Just strolling down the sidewalk or watering his lawn he had a kind of swaggering walk—shoulders back, stomach out, feet angled out to either side in a reverse pigeon toe. No one actually born in Brooklyn in the twentieth century walked like that. Paulo was as Old World as grappa.

Around the house Paulo was a happy-go-lucky guy—always whistling to himself, singing, narrating what he was doing in the mixture of hyper-speed Sicilian and slow English that earned native guys like him the behind-the-back handle "zips." He loved kids and played with me sometimes when I was young. Paulo had two daughters and for a while I guess I was a stand-in for the son that he probably always wanted but never got. We played a game together that Paulo called "*focu*" (Sicilian for "fire") that mostly involved us chasing each other around the outside of our semidetached houses. But Paulo had an edge. He was always fiercely competitive in the checkers games we had on his porch, and quick to loudly announce he had beaten his eight-year-old neighbor. When the mood struck him, he would go around to the back of the house where his daughters kept a rabbit hutch, remove one of the bunnies from the cage, snap its neck in a single shake of his arm, and deposit it on his kitchen counter. Lunch. It didn't rattle him one bit.

If his wife spoke a word of English or any other language she never felt obliged to show it. She was always in black, scowling like she was born in mourning. Their daughters were beautiful girls. Olive skin, deep brown eyes, long dark hair like burnished mahogany—they were the apple of their father's eye and the object of desire of every guy in school. Paulo ran his home like a castle where those girls were concerned. It was like they lived on the right side of the tracks and the tracks ran around the outside of the house. When his daughters were done at school and their retail jobs afterward, they went home and they stayed home. Selling lemonade together on the corner of Avenue M when we were little was one thing, but once we all got older, no amount of hormones in the world would've made me ask either of them out. It was just understood. I pictured Paulo and the rabbits.

Eventually, Paulo bought his family a big place on the water in Mill Basin and they moved away. How a roofer could afford to move into a five-bedroom home with an in-ground pool was the subject of some very quiet talk among the people he left behind in Canarsie. You really only had to look at his Mill Basin neighbors—made guys, mob lawyers, Canarsie crew stars and their families to start forming ideas. Paulo, the rumor went, had a side business, closer to what he did to those rabbits than what he did with a hammer on construction sites. The word was that he'd been imported from Sicily to use that skill on someone who pissed someone else off. The money was good, the work didn't rattle him and he decided to stay. He sent for his wife in Sicily and started a family in Canarsie.

By the time I was working in Alphabet City, Paulo had achieved what he set out to do. He married his eldest daughter off to an Italian guy who had passed inspection in a huge wedding staged in a rented tent in their sprawling backyard by the water in Mill Basin. Paulo installed his daughter and her new husband into a similar house just down the street, and bought her a wedding boutique to operate while making her papa proud and her mother hint at a smile with a dozen or so grandkids. That was the plan, anyway.

One morning in the late eighties a man walked into the boutique. If you saw him come through the door you probably wouldn't remember much about him—what he wore, how tall he was, what he looked like, other than a pair of dark glasses covering a lot of his face and a bright smile he occasionally flashed below them. The man browsed the glass cases displaying crystal and bone china, his gloved hands clasped behind his back, then flipped through a sample book of wedding registry patterns and sets until he and Paulo's daughter were both alone in the store. When they had the place to themselves he locked the door, pulled out a butcher knife and began stabbing her. Paulo's daughter was petite but she was her father's child to her last breath. She fought and twisted against the knife, tried to push the man away, tore at his face, yelled for help, and demanded to live, but the man just kept pushing the knife blade in and out of her until she was silent and still. The medical examiner logged over eighty stab wounds in her.

Detectives found nothing missing from the store, the register, or Paulo's daughter's purse except her car keys. A short while later they discovered her cream Mercedes ragtop parked across the street from Paulo's old house—the one next door to my family's old place—a home neither Paulo nor his family had set foot in for more than seven years.

I was out in Canarsie at the Six-nine Precinct interviewing a robbery perp a few years after it happened. Out of curiosity I took a look at the investigating officer's case file on my old neighbor's homicide investigation. The file itself was a mess—badly organized and typed up—a textbook example of sloppy police work. I could handle that but I couldn't handle the pictures. I knew her, I knew the store, and knew that no one anywhere needs to die of eighty stab wounds or see what that looks like. According to the Six-nine's detectives, despite the blood on the counters, the carpet, the door to the store, in Paulo's daughter's Mercedes, and on the sidewalk, there was only one partial fingerprint successfully lifted. The FBI database supposedly identified it as belonging to a Sicilian national, whereabouts unknown.

The grieving father offered a huge reward to anyone who could identify the killer. He even hired a famous private detective to do his own investigation, but the case remains unsolved. I don't have any more actual insight into what happened than anyone else. But I do have a feeling. It feels like a message. An anonymous Sicilian assassin cuts the thing you love most out of your life and leaves a reminder about it a few yards from your former house before shifting into park, stepping out onto the sidewalk, and vanishing? What that says to me is no matter where you go, remember where you came from. No matter what you do, remember that there's someone you're doing it for, and doing it to. On the right side of the law, the wrong side or, like nearly everyone I encountered during my time as a cop in Alphaville, somewhere in between, every one of your choices and acts has a potential consequence—good, bad, or outright tragic—if not today, then tomorrow. If not where you started out in life, then where you wind up farther down the line.

B

Avenue D

Big Arthur is a different story than his brother Michael. He's physically even more of a monster, but with enough brains to stay off the spike and to avoid getting caught dirty. He also must have some heavy friends because now that his four-year manslaughter sentence has ended, he returns to the neighborhood in a brand-new burgundy Alfa Romeo. Arthur makes a point of circling the block where I stand a few times the first day he's back. I guess we both have a reputation.

Within twenty-four hours of our staring contest Arthur's strong-arming corner dealers into kicking back dope and money to him and giving up the spots they've been working while he was upstate. A bunch of Arthur's boys from the East Williamsburg and Red Hook projects on the other side of the river start dealing on the avenue. Arthur's plan appears simple—rip off anyone with material and money, redistribute the material to the dealers he's hooked up in Brooklyn and buy even more dope with the money he takes. Overnight our snitch network becomes a Big Arthur Washington complaint department. The Avenue D heroin racket suddenly starts to resemble Dodge City lawlessness for the first time since I've been here.

A growing trail of busted jaws, broken windshields, and

dead bodies all lead back to Arthur, but we only ever hear about it when it's over. He's rattling everyone from the lowest junkie to the most profitable corner guy looking to climb the ladder to the next tier of perpdom. He's also fucking us up. He can't be the man with the way he's acting, and the shit he's pulling are all sad stories after the fact for us, not heads-up tips like we've been working with a lot of the time up to now. When business is good, nobody thinks twice about ratting each other out. With business in turmoil, mouths stay closed except for bitching. With Arthur on the rampage, good people like Venus stop coming around with anything other than another fucked-up Big Arthur story.

First day back Arthur walks up to one of the more profitable Third and D dealers, pulls a big Belgian automatic from his pants and jams it in the guy's face.

"Give me everything, motherfucker," he growls. "Your money and your shit. All of it or I'll fucking kill you." It doesn't really take balls to duck away from a gun. Fight or flight—running from a gun barrel is a natural instinct, one that usually results in an unnatural death by gunshot wound. Whether or not the dealer has balls I'll never know. But in the moment he succumbs to the flight instinct he clearly has luck to spare. Arthur squeezes the trigger the second the guy flinches. Nothing. His gun is jammed. Arthur looks at the gun, thinks of the Schwarzenegger movie he saw it in and the lunch bag of twenties he traded for it, swears, and watches the dealer take off like a bat out of hell down Avenue D toward Houston Street. Arthur takes off after him, yanking at the slide on his gun, trying to unfreeze it and keep his promise. Arthur is big and he's fast. Picture Dave Winfield crossed with the Tasmanian Devil. The dealer is a five-foot-two chain-smoker whose idea of a workout is to stand on

tiptoes and scream into the face of his runner for not picking up a hot café con leche along with a fresh bundle of smack.

The dealer runs, Arthur runs. The dealer gets winded and Arthur sinks to one knee in the middle of Houston Street. Whack! *He smacks his still jammed gun on the pavement and tries the slide again. Nothing.* Whack! *He hits it on the ground again. Still nothing. Arthur slaps the gun down onto the pavement alternating sides over and over until finally,* click—*a dented .380 round pops loose and hits the street with a dull ting. Arthur stands up, chambers a new round and fires twice in the air. He drops his arm, takes aim, and knocks the dealer off his feet in midstride with a clean shot through the guy's shoulder. Arthur calmly crosses Houston Street, walks up to where the guy is leaking blood from his shirt collar, and shoots him a second time. He then helps himself to the deck of dope he's just seen the dealer take from his runner five minutes before, and a fat wad of bills rubber-banded together and stuffed deep into the now dead guy's windbreaker pocket.*

Four

"Is this for real?" I was sitting in the backseat of Mr. Daley's brown station wagon. Mr. D's son Robby, a lifelong friend and brother to one of my best friends, was in the front seat, WNEW was playing the Moody Blues and the three of us—Mr. Daley, Robby, and me—were all in uniform. Mr. Daley had twenty-five years on the job, ten with NYPD Emergency Services Truck 1, and all the commendations and decorations to prove it. Robby and I each had a few months in at the police academy and were both in the generic uniforms assigned to academy recruits—dark blue trousers, light blue shirts, shiny thick-soled oxford Herman Munster shoes, and little metal nameplates pinned under our left pockets.

Most days I took the double L from the Rockaway Parkway Station at the end of the line in Canarsie to the Third Avenue stop in Manhattan and walked six blocks up to the NYPD academy on Twentieth Street. A lot of days Rob rode with me. I never really minded the train or the walk to the academy. You never knew what entertainment the streets of New York would provide. One morning on the way to Twentieth Street, I saw a former great white hope heavyweight boxer whose career I'd followed buying coke in a doorway.

Today, Mr. Daley gave us a ride. It was six thirty in the morning and we'd numbly listened to the radio, the sound of shocks and potholes on the BQE, then the growl of tires on the metal grating roadway on the Manhattan Bridge before turning onto the FDR Drive, a stretch of six-lane highway running along the eastern edge of Manhattan island.

Traffic was heavy and slow on the FDR and we exited at East Houston Street for a shortcut up Avenue D, paralleling the drive to Fourteenth Street, then to Third Avenue and on to the academy's Twentieth Street entrance. Avenue D is the last letter in Alphabet City—the final north–south residential road on the map before the multilane FDR, the strip of public borderland beyond called East River Park, and the river itself separated from a concrete promenade at the park's edge by a metal railing and a twelve-foot drop to shoreline rocks and foamy brown water.

I'd never driven this far into the Lower East Side before and the light from the east over Brooklyn and through the buildings was warm and clear and easy on the eyes. I automatically exhaled as the projects went by on our right. With sunshine obscuring and highlighting details at the same time, the buildings and the grounds below looked all right. Nice. The view up on the sun breaking out over the projects' rooftops, and the low iron fences separating some ragged-looking little hedges and patches of turf from the parking cul-de-sacs between each cluster of towers reminded me of the Bay View Houses just inland of Jamaica Bay in Canarsie. It wasn't Scarsdale or whatever but it looked livable. Yeah, it looked okay. Except for one thing. Every couple of towers there was a handful of guys in expensive leathers herding a little clustered mob of people into a line. It took me a second to realize what they were doing. And to get really pissed off.

"You've gotta be kidding me," I said to Robby's father. "Right out here in broad daylight?" The rough lines were groups of tensely milling junkies waiting to score. The herders were dope dealers.

"E.T., E.T.," I heard one guy in an eight hundred-buck shearling coat yell. A few people in line moved forward. The shearling guy stopped them with a hand gesture. It seemed like a fucked-up ritual. I found out later that smack dealers were just as into marketing as anyone else in retail. They often named their "brand" of dope after a popular movie or song title, a TV or movie character, or a video game like Pac-Man or Donkey Kong. I also learned later that the brands were total bullshit and that most of the dope trading hands for cash at street level came from the same sources.

"School taught one and one is two, but by now, that answer just ain't true . . ." The radio sang a familiar song and I sat in a familiar car with people I'd known my whole life. We were on our way to the same destination I'd arrived at Monday through Friday for weeks. But what I was looking at out there on Avenue D was a completely new world to me.

"What the fuck . . . ? It's six A.M. for Christ's sake!"

"Yeah, this is where they buy it," Mr. Daley said, glancing quickly at the fucked-up pageant to our right. He'd seen a lot in his career with the SWAT team and what was blowing my mind didn't faze him for a second. "It's been like that for years."

"Yeah, but come on, broad daylight?"

"It's a shitty neighborhood," Mr. Daley offered. It didn't look that shitty to me, but I didn't want to be rude.

"Well, with those scumbags dealing in it, it is," I said.

"It's concentrated here. Contained like the measles." He sighed. Anyone with a police career as long and distinguished as Mr. Daley had to resign themselves to departmental and City Hall double standards. "The mayor and the commissioner don't really care, as long as it doesn't spread out to nicer neighborhoods. They've got other stuff to worry about, I guess. There's always going to be drug addicts."

I didn't know it then but the ragtag bunch of addicts we passed represented neighborhoods all over the city and the country. A lot of them were just straight-up junkies like Mr. Daley said—their days and nights were an endless cycle of scoring dope, getting works to shoot it with, a safe place to do it, and enough money to buy more dope. They came here to score, but they went anywhere and did anything they could think of in any neighborhood to get the money to buy more dope with. Shoplifters, second-story men, Dumpster divers, and bike thieves who'd sell whatever they could find off the sidewalk in front of Cooper Union at Astor Place jostled to make the hand-to-hand deal their brains screamed for, alongside whores, muggers, and former dealers who let themselves get strung out on their own shit.

Those skells were elbow to elbow, and in some cases later needle to needle, with everything from East Village club kids and punk rock bohos looking for something to take the edge off an all-night coke binge, to commuting breadwinners— Jersey lawyers, Long Island truck drivers, Connecticut carpenters, city employees from Riverdale, schoolteachers from upstate, college professors from NYU—needing the day's score. An early morning trip to Avenue D meant they could get through a workday without having shakes, sweats, or any other tell to their coworkers and families that their "allergies" or "touch of flu" was actually their strung-out brains shaking down their bodies for more heroin.

I didn't know any of that yet—I simply could not believe this shit was going on less than twenty blocks from where I was going to spend the rest of the day being drilled in methods created to wipe out lawbreaking on this scale. Sitting there in the car I just tried to wrap my mind around it. Why didn't somebody send a half-dozen paddy wagons down there, or just fire a fucking shot in the air, or get on a bullhorn and tell them to disperse or just say no or something— anything? I was only twenty-one but by that age I'd seen and done enough to know at least half of the score when it came to double standards. These motherfuckers in expensive coats were forcing a bunch of pathetic fellow humans to beg for drugs out in the open. It was like they didn't think they could be busted. The truth was, they couldn't.

In the late sixties an unlikely pair of cops named Frank Serpico and David Durk made the rounds at Police Headquarters and City Hall trying to get anyone big enough to help them. Serpico, whose niece I knew from school in Canarsie, was an Italian-American from Brooklyn. He got into a Greenwich Village lifestyle and wore a beard and an earring back when that kind of thing drew dirty looks. Durk was a clean-cut Jewish family man with an Ivy League education. Both cops worked in vice. They may have seemed like an odd couple but they had a few things in common— badges and guns issued from the same HQ, a shared oath, similar duty assignments, and the fact that they both loved being cops and detested the corruption they'd seen firsthand on the job.

Together Serpico and Durk documented multiple instances of cops taking bribes and payoffs to look the other way while heroin dealers and numbers runners plied their trade. They didn't want or intend to rat out individual cops. Their sources were anonymous and they expected that the official wheels of justice would grind up the guilty. But neither of them got any action from City Hall. At the *New York Times,* however, it wasn't just a different story, it was the lead on page one. The *Times* put what the two cops tried to land on the desks of the people who should've been taking care of it smack in the middle of breakfast tables, diner counters, and straphangers' laps across the city and in every newsroom in the country.

Mayor Lindsay's office, the Essex County DA, and especially the NYPD had ostrich-size egg on their face. What was most galling to average readers and people in power who were good at kidding themselves was that cops could take money from drug dealers, a nearly invisible, totally repulsive occupation on par with child molester in the minds of most Americans. Mayor Lindsay wiped yolk from his eyes and did what any politician on the road to a presidential campaign would do under the circumstances—he cleaned house, replaced his police commissioner, and appointed a fact-finding commission. After a few months of rattling papers and making statements, the commission, under the chairmanship of Judge Whitman Knapp, began a series of hearings exploring some of what Serpico and Durk had charged.

When the hearings and the media circus finally ended, the commission issued recommendations that the department turned into a tangled cat's cradle of too little, too late edicts and guidelines designed to force cops to be honest.

They also increased the size and powers of the NYPD's Internal Affairs Bureau. The assumption was that cops couldn't be trusted to stay clean on their own.

The scandal hadn't taken place within the housing or transit police rank and file, and both of those departments dodged that PR bullet. But among street-level, everyday NYPD uniform city cops a new edict came down—do not make street drug sale arrests. Policing drug dealers would now be the exclusive domain of various task forces and specialized teams within the department's narcotics division.

If a regular city cop saw, say, a guy with a needle sticking out of his arm selling a quart-size ziplock of heroin to Mickey Mouse on the corner of Second Street and Avenue D, the officer was not to interfere. Instead of pulling out their cuffs, he or she was to grab their pen and make a note of all the pertinent information surrounding the incident— descriptions of the principals, the events that transpired, and the location where it all took place. Having jotted down which arm the hypo was dangling from, the fact that Mickey had on white four-fingered gloves and used a squeaky laugh, which direction they arrived from and left from, et cetera, post-Knapp procedure dictated that the officer was then supposed to fill out an OCCB report documenting all this 411, and file it with their precinct captain to forward to the Organized Crime Control Bureau at the Seventh Precinct on Pitt Street. The form would be processed within a week or ten days, turned over to the narcotics division within OCCB, and a follow-up investigation would begin. Never mind that the dealer and Mickey were probably in Disneyland by then.

The prize I had won by passing the civil service application process for joining the NYPD was an all-expense-paid (literally—when you're accepted to the police academy you go on salary) admission to a half-year course of cop training in a school building on East Twentieth Street. That facility combined a military-style boot camp with class work, lectures, and training field trips along the lines of Army Officer Candidate School and ROTC. We didn't cover any of the Knapp and Serpico-Durk history and policy at the police academy. There was plenty of other topics under discussion there.

Investigators went through the formality of asking around among my friends and family, former bosses, and coworkers if there was anything they needed to know about me, gave me a piss test, and I became part of 83-58—the New York City Police Academy class of 1983, company 58. What I'd taken was technically a transit police test, but passing it qualified me for training in transit, housing, or as a city cop in the regular NYPD. Where my number was on the list and where the city was in retiring and hirings lined up so that I'd been selected for the Housing Police Department same as my father. In my company of forty academy PPOs (probationary police officers) I was one of about seven assigned to the New York City housing police. The rest were either on track to become city cops or transit police.

City, housing, and transit all received the same treatment and education at the academy. Once we graduated, we'd have equal police powers and equal opportunity to advance or screw up in the eyes of our parallel chains of command and bosses in adjoining offices at One Police Plaza downtown and housing headquarters on Ninety-ninth

Street in Harlem. The specialized stuff within each department and operations that procedurally distinguished the three subdepartments would come later during field training within the individual precincts' jurisdictions (a "police service area," or PSA, in housing cop parlance; a "transit district," for transit police) to which we'd be assigned. On day one at the academy prospective housing, transit, and city cops all dressed in the same blue shirts, dark blue trousers, and spit-shined black shoes stood at attention and sweated gallons lined up side-by-side on a broiling hot muster deck located on the roof of the academy building.

"You are now part of the greatest police department in the world," an instructor yelled in his best Paris Island bark. "You will pay close attention to detail, but you will screw up. When one screws up, you all screw up." After roll call we marched double time, still at attention, to the academy gym. Instructors took places alongside boxes and piles of textbooks, notebooks, equipment, and supplies that we'd need during the half-year course. Whistles blew, instructors yelled, shoes squeaked and we scrambled in a circuit from instructor station to instructor station with our gym bags open. At each stop, somebody shoved a notebook or piece of gear into our bags or smacked something into our hands. Each teacher slam dunked whatever they had as hard as they could. The object for us was to get all of our stuff in one fast moving, full-contact shopping trip—kind of like the old *Supermarket Sweep* game show. For the instructors the object was to make as many of us as possible fall down, trip up, or drop our books, gear, and bags so that they could berate us. The guy with the *Patrol Guide* was a gorilla. He had to be—the rookie cop's bible must have weighed twenty-five pounds. The way he handed them out dropped recruits left and right. I lined up with him, swung my bag around to catch the book, then faked left to the outside like Riggins taking a handoff from Theismann. Before he could change the pitch to catch me off guard, I had the book and was gone and he was spiking the next guy.

Academy training was divided up into a three-course classroom program of law, social and police science, driving instruction at Floyd Bennett Field near my neighborhood in Brooklyn, firearms training at a firing range in Rodman's Neck in the Bronx that the city borrowed from the army after the war and never gave back, and gym training. Some guys took the whole thing as a kind of joke. Others took it completely seriously. Most of us, though, took it for what it was— part education, part hazing, and part necessary formality before the real training began on the beat we'd be patrolling after graduation.

"Never tell anyone about what you learn in this here academy," the police science instructor would remind us at least once a week. "If the skells and perps learn this shit they, not us, will have the upper hand." The academy curriculum did indeed include lifesaving info. "Car stops are always dangerous," an instructor said during the first week. "Always let Central [the bank of radio operators dispatching and keeping tabs on every cop working a given shift] know when you're doing one. Never pull up directly behind the stopped vehicle. Leave your door open when you can. You can and may one day need it for cover. Place the bulletproof clipboard against your chest while approaching the vehicle and have your other hand on your firearm. When you walk up to a car after pulling it over, slap the side of the car. It'll shake up the driver and divert his attention for a second that can potentially save your life."

A lot of academy routine and curriculum seemed designed to keep the department's ass covered once we were out on the job. Firearms training centered on how not to shoot yourself or get shot while reloading. I'd only ever fired a gun once and that was into the air from inside a friend's car hauling ass down the Grand Central Parkway, so I was grateful for the target practice. But the bulk of the two-weeks gun training was devoted to making yourself as small a target as possible, not hitting bull's-eyes. Driving strategy was about how not to total a car that the department had successfully lobbied Albany to pay for. I was never a crazy driver, so I paid attention, avoided the cones and enjoyed the short trip home from the closed course after each session behind the wheel. Gym was pass-fail and centered around running and endurance drills that demonstrated whether you could or couldn't hump yourself from corner to corner on your own. I was in fine shape so it didn't bother me. Trainees that couldn't manage the two-mile runs around the perimeter of the gym (fat or skinny anyone could get dizzy running the same loop sixteen times) got an earful from their supervisors.

"Your partner is dead!" they'd yell at anyone who faltered and dragged themselves to the center of the room to dry heave and sit out the remainder of the run. "You couldn't finish the run! You couldn't save him! He's dead! You let him die!"

I learned one lesson at the academy that I would take out on the street with me for the rest of my career in law enforcement—a lot of cops spend their entire careers looking for ways not to work. In the mind of some cops yelling at a hyperventilating fat guy in NYPD sweats beats the hell out of walking a beat in the South Bronx. The academic and athletic instructors at the police academy were uniform cops. But they'd wrangled and finagled light, no-hazard duty teaching the same stuff out of the same textbook to different PPOs until retirement. It was a warm, dry, safe, easy gig with regular hours and very little supervision and scrutiny. Whoever coined the phrase "those that can, do, those that can't, teach," might've been an NYPD academy trainee.

My social science instructor was a guy named Curran who'd made the sergeant's list and used some pull inside the department to ride out the wait for his promotion behind a lectern at the academy. I guess it was a long wait because the textbook and subject matter at hand had apparently become so boring and familiar to him that his two-cent asides along the way were usually longer than the assigned business we were supposed to cover. I got the impression pretty early on that Curran had lost his nerve and couldn't handle the street anymore. His little asides always seemed to be pointing back to whatever it was that had scared him out of real police work and into the academy. Like any other school situation, I got good at turning my brain off for the bullshit and back on again for what was going to be on the test. I was letting my mind wander one afternoon as Curran killed time with an aside about his years courageously walking a beat in the Seventy-fifth Precinct in Brownsville, a tough, primarily black and Hispanic section of Brooklyn about fifteen minutes from where I grew up, until he mentioned another beat he'd walked.

"I would rather go back to the Seven-five in Brownsville," he was saying. "I'd rather walk a beat in one of the roughest black and Spanish precincts in the whole city, than walk a beat on Flatlands Avenue in the Six-nine." Wait, what? The Six-nine? That was Canarsie. I raised my hand.

"Officer Curran, why is that exactly?"

"I'm getting to that, Codella." Curran launched into a spiel about how the kids on the streets in Canarsie, in his opinion, had less respect for police and the law than the kids in the surrounding neighborhoods. I was on my feet before he was done.

"Then why are the murder, robbery, and violent crime stats so much worse in the Seven-five?"

"This is just my opinion," he said, "based on what I observed when I was working in the Six-nine." His opinion may have been worth something in his local bar, but he was instructing a classroom full of guys most of whom had never been to either place and were forming judgments from what their instructor was telling them. What if one of the Long Island or Rockland county-born future cops I was surrounded by wound up posted in the Six-nine or the Seven-five? Was Curran's opinion supposed to give them some kind of advantage or insight?

Yeah, Canarsie could be rough. It was so far out at the end of the line and so insular that the first black families that moved in there in the late sixties had a particularly hard time. Some retard even firebombed a real estate office that broke ranks and sold to blacks in the neighborhood. But what Curran was talking about was a situation from a few years back where a Canarsie headcase named Crazy Sal de Sarno had run over a beat cop named Sledge. I remembered it well. My friends and I all hated Sledge—he made a big deal out of everything, loved breaking up groups of kids hanging out as much as we loved to hang out, and generally had no clue how to handle minors in a tight-knit neighborhood. Nobody liked Sal, either. As his nickname indicated, Sal de Sarno was nuts. He lived by himself, like some kind of Brooklyn caveman, did lots of coke, and arbitrarily busted into stores, houses, and cars when he needed money.

In January 1980, Sledge was doing routine traffic stops on Flatlands Avenue on his own. For whatever reason his partner hadn't shown up for their shift. The city was running on empty financially and even though Sledge shouldn't have been solo, manpower being what it was, he had to go on radio car patrol, partner or not. Because of its proximity to the bay, Canarsie can be as cold as Chicago in the dead of winter. Nobody in their right mind would have walked a beat that time of year if they could help it. Pulling Sal de Sarno over probably seemed like a good way for Sledge to get back inside where it was warm and dry. There was a 90 percent chance that Sal would have drugs or stolen property on the seat next to him and that Sledge would have a collar.

When Sledge came around to the driver side door of Sal's car he found out exactly what Sal had. Without a word Sal, unrolled his window, emptied a .38 into Sledge's brass-buttoned coat front and hit the gas. Somehow Sledge's belt got caught on Sal's car bumper. Sal dragged the dead or dying cop a dozen blocks at about eighty miles an hour down Flatlands Avenue before the belt snapped and what was left of the poor guy fell away.

True to his nickname, Sal broke into a house and held a woman hostage until the police surrounded the place and he gave himself up. About the only rational thing Sal did in his life was plead to second-degree murder and a few lesser charges, but he's still in prison and probably always will be. Every time he comes up for parole the PBA and Sledge's widow lobby the parole board good and hard.

Holding a neighborhood and its residents responsible for Sledge's murder is like holding a beach responsible for a shark attack, and I told Curran as much.

"Maybe it's just that people in Canarsie are better at smelling fear on a beat cop who's lost his nerve and is looking for a job on the inside," I offered. Curran's "experience" was why he was here in the academy and not meeting and greeting the people of Brownsville that he missed so much.

A few days later Curran made a point of volunteering me for a frisking demonstration. He pushed me against a wall in the front of the classroom and bent his head into mine.

"Give me a little fight," Curran said, as he shoved my head toward the blackboard. "C'mon, give me a fight!" No problem. I shoved back. Curran swung his shoe hard against my anklebone and pushed my legs out to a spread eagle. It hurt like a bastard but I didn't say anything. Typical. The "little fight" was his excuse to give me a limp for a couple days. He'd manipulated me the same as he manipulated the system so that he could be here in the academy collecting a paycheck for parroting a textbook and beating up on guys half his age without risking getting hit back like he would on the street.

"Choose partners!" One of the mandatory gym drills was a boxing glove workout designed to give those recruits without any fighting experience some sense of how to throw and take a punch. Each company numbered about forty guys.

Out of those, one guy was chosen to be company sergeant. The company sergeant was supposed to be a sort of team captain, but with real duties like picking up and distributing paychecks to all the recruits in his company and generally acting as liaison between the academy brass and his or her PPOs.

It was hard for me to believe at first but a lot of PPOs in my class had not only never hit or been hit, but in a few cases had never really even been in the city before. Go figure. I'm not saying that every future cop needs to have trick-or-treated at Little Vic Amuso's house, rolled a pimp, and done a burglary for hire (the department's background checks have actually gotten a lot more detailed since my day and I might not have made the academy if they were as thorough back then) but some of these guys and girls I knew from that academy seemed like lambs going to slaughter.

Unfortunately, the guy that had been selected to be 83-58's company sergeant was one of those unsullied individuals who'd chosen a police career in a city he hardly knew. Without anyone asking, our sergeant had proudly told us all on the first day that he'd only ever been in the city twice— once to take the exam and again to get sworn in and line up for our first roll call. He was raised on the not very mean streets of Northport, Long Island, a suburb mostly known for some teen Satan worshipper murders and that had no social or physical resemblance to any beat he was likely to walk anywhere for the NYPD. Simply put, he was an asshole— a rod-up-his-ass racist jerk always looking to make life hard for the people he thought he was better than. Which was everybody, I guess. Since he was an Irish white guy from the 'burbs, anyone of any other ethnic background or community was beneath him. He was recruited on the city cop list so that meant any transit and housing cops like me in his company were beneath him, too. He was always finding extra duty for us and forgetting to pick up or give us our paychecks. Everyone in the company hated him, housing, city cop, and transit trainee alike.

The academy had strict rules of conduct. You marched in formation from class to class. Uniforms had to be spotless (even though the gym locker rooms were so old and small that no one ever could get dry after a shower) and in good order at all times. Tie clips were to be at regulation height, book bags all needed to face the same way. If a superior saw you on the subway coming to and from Twentieth Street with a button unbuttoned or a scuffed shoe, they could issue you a "star card" that gave you demerits and cut into your class ranking. If the academy higher-ups got wind of anything questionable happening on your own time, you were on the carpet that Monday. Fighting was 100 percent forbidden.

Suited up in the same group as my company sergeant, the boxing drill became an opportunity. I'd fantasized a few times about smacking the fucking jerk when he yanked my chain about my paycheck or said some racist bullshit that made him feel tough and look like a moron. He reminded me of the wannabe wiseguys I knew from high school who were at home or furtively doing coke in the bathroom at the Nut at the same time I was pulling on my gloves at the academy. It was clear from the way our sergeant carried himself— flatfooted with his weight evenly distributed between both feet—that he had no idea how to handle himself physically and what I'd just seen of him warming up, shadowboxing leading with his chin and not protecting himself clinched it. As we partnered up for the boxing drill, I quietly slipped out of my row and into his. Every other recruit stepped aside and let me.

When the company sergeant looked up and realized who he was about to spar with, the smug smirk on his face vanished. The first part of the drill involved each of us taking turns punching the other guy's gloves. I let him go first. He lunged and alternated punching at me pretty tentatively, like a kid throwing a baseball for the first time. Then the whistle blew. It was my turn. I started hitting his gloves. Hard. He didn't roll or move with the blows. Instead he took the shots with his whole arm, extending it farther and stepping back awkwardly at each impact. I could tell I was hurting him. The second part was a short sparring session. This time I went first. I grinned through my mouthguard, faked a jab, and caught him full in the left side of the head. It was almost too easy. He was scared shitless, rooted to the ground, and took the punch full in the temple. His head snapped back and the rest of him followed it. The whistle blew and Sergeant Long Island was out cold on the gym floor.

The gym instructor ran over to scream at me, but he was drowned out by the rest of my company clapping and cheering. The instructor decided to call the exercise off and told a couple of recruits to drag the company sergeant over to the side. Our sergeant was never late with a check again. A few years later they stopped doing full-contact drills in the academy. I later heard our former sergeant turned in a veteran cop during his first year in a rookie precinct post for some minor infraction. The other cops there made life so hard for him he had to join the Internal Affairs Bureau to stay on the force. No one else would have him.

If you subscribed to the academy party line, he did the right thing when he ratted on a guy at his rookie precinct. Instructor after instructor drummed into our heads that no matter what the circumstances, no matter how difficult it was, if we saw another officer doing something against the rules—anything from fudging an overtime slip to taking a bribe—it was our duty to report it. But this one-size-fits-all message was hammered home by the same instructors who, like Curran, had completely given up on actual police work, and who sat idly by as various "experts" addressed us on topics like organized crime that those of us with any prior knowledge on the subject knew were barely credible. Like I said, the academy was a joke to some and was a seminary to guys like my company sergeant on their way to a paper precinct and twenty years of self-imposed misery as part of a brotherhood that hates them. For a small number of guys like myself it was a chance to get the official version of what was expected of you until you figured the rest out on your own with the help of that small minority of other cops who knew the score and liked the work.

Avenue D

Gio and I make pulling Big Arthur Washington over and spread-eagling him on the hood of his Alfa in front of the whole neighborhood our 1987 summer project. We look for him every day we work the D in plainclothes and find him plenty of times, but the motherfucker is always clean.

"Rambo, you guys ain't ever gonna find anything on me," *Arthur says to me each time as he calmly picks up the contents of his pockets off the sidewalk. "I ain't going back to the joint. Not ever." I still can't figure it. Dope sales run like clockwork until Arthur shows up then all hell breaks loose. The organizational shadow I'm just starting to figure out seems to have vanished. Finally, a corner dealer named White Boy Ronnie reaches out to us about Arthur's rampage. Ronnie's a kid from a dairy farm in the Midwest who comes to the Lower East Side and starts dealing on the avenue instead of starting a band or whatever the hell it is kids come from a place like that to a place like this to do.*

Ronnie is an Op 8 regular collar before Gio and I joined, but the other guys in the squad never make him useful as a snitch. Most of the young, lower echelon dope dealer kids doing hand-to-hands on the D have more professional jealousy for the dudes in the Third and D crew than professional ambitions to work their way in and up to become a member of the club. Ronnie's different. He's one of those guys who sees himself on top in a few years. He takes a liking to Gio and me and starts feeding us info now and then. My guess is he thinks he can use us to collar and hassle his competition and I'm only too happy to let him believe we'll let him get away with it as long as he keeps us fed with info. It's pretty nervy—he's as likely to get shot for the stuff he tells us by the Third and D crew, as get collared by us or the Feds who increasingly come into PSA 4 to serve warrants and pluck out dealers that come under their microscope. That's his fucking problem.

Like everyone else, Ronnie wants business to go back to normal. He tells us he's worked it to stay on Arthur's good side and has even middle-manned material to him. Since he and Arthur are close, he offers to let us know when Arthur is carrying a gun so that we can catch him dirty and get him violated back to prison. Ronnie also lets a new name slip: Davey. Come again? Davey Colas or Davey Blue Eyes as Ronnie calls him is apparently someone very heavy and very dangerous. Ronnie is pretty much a wiseass about everything but when we press him for details on this Davey guy he looks like he's going to cross himself. Or shit. Apparently Davey and Arthur go way back and somebody owes somebody else in their business partnership big time. I figure we'll find out more when we bring Big Arthur in with a solid weapons charge and offer to violate his ass back upstate for two decades unless he tells all about this Davey guy.

But before Ronnie can come through for us, Arthur seals his own fate. A week or so after my conversation with Ronnie, the whole avenue is buzzing about Big Arthur's latest move. Appar-

ently, Arthur sees one of the heaviest main dealers, an Avenue D native nicknamed Dougie Dee walking out of a bodega on Pitt Street one evening with his wife and daughters. Arthur doesn't have a gun, but he has his mouth and his balls, and he goes out of his way to fuck with Dougie. He knows full well like we do that Dougie Dee isn't a killer like some of the other main guys and would never carry a piece when he is with his family, so Arthur hassles him bad in full view of a busy project block full of eyes and ears.

"That your bitch-ass dope I grabbed yesterday, Dougie?" It was but Dougie Dee doesn't answer. "That shit sold real good. My boy in Brooklyn, he sold that shit out in like half a hour. You think you coulda sold it that fast, bitch? Yo, let me know when you open another spot, I gotta grab some more of your shit, nigga." Dougie takes his wife by the hand and walks faster. "Where the fuck do you think you're going? I'm talking to you, bitch!" Dougie's wife and kids look at the ground. Arthur lets them get across the street and then comes after them again. He makes a show of sneaking up behind Dougie and smacking him in the back of the head. "Ohhhhh," Arthur said, "that hurt? Get the fuck out of here, punk ass! Go the fuck home and find me some more shit to sell!"

Arthur's bravado is beginning to border on the insane. Yet everything I hear and see makes me believe that as over the top as he acts, Arthur knows what he's doing, or at least thinks he does. He isn't setting up shop on Avenue D as much as he's diverting material to Brooklyn. Whatever the fuck Arthur's plan is, it doesn't involve taking over the lucrative PSA 4 drug franchise as much as leaching off it to stake a claim of his own across the river. Arthur has a pass and what we're finding out is that it was issued by Davey Blue Eyes. This guy Davey has declared Arthur off limits. Nobody ever would've told us except that Arthur is fucking up too many livelihoods and lives.

After calling out Dougie Dee in front of the neighborhood and humiliating him in front of his family, Arthur's ticket only has a few more punches left in it. Armed with a name, we start asking about Davey. Shit-scared of Arthur, people start telling us. Slowly, Ronnie, Venus, and others start saying the name more and louder. The word is that this guy Davey gave Arthur the Alfa along with carte blanche to do as he liked when he got out of the joint. What we hear is that Arthur either stood up and did time for Davey, or he had something on Davey that bought him slack. But the slack had run out. Whatever arrangement Arthur has made with Davey is apparently at the breaking point.

I doubt Arthur is thinking about Dougie when he comes out of the same bodega himself a half a month after humiliating Dougie in front of his family and the Third and D crew. Mobile phones are still a novelty and payphones are the way that dealers keep in contact with the people they need to talk to. Arthur has just finished using the coin-op phone next to sacks of rice inside the store. A Pitt Street regular named Pito sees Arthur go. He does what he's told to do the day after the smacking incident—go to the nearest corner phone and call Dougie Dee. Arthur comes out of the store but before he can get to the double-parked black BMW he just bought for eighty grand cash, Dougie Dee calls out to him. Dougie has company. It's not his wife and kids.

Dougie isn't a killer but the guys flanking him—Londie, Macatumba, ChaCha, and Jimmy Rivera are some of the baddest bad guys on the D and are rumored to have done dozens of shootings. Londie for sure. Arthur goes pale for a second. Londie is holding an Uzi. Londie hands it to Dougie who momentarily struggles with the small gun's awkward weight and heft.

"Shoot the motherfucker," Londie tells him. Dougie Dee fingers the trigger and points the Uzi's tiny business end up at Big Arthur's chest.

"This motherfucker gots to go!" Macatumba yells. Dougie is shaking.

"Fuck all y'all," Arthur shouts as he breaks into a run. Dougie fires. Submachine guns look easy to shoot on TV because bullet-less blank cartridges cut down on their weight and make the shooting mechanism work less violently against the person squeezing the trigger. But in real life an Uzi belches clouds of burnt gunpowder gas and several pounds of lead bullets per clip out of a tiny barrel and is surprisingly difficult to aim if you're not ready for it. Personally, I hate shooting machine guns. The motion and noise gives me a headache. Dougie's a first-timer and clean misses with his first burst. He then rakes the gun back across Arthur like a fire hose, holding the trigger down the whole move. Lead tears chunks from Arthur's arms and ass, but he keeps running.

Macatumba quickly shows Dougie how to change clips. Dougie's into it. The other dealers all have guns out and are firing. Crime scene detectives later count over thirty shell casings on the sidewalk and street. Bullets lodge in Arthur's back, punch through his legs and ricochet around him but he's still going. Thick gobbets of his blood smear and spatter in front of and behind him. Big Arthur makes it to the ground floor of his mother's building before he falls to his knees one last time. A second later, the guns have stopped, smoke is drifting past the upper floors of the projects and Arthur is the only person left on the street. A few breaths after that he's dead.

Within forty-eight hours of Arthur's last run, every one of his buddies with dope spots in the Brooklyn projects is dead, too. Most of them are shot in their apartments along with anyone unlucky enough to be there with them. As usual, we don't hear about it from our informants until after it's happened. But what we do hear about the murders, is that they've been done under orders from the same guy who gives Dougie, Londie, Macatumba, ChaCha, and Jimmy Rivera the greenlight to cut Arthur in half with nine-millimeter rounds— Davey. Davey Blue Eyes. We don't have our man yet, but we have his name. We start using the name in every conversation with every snitch, dealer, and user in PSA 4 and start learning that this Davey guy has more juice than anyone in the dope business on Avenue D or anywhere else in the city.

Five

"Central?" I said into my radio on a cold March night in 1984. "Can you raise post one-four-five?"

By the late seventies nearly 30,000 new residents were pouring into the NYCHA's 2,500-plus buildings a year with crime skyrocketing accordingly. To meet the ever-growing demands made on the housing police and the city cops who reluctantly followed perps into the city's buildings, Housing PD tactically reorganized into nine individual PSAs all under dispatch control of the same 911 system the rest of the city's law enforcement and emergency services responded to. The beat I drew my first year wearing a badge was PSA 1, the New York City housing police service area covering most of Coney Island.

My first year in PSA 1, I was teamed with two other rookies, Louie Corsini and Philly Mazza. They were good guys, didn't bust balls (mine or anyone else's) unjustifiably, were genuinely curious about the job, and not afraid to get out there and work. They also had no problem embracing what you might call the gray areas of procedure and conduct that were, we quickly learned, a part of police work overlooked in the *Patrol Guide*.

Tonight's assignment was a foot patrol of the Marlboro Houses with two other rookies. There had been a series of shootings and robberies inside the buildings themselves and in the barren, poorly lit public spaces in between. The game was to be seen and maybe get lucky and catch one of the local bad guys in the act of making it tough on his law-abiding neighbors.

I only had a couple months on the job but more and more I found that I liked having some breathing room and solitude on night patrols. A single uniform rookie may not exactly be the most potent crime-fighting weapon, but I felt like I saw more, learned more, and was focusing and fine-tuning my abilities and instincts better when I periodically walked the quads, gardens, and halls of the New York City Housing Authority's buildings in Coney Island solo. I liked it that way and it was fine with my partners. While Philly and Louie walked through the Marlboro Houses' bleak court-yard and piss-stinking halls together, I strolled a different part of the same beat on my own.

Our shift was winding down and I felt like checking in with Philly and Louie before we went back to the PSA Command. My first weeks in uniform on Coney Island had yielded some domestic disturbances, the aftermath of a few fights, and other fairly mundane duties. Tonight hadn't been much different. Most of the calls I'd responded to were "aided cases"—basically medical calls to 911. People in New York City housing projects call 911 a lot. Often the EMS guys got the runaround—my husband's too drunk for me to get him off the floor by myself; I have this headache that won't go away; I can't find my medicine—that kind of thing. But no matter how sketchy the call, EMS was paid to respond and the rules said a cop had to check in, too. Tonight I'd done a lot of standing around trying not to look embarrassed as EMS techs either humored or ignored what were for the most part very lonely and very unhappy and probably not very sick people who had used the only tool they had available to them to reach out. Just to liven things up, I'd also shooed a nasty drunk who'd pissed his pants off a corner.

It had been a cold, quiet, and just plain boring night and calling Louie was shaping up to be a highlight. But before I got a radio response I saw one of the other rookies we'd been sent out with break into a dead run. A tall, black male in a long jacket ran in front of him. The running cop raised his radio to his mouth.

"Ten eighty-five forthwith, unit in pursuit!" I recognized his voice—Donny Cannon, another rookie who liked to patrol alone. One of the old guys at the Command had tried to hang him with the nickname "Boom-Boom" after a guy in the Top 40 in the sixties named Freddy "Boom-Boom" Cannon, but to Donny's relief, he hadn't made it stick. Without a second's thought I joined the chase, keying my radio as I ran.

"Central foot pursuit, twenty-two fifty West Eleventh, male black." Cannon still had his thumb on his call button. I could hear him panting and the sound of his shoes on the pavement.

"What do you have at twenty-two fifty West Eleventh?" Cannon just ran. "Unit in pursuit, what do you have at twenty-two fifty West Eleventh?" I ignored the call, too. The dispatcher wasn't going to find out what was happening until I found out what was happening. Any other cops in the vicinity would come running anyway. I just chased. There was about twenty-five feet separating Donny from the perp and twenty-five yards between me and Cannon. All three of us ran like hell keeping about the same distance as we went.

Bang! The perp ran inside the nearest building lobby slamming a heavy steel door behind him. *Bang!* Donny followed. *Bang!* It slammed behind me as I followed the two of them. My radio squawked again.

"Unit in pursuit, what do you have at twenty-two fifty West Eleven?" Central wouldn't let it go. Three more bangs as each of us exited the back of the lobby. I ran out through a garbage strewn back hallway and retched from a smell that was like a cross between shit and onion soup mix and from the sudden exertion in cool air.

Outside in the shadows, the perp leapt over a bench and into the courtyard center of the Marlboro block. He must have sensed that he was gaining yards or had an exit strategy in mind, because he was hauling ass like Walter Payton running to daylight. My heart pounded and the distance between me and Cannon stayed the same as our quarry pulled ahead. Then—*BOOM!*—a shot rang out, the sound echoing between the high-rises. Cannon's guy crumpled forward, chest-first and hit the ground like a sack of potatoes. Fuck me, Cannon shot him in the back! Just because he was getting away? Wait, no, his weapon was still in his holster. NYPD service .38s have a distinct *pow* that even rookie cops recognize a mile away. The shot that dropped this guy sounded like a bomb blast. Cannon stopped running and drew his service pistol. I looked around the four-sided wall of buildings that formed the courtyard we were in. Marlboro had distinctive floor-to-ceiling balcony grills that looked like they were designed to keep residents from jumping. Mostly they kept the size of things people could throw down to brick and bottle dimension. They'd probably be perfect for sniper cover. Donny Cannon slowly approached the pile of bad guy half in shadow a few dozen feet away. I followed, gun drawn.

Cannon and I moved forward warily, each of us quietly trying to get our breath back, with our guns pointed, and our eyes fixed on the still hands of a guy that was breaking the five-minute mile a moment ago. When I got within a few yards, I saw a sawed-off shotgun lying on the ground next to the perp. One of its barrels was frenching smoke. I also saw that his face was blown off. What had been huffing, puffing and cursing all the way to this spot was now a mess of dark arterial blood, fragments of bone, and glistening lymph. Cannon reached out with his foot and flipped open the guy's coat. His lifeless head turned a little. Okay, only half his face was blown off. It didn't make him any less dead or me any less sick to my stomach.

Inside his jacket was a sling made with a wire coat hanger. It was attached to the gun.

"He shot his own fuckin' head off," Cannon said, incredulously. I bent down and took a good look at the shotgun and the ghetto-rigged shoulder holster. Cannon was talking through it. "I'm chasing him, and he blows his own fuckin' head off."

This guy may have been an athlete, but he wasn't much of a gunsmith, or whatever you call the people that make holsters. Apparently as he kicked into high gear across the courtyard his low-budget holster snagged the trigger on the sawed-off and his own gun delivered a load of twelve-gauge buckshot to his face from about a foot away.

Within a few minutes there were five more cops on the scene and a patrol car. Within an hour the guy was on his way to the morgue. A short while after that, Louie, Philly, Donny Cannon, and I were all in the locker room at the PSA 1 Command changing back into our civvies at the end of our shift. Cannon couldn't let it go. Neither could I, but I kept it to myself.

"My first DOA, first sawed-off shotgun, and first foot pursuit," he said for the fifth time. Every time he said it I pictured the dead guy's non-face again. One of the purple-nosed dinosaur veterans that kept calling Cannon "Boom-Boom," peered around the corner as he pulled on permapress western-wear slacks.

"Yeah? You know what you got there?" he asked us with a shit-eating grin.

"What?" I asked.

"A hat trick!" He laughed.

I used to ride my bike to Coney Island as a kid. By day, and within the confines of Luna Park and later Astroland, the last of the brightly lit and rusting thrill ride collections surrounding the Wonder Wheel, the Cyclone, and a few other old-time attractions, it was cheap fun. The parade had very much gone by and you could fuck things up and get away with it within the rusting steel and rotting wood of the rides and the boardwalk. The Cyclone's reputation as one of the hairiest and scariest roller coasters is well deserved. I swear the first drop is nearly vertical and the fact that the whole thing feels like it's going to collapse and send you and your car sailing out over the boardwalk and crashing into the beach beyond just adds to the panic when you're on it, and the relief when you arrive back at the start more or less in one piece.

The Cyclone was bought by the city, condemned, saved, and reopened in the mid-seventies. I always thought the items in the paper each year about last-minute insurance okays at the beginning of each season and of various injuries and lawsuits brought by riders who took a beating on the Cyclone worked as PR for the guys that ran it. It helps to be crazy to ride it, and Brooklyn and the world beyond have enough crazy people to keep the Cyclone running indefinitely. During my time in Alphabet City, a guy that ran a junk shop on East Tenth Street and his punk rocker girlfriend were even married on it. They took their vows while it was parked at the start. Then, after the "I do's," the Cyclone's operator pulled the big lever and the couple's married life began with a fifty-three-degree, seventy mile-per-hour plunge to earth in a car and on a track older than their parents.

In the mid-seventies when I went to Coney Island with my friends, you didn't want to stray too far from the boardwalk after dark. Even in daylight, on the beach or the rides, you had to keep your wits about you. If you wanted to fuck around, Coney Island was fine. But if you wanted to take a date to the beach you would skip Coney Island unless you don't mind picking up garbage before you lay down your blanket and dealing with a real-life freak show while you're there. The Marlboro Houses and the other NYCHA buildings that Philly, Louie, and I worked in PSA 1 were a big part of the reason why.

Coney Island isn't an island at all. In 1918, a project undertaken by local amusement park operators and the city to fill in the creek that had cut Coney off from the Brooklyn mainland finished a job that nature had been working on for centuries. The beach and boardwalk at Coney line up almost exactly west–east, giving it nearly perfect all day sun exposure during good weather. But the Coney Island I worked was one filled with the long shadows of public housing highrises. And that wasn't nature's plan, it was Robert Moses's.

Moses was New York City's "master builder"—the municipal architect who, for better or worse, shaped much of the five boroughs in the second half of the twentieth century, through mammoth public works projects like the East River Drive, Tri-Borough Bridge, Lincoln Center, and NYC's best public beaches (one of which is named after him). Moses came from money and was a second-generation crusader with rigid and passionate ideas about how low-income New Yorkers should live. Like his mother, who had advocated for a prior generation of New York's immigrant poor, Moses hated slums. He also hated anyone—from FDR to Frank Lloyd Wright—who resisted or disagreed with his ideas or who he suspected of having any kind of socialist agenda when it came to public works. And he hated Coney Island.

A child of the era of deadly flu, tuberculosis, cholera, and other epidemics caused or made worse by overcrowding and pollution, Moses saw Coney Island's crowds jammed into the dirty surf as a public health menace. "Her Grace," as his political opponent turned reluctant ally Fiorello La Guardia called Moses, also blamed the living conditions of Coney Island's locals for the area's deserved reputation as one of the street crime capitals of the five boroughs. Moses's solution was to use eminent domain to condemn and dynamite the shanties, bars, and tenements in the neighbor-hood's western tip. What went up from out of the rubble were housing projects. Lots of them. Every decade from the forties on saw another addition to Coney Island's growing array of low-income living possibilities. And each in turn provided more evidence that Moses and the New York City Housing Authority he took over in the forties had only really repurposed an overcrowded, crime-infested ground-level tenement environment into the same thing pointed dozens of stories into the air.

Each decade since the fifties the NYCHA tried out some new architectural experiment on the mostly immigrant poor streaming into Coney Island, as native New Yorkers who could afford it headed for the suburbs in droves. Mo-ses's first attempt at cheap rent utopia was the Gravesend Houses, a cluster of low-rise brick buildings nearly identical to the Breukelen Houses in Canarsie. The first residents of Gravesend were working-class Italians, Irish, Jews, and blacks. Gravesend was followed by tower complexes like Marlboro that filled primarily with newly emigrated His-panics. Slowly but surely the first generation of Gravesend residents either died off, headed for the suburbs, or dug in. The NYCHA relaxed their rental qualifications and the buildings began to fill with a disproportionate number of the jobless, the disenfranchised, those from broken if not outright shattered homes, and legions of kids growing up bored, pissed off, and hungry for a quick buck. A portion of that new population turned to drug dealing, armed rob-bery, and pretty much anything else they could get away with. More than anything, though, they turned on each other. Street fights, gang clashes, and race riots along just about any ethnic line, but particularly between the old-time white residents and the new black and Hispanic immigrants posed a daily threat to law, order, safety, and everything else Louie, Philly, and I were hired to maintain.

My first day on the job began in the PSA 1 Command locker room. I remember pulling up a stiff new pair of dark blue uniform trousers, pulling on a regulation dickey to protect my neck from the winter weather, strapping on my new black leather gun belt, and snapping the same four-inch .38 caliber Smith & Wesson that hadn't exactly earned me marksman cred during training into its holster. I pinned badge number 2389 to my department-issued wool coat, and thought of how, according to some friends already on the job, supervisors on patrol would feel a rookie's shield in winter time to see if it was cold.

The locker room at the PSA 1 Command was loud. Old hairbag dinosaurs took up as much room as they could while slamming their locker doors and shouting jokes and curses at each other. In the corner, I watched one old-timer who looked like he'd been soaking in brine for the last ten years lay down a twelve-inch-by-twelve-inch piece of carpet he kept in his locker. As he removed his street clothes he balanced on the carpet square one foot at a time, careful not to let his clothes or feet touch the dusty locker room floor. I wondered whether he'd done that before roll call on his first day. I doubted it.

Louie introduced himself to me with a tap on the shoulder.

"It's gonna be me, you, and some guy named Philly working in the same training squad," he said, shaking my hand with a tight grip.

"How do you know?" I asked him. Louie smiled.

"I waited until the sergeant put down his clipboard then took a peek at it. How else?"

After roll call we broke up into groups that the sergeant read off from the clipboard. Louie and I introduced ourselves to Philly and we waited to meet our field training officer. Every rookie cop was assigned an FTO, a veteran uniform cop charged with teaching a trio of new guys how to do the job and not get hurt. You couldn't be a field training officer unless you had a lot of years on the job. But a lot of the cops that qualified for FTO assignments had worn the badge for too long and either didn't care or didn't remember how to teach newbies like us how to do what we were supposed to.

Our FTO introduced himself. It was the same guy I'd watched balance on the piece of carpet in the locker room ten minutes earlier. His name was Jack Genova. Jack was fifty-five years old and looked every second of it. He had thirty-five years on the job and from the minute we met was laying down his law on how a cop needed to behave and what we needed to know to make it as far as he had.

"A good cop never gets wet, hungry, or horny," Jack lectured. Lou, Philly, and I nodded as he led us into the cold, down the floodlit pavement outside the Command. "Another thing, if you're gonna do anything off your post, always let at least one other cop know where you are in case anyone looks for you. Never bring your wife or steady to any cop rackets, and God forbid you do, make sure she don't talk to anyone's project *goomata*. And," Jack concluded for the moment, "if you're off your post with a hot piece of ass, make sure you let your old FTO know. I wanna check her out, too." Jack laughed, slapped Philly on the back and pointed and winked at Louie like some horny uncle. I thought he was bullshitting. We each found out later that he wasn't. The uniform was a chick magnet, something we all experimented with. Jack's single years were behind him. If he'd cheated when he was younger, those years were over, too. But Jack still loved looking at girls and lived vicariously through us as much as we'd let him. Sometimes I think we let him more than we should have.

It was early January with about four inches of sooty snow on the ground. Jack led his litter of rookies through the Sheepshead Bay/Nostrand Houses. His head turned to follow a pretty young black chick's ass as she hurried inside for warmth. Jack whistled and replaced a spit slicked toothpick in his mouth with a new dry one. We approached a building lobby but Jack led us around to the manager's office on the side. He pulled out a set of keys big enough to tip a boat and, without saying a word, unlocked and opened a door to the office. Inside, he pointed at the key he'd just used.

"This key everyone wants. It fits every housing authority manager's office in the city." He led us into a plainly decorated office. "When you guys get some time on, you'll have your own keys," he said as he pocketed the ring and took off his heavy winter uniform coat. We stood and stared at the few desks, chairs, file cabinets, and small TV set on a wooden stand that was all that there was in the room.

Jack folded his coat like a Marine folding a flag. "We're not supposed to be in here," he said. "Don't make a mess and fuck things up for us." He gently removed his gun belt and placed it gingerly on a desk next to the chair he'd chosen to occupy for the rest of the shift. Seated, he looked up at us, still standing, dressed for the cold, unsure what the hell we were supposed to do. Or not do. After what seemed like an eternity, he addressed his pupils again.

"This is the quietest project in all of PSA 1. There won't be shit going on, especially with this bad weather and all, so we'll take it easy today. Anything happens, we'll answer our radio jobs. But we won't go out hunting for collars. You guys understand?" We nodded. "Tomorrow when we get assigned to a tougher, more active area we'll hunt up some arrests and I'll show you guys how it's done." Louie smiled. Philly shrugged his shoulders. I shrugged at Louie.

"Whatever, Jack," I said.

"Tomorrow's another day," Louie added. Jack started to fiddle with the television. I grabbed an old newspaper from the trash, folded it to the sports page and sat in front of it. Another story on Tyson and Cuss D'Amato. I wondered how long it would take for my shield to reach room temperature.

Jack turned out to be a no-nonsense guy who, despite the years and the miles, was still into making arrests and teaching young cops. He was a character, for sure. Even for a cop he had a weird sense of humor. But he was known around the Command as a cop who always did the right thing and knew the job—the real job: how to make collars, cover your ass when you needed to, and not get hurt or let your partner get hurt. It turned out that Jack had worked with my dad back in the day, and he took a particular interest in my training. I owe him a lot for showing me the ropes in PSA 1.

Jack also knew the things that good old-time cops always knew—where a uniform could get a good deal on anything in the city: a discount on a meal, a half-price tune-up for your car, a complimentary tux rental for a wedding, a break on the price tag on jewelry for a girlfriend, or a free massage in a dozen massage parlors from Staten Island to the Bronx.

Jack knew how to make the job work for him and how to do the job he was paid to do. Jack taught us how to patrol a housing project the right way.

"Always make sure to take note of the building address, and write it in your memo books. Just in case you need to call for emergency backup, you'll know where the hell you are," he told us as he led us through a building lobby to a bank of elevators the next night. Some of the NYCHA projects had address numbers that defied logic. The only way to be sure where you were and be able to communicate that to Central and in turn to any potential cavalry was to remember what it said on the outside of the building you were in. Jack punched the call button for the elevator and shut off his radio, gesturing for us to do the same. The elevator arrived. As the door opened the smell of piss was overwhelming. Jack smiled and shook his head, "Like a damn toilet, huh?" Philly nodded then covered his mouth with his hat.

"Fuck," Louie coughed up.

"You'll get used to the smell." Jack smiled again and pushed the button for the top floor. "You guys will get used to all kinds of shit you never knew existed."

Jack literally taught us the job from the top down. The elevator arrived at the last stop and we climbed some metal stairs to the roof itself. Every NYCHA lease says that tenants aren't allowed on their building roofs. But that didn't stop anyone. The first place to look on any building patrol was on top. First with Jack and then later on our own, Louie, Philly, and I would walk the upper floor hallways, roof landings, and roofs checking for trespassers and junkies. Even if we didn't find anyone shooting up dope, or smoking cocaine, there'd be empty glassine envelopes that once held ten-dollar doses of heroin or our feet would crunch discarded tin foil that the coke had been packaged in. It wasn't unusual for us to find used needles with blood still in them. Hardcore junkies jacked the plunger in and out to get a potent mix of dope and blood going from syringe to vein.

The smack high itself and the baby laxative that dealers used to cut dope and coke were rough on the bowels. Piles of human shit, ten times worse smelling and harder to get off your shoes than dog shit if you were unlucky enough to step in it, were everywhere. Jack also taught us to smash any empty bottles we found lying around into small pieces with our nightsticks. It might've taken a nickel out of the pocket of some fixed-income resident barely squeaking by, but it meant no one would use a bottle as "air mail" and drop it on any of us as we walked a beat below.

If there was no one up there to arrest, we'd split up and take the stairs down floor by floor. Most projects had at least two staircases. In order to catch anyone who didn't belong in the building or who was fucking around (or just fucking) on the stairwells, and maintain the deterrent presence that our uniform, badge, and gun were supposed to provide, we needed to turn our police radio volume way down, and each go down separately. A stair walk was an adventure in itself. Along the way down the stairs you could trip over a sleeping derelict, interrupt a rape or robbery, or ruin somebody's day by arresting them before the blow job they'd paid for was over. Jack taught us how to bang our nightstick on every floor as we passed it and listen for each other to send back the same message.

"Just rap the stick loud on the cement wall," Jack said.

"For cops it's a reassuring sound. Listen for your partner's nightstick bang," Jack reminded us. If we didn't hear our counterpart marking time on the way down we knew that they'd found something and that we should come running.

By the book policing required that you measure everyone you encountered solely by whether or not they broke the law. But effective policing challenged you to do some balancing of the scales of justice yourself. One of a cop's most effective tools was his or her ability to choose who to bust and who to let free. Later, in plainclothes in Alphabet City, that ability would make it possible to turn bad guys to my own use, create informants and gather the information needed to make bigger, farther-reaching arrests. At the heart of that more sophisticated decision making was something that Jack insisted on. No matter how shit scared you may be walking your beat, and no matter how shocked, surprised, or confused you were by the rich pageant of questionable choices and fucked-up behavior you encountered, you the cop had to command one thing—respect.

Even though I'd mentally prepared myself for who or what might be around a corner, up some stairs, or through an open roof door, nine times out of ten what I found there would make my heart race and the adrenaline pump through my veins. It always gave me the rush I was looking for, and it was the thing I loved most about the job. Jack didn't care about that anymore. What he required, and what he got, was a measure of respect from everyone he encountered in those winging-it, what-the-hell situations. He made it his personal mission to teach us to get the same respect in the same circumstances. Growing up in Brooklyn, I knew this already. What Jack reminded us was the same story my father taught me in Canarsie. If you don't punch the school-yard bully in his face the first time he tries to take your lunch money, he'll be eating on you every day for the rest of the school year.

My first collar was a gift from Jack that underscored his point. Philly, Louie, and me were beginning a foot patrol in one of the worst projects in all of New York City, Carey Gardens. A sprawling seventeen-story clamshell of brown brick towers that was some sixties city planner's idea of a good place to live when it was built, "Carey Garbage" as it was now known to the gangs of thug kids that lived and got their kicks there, was completed in 1970 and quickly sank to the bottom of the public housing barrel. As we passed the entrance a group of black and Hispanic teenagers slowly dispersed from the front of the building. It was a game we all played—they knew we'd give them a hard time, maybe roust a couple of them and make them empty their pockets if they didn't break it up, and we knew they'd take as much time as they thought they could get away with clearing out. I'd played the game from their side with the late Officer Sledge. But while all the other kids slunk off, one kid stayed put on the stairs. Jack led us right up to him. Without a word to the kid, Jack turned to me and said, "Okay, Mike cuff him up."

"Cuff him up?" I asked. Philly, Louie, and I looked at each other. Was this a threat or Jack's sense of humor? "Yeah, cuff up this little pain in the ass," Jack insisted. I pulled out my cuffs. The kid turned around and assumed the position with practiced efficiency—head sloped, feet shoulder width, hands behind his back, palms together like saying an upside-down prayer.

"What the hell did I do? I was just hanging out. All's I did was stand in front of the damn ass building," the kid muttered. He had a point. I clicked the cuffs closed on his wrists and turned him around to face us.

"Yeah? Cut the bullshit," Jack said. "Is this the first time you ever saw my face?" The kid shook his head no. "Then, you know what you did. No hanging out in front of the building." Louie took out his police radio and called for a unit to pick us up and transport us back to the station house.

"Central, please have an RMP [a squad car] respond to twenty-three forty-eight West Twenty-third Street, front of [the address of the project and where to find us in the building]. FTO and three units holding one [Jack along with Louie, Philly, and I with a single bad guy in custody]." A short time later a police van picked us up.

Inside the Command, I took Jack off to the side and asked him what the kid did. After all the lessons and role-playing in social science at the academy, I didn't understand the collar, and for sure didn't want to start my career locking up guys for nothing. Jack walked me back to where Philly and Louie were standing.

"Listen," he said to all of us, "when you come up to a building these guys know they shouldn't be hanging in front. If they give you the respect you deserve, they leave. If they don't, well then you either make 'em leave, or you lock 'em up. This guy has been told before to leave, by me and by a bunch of other guys. If we don't lock him up, we make ourselves look like assholes and make it that much harder for the next cop to deal with this guy. You rookies bear the mark. You look young and sometimes you look scared. From now on this kid, and the kids that watched Mike cuff him up know that young, scared, or whatever, you're for real. The bottom line is, it's all about respect."

As I filled out a summons for disorderedly conduct, I felt bad for the kid. It actually made me a little sick to my stomach. The letter of the violation said that a person could not obstruct pedestrian traffic, which the kid did, I guess. But the whole thing reminded me of getting hassled by cops when I was this kid's age. As I scribbled, Jack did a warrant check on our young perp. It turned out that he was over eighteen and had two outstanding felony warrants. My suspicion that we'd grabbed an honor student and ruined his life instantly vanished. This guy was a wiseass and a perp. Moreover he was stupid. He knew the deal and still felt the need to test Jack and us even though he had two felonies hanging over him. Fuck him.

Jack knew the system and how it worked and didn't work. He showed us how to use our discretion to kick ass when we needed to and to cut slack when it made sense to do that, too. Sometimes both. After we dumped the kid off at Central Booking he told me, "If you feel like it's the right thing to buy a perp a sandwich while they're being processed, do it. You never know, he may be the one who calls nine-one-one and saves you or your partner's life someday."

"We're gonna make some overtime on this one," Jack explained to me. "We might be in the system all night."

"That's cool with me, I could use some extra cash," I answered. And so it was. Jack and I spent the better part of the night processing my first collar, one that I didn't even know was a collar, while adding a few bucks to our paychecks in the time-honored tradition of cops everywhere. Did I say

Jack taught us the job from the top down? Some of the lessons I learned were from the bottom line up.

Avenue D

While the neighborhood dealers cool off and quiet down, I work my informant contacts armed with a new weapon, the name Davey Blue Eyes. I put it to dealers, to junkies, that kid with the bat who hit an eyeball homerun—anyone and everyone who may have something to tell me about Davey Blue Eyes, where he came from, and how to bring him down. Initially I piece together the bio of a guy powerful enough to grant Arthur the freedom he abused to the point of extinction and then sanction Arthur's execution along with a half-dozen Brooklyn bad guys, their families, and whoever was over to watch the game when the assassins came to call. Who did the killings didn't really matter to me as much as who is operating a traffic light that went from red to green and allowed Arthur's victims to become his executioners and Arthur and his boys in Brooklyn to become a cluster of snapshots, handwritten notes, and botanica candles in front of the project buildings they grew up in.

Backseat, rooftop, stairwell, and interrogation room conversations with Venus, Ronnie, and dozens of others gives me a composite picture of a guy that sounds like Lucky Luciano's heir. What I learn is that in the Avenue D heroin trade, Davey

Blue Eyes's word is law. Half Italian, half Puerto Rican, project born and raised, Davey, like Charlie Lucky, is a product of the Lower East Side. By the time he joins the Marines at age sixteen, he's already no stranger to guns and ammo. One story I hear repeated several times involves teenage Davey holding up another dealer at gunpoint in a back row pew in St. Mary's on Grand Street during midnight mass on Christmas Eve.

The Marine Corps introduces Davey to heavier weapons and hard-core military tactics. When he returns to civilian life, he brings a flair for reconnaissance and a belief in superior firepower back with him. That's not all he comes home with. Davey doesn't just emerge from the Marines a marksman, he comes out with ordnance connections within the Corps that help him set up shop as a bona fide gun runner. Handguns are never a problem to get in Alphaville and even if you're not connected, you or a friend with a cleaner record can just drive south to Virginia and pick one out at a sporting goods store. But Davey puts government-issue machine guns and grenades—stuff that couldn't be had legally anywhere at any price—within reach of any local gangster who can pay.

Davey's uncle is a connected guy who deals dope from a headquarters in a body shop near the boat docks in Mill Basin in the early eighties. Davey apprentices with his uncle dealing, collecting and, thanks to his interest in guns and the things he accomplishes with them, enforcing and regulating when his uncle encounters thieves and rivals. While I'm learning how to drive a patrol car at Floyd Bennett Field, Davey is running dope for his uncle a half mile away and forging his own links with a group of Chinatown-based smack wholesalers walking distance from his birthplace in the projects in the Lower East Side.

Visible is vulnerable and Davey makes a practice of being

nowhere. "You know, him, yo. You seen him around," snitches tell me, but if I have, I don't know it. Davey's Third and D dealers can chimp around in fancy cars, jewelry, and clothes, a debarked pitbull panting beside them and a stripper with a cast-iron septum cooing in their lap, as long as they stay earners and as long as they stay loyal. The flash life wasn't for him, though.

There's bound to be some chaos in a retail drug operation as huge as the one Davey sets into motion. His roots are deep and the people he puts to work know their connections with him are till-death-do-us-part solid. Davey doesn't try to micromanage every aspect of his ant farm. He just taps the glass or grabs the Raid when he needs to. But there are always some things that call for a clear message, delivered personally.

A year or two prior to me arriving on the D, Davey discovers a pair of upper tier main dealers he's known since grade school are stepping on already cut dope he fronts to them. They'd set a price knowing full well that if they sold for more they needed to kick back to Davey as a courtesy. Or life insurance. Not good. Davey takes care of the two personally. In broad daylight, Davey climbs the roof of a library building on East Houston Street, assembles the high-powered Barrett rifle he qualified with in sniper school in Hawaii and waits for his soon-to-be ex-employees to cross the street from Avenue D. Both die from single bullets the size of an adult pinkie finger vaporizing their heads in broad daylight. On-scene forensics find teeth scattered a half block away from the impacts. Davey's so sure of his timing and tactics, he doesn't even bother with a silencer. In two trigger pulls he joins the ranks of Lee Harvey Oswald and water tower sniper Charles Whitman by showing, like the drill instructor in Full Metal Jacket said "just what one motivated Marine and his rifle can do."

Six

Once the prescribed six weeks under FTO Jack's wing came to an end I was free to use what I'd learned from Jack and the other vets I worked with to make collars on my own. Every day was a tug-of-war between discretion and compromise on one side, and a twenty-two-year-old's natural desire to see action and get his kicks on the other. Protect, serve, and have fun. Don't be an asshole, don't pull anything stupid, don't get caught if you do, and if you fuck up, deal with it. "Behave-a yourself." Do your job the best way you knew how. The outrageous circumstances—harsh weather, violent behavior, drug-addled human misery and acts of cruelty in an overcrowded skyscraper—were simply the lay of the land.

A group of black Muslim militants decide they're going to have their own police force in a neighborhood high-rise complex? Okay. More power to them. They patrolled some private buildings that surrounded the projects and weren't part of the Housing Authority, so as long as they stayed off our post and on my side of the law, and showed reasonable respect it was okay with me. Unfortunately, in every one of these organized groups of tough guys all raised in this very tough environment, there was one doing double time by working for bad guys. Positioning a housing cop downstairs with the black Muslim security guards when we did venture into one of the buildings they protected became as routine as dodging bottles, stepping around human excrement, and fighting off hypothermia on rooftops so windswept you had to lean in to keep from being knocked down. That way, we were sure that none of them could call up to whomever or whatever apartment we were sent to investigate and warn them we were coming.

When the residents of Coney Island's housing projects weren't preying on each other, they were preying on the cops sent into their buildings to protect them. Early in my rookie season in PSA 1 I was returning from Central Booking in a patrol car. I'd made an arrest earlier in the day—a drunk-and-disorderly scumbag hassling a couple of young Puerto Rican moms pushing strollers—and was due back at the Command to fill out more paperwork and end my shift. Our Command—the actual precinct house—was located in the ground floor of the Site Four and Five Houses. Site Four and Five was a multistory poured concrete rabbit warren so sprawling and generic that even seasoned cops would get completely lost in its hallways or not be able to give the correct address for where they were when calling Central for backup.

As I pulled into the Command parking lot I caught a white flash out of the corner of my eye and an entire refrigerator smashed into the ground like a meteor about a dozen feet ahead of my car hood. It sounded like someone had dropped a garbage truck. I froze until it dawned on me that if a stove was coming next, a patrol car roof was probably not going to stop it. Anyway, I couldn't move forward with the smashed fridge where it was. I cautiously got out of the car and, looking overhead the whole time, muscled the smashed Maytag onto a narrow stretch of sidewalk before I ran back to the car and hauled ass back to the Command.

"Some people will never like you in these projects, no matter what you do," Jack told Louie, Phil, and me early on. Like most of what Jack said, his observation about the people we policed was true. My Maytag encounter just underlined it.

It went both ways. Future lawbreakers take note: The system isn't a faceless, remorseless, hostile mechanism. It's a chain of people just like you doing their jobs. Everyone you encounter on your trip through the criminal justice system is shaped and controlled by the same stuff that made you break the law in the first place. Along the way to your final disposition—in jail, on parole, free to go, whatever—you will encounter people who are potentially as stupid, mean, crazy, guilty, noble, compassionate, smart, and every flavor of humanity in between as you are or aren't. The only difference between you and the cop that cuffs you is that he or she has the law on their side.

Make a cop, DA, judge, court officer, EMT, doctor or nurse's already mind-rippingly hard job harder, and you're making their life harder. Many of them will gladly return the favor. If you run on the cop that's arresting you, he's very likely to make it as difficult for you to get up once he's dropped you, as you made it for him to catch you. Beat up your spouse or your kid? Maybe your arresting officer grew up in a household with an asshole like you at the head of it. Or maybe the cop is an asshole like you that beats his kids, too. If so, you'd better watch every gesture you make. With you in cuffs the very real, very imperfect person or persons who have taken you into custody have found a way to potentially make things right with their past or their conscience even if just for a night, an hour, or a second. Maybe they'll make you stand next to an empty bench for half the night while they fill out paperwork instead of sit. Maybe they'll do something much, much worse.

Not long after our time in finishing school with Jack ended, my assigned partner and I responded to an assault call in the Surfside Houses. It was a "family dispute," two words a housing cop hears, says, and reads about as many times in their career as a priest encounters "amen" in his, that had boiled over into a stabbing. The husband in this particular troubled household had been using his wife for a punching bag until the missus got fed up, or in fear for her life, took a steak knife, and plunged it into her husband's thigh. My guess is that she was aiming for his balls. In any case, she'd been arrested for assault. We were sent to the happy couple's apartment to get follow-up statements from the husband. But when we arrived on the scene we discovered that he had already been removed to Coney Island Hospital.

"Help you, Officers?" A scowling doctor intercepted us at the nurses' station on the floor we'd been sent to when we inquired about the guy on our patrol car radio on the way to Coney Island Hospital. The MD seemed particularly pissed off. I figured the poor son of a bitch screaming from one of the treatment rooms probably had something to do with it. We explained to the doctor who we were looking for and he directed us to the alcove where the screaming was coming from. My partner pushed back the curtain and we went in. What we saw inside kept me from having a hard-on for a week.

The guy with the steak knife in his thigh had apparently pulled every stupid move in the book from the minute EMS arrived on the scene. He'd cursed out the cops, and the ambulance guys at home and in transit, fucked with the ER staff and every one of the doctors and nurses that examined his not altogether life-threatening wound. After knocking equipment over, trying to leave multiple times, bellowing about his rights and demanding to see his wife, his lawyer, and his mother to the point that even the sedated patients on the same floor were murmuring "shut up," someone on staff with access to a catheter took justice into their own rubber-gloved hands. The guy lay there in front of us with a tube sticking into the head of his dick that I swear was the width of a roll of quarters.

"Oh, we'll come back later. I can see that you're, uh, in pain," my partner stammered. We got out of there as quickly as we could, hoping that the image of what we'd seen wasn't burned into our memories forever.

One particularly cold night Lou, Phil, and I were freezing our asses off together outside a building complex on Neptune Avenue and West Thirty-fifth Street, nearly opposite where the Cyclones ballpark now stands. The only people dumb enough to be prowling around in that deep freeze were the three of us. Louie was obsessed with three things—the law, which he could quote chapter and verse, proper radio call jargon, which he had down from the day he put on the badge, and girls. Tonight it was girls.

"What about that window? There's a red light in it . . ." One of Jack's more casual briefings had touched on the fact that there were known to be prostitutes working out of individual apartments within the NYCHA buildings in PSA 1. Freezing and horny, Louie was playing spot the whorehouse and pointing from window to window up in the howling night sky.

"Let's get inside for a while," I said. I hadn't felt anything in my toes for long enough that it was starting to worry me.

"Great," Louie said. "We can go from door to door and listen for signs of struggle."

We went in the back entrance of the building. None of us had "the key" yet, but it didn't matter. The door was nearly off its hinges. Once inside we rubbed our hands and stomped our feet and tried to warm up as best we could for as long as we could.

"Damn, it's cold as a bitch," Louie said. His expression changed as he looked down at the floor. Philly and I saw it, too. There was a small piece of a grating missing from an access panel in the floor that maintenance guys used to get into the cavernous cellars of buildings like this one. We bent down to see what had happened and suddenly heard the sound of some kind of echoing commotion.

"What the fuck is going on down there?" I whispered.

"Fuckin' trespass and burglary for a start," Louie said. Philly nodded.

"Let's go down." There wasn't much clearance on either side of the hole. But I was pretty sure that I could wedge myself through. "I'll go first," I said and shoved my gun deep into my holster and turned my belt halfway to the side so that it wouldn't hang up on a corner on my way down into the basement. I hoped my .38 wouldn't blow my dick off.

The hole turned out to be more like a shaftway or duct like the ones Bruce Willis snuck around in *Die Hard*. After an eight-foot descent I emerged in a dimly lit basement whose half-football-field-long walls and low ceiling were lined with pipes, wires, and electrical conduit. Five thieves were tearing out copper wiring and fixtures on the far wall. As Philly and Louie dropped down the shaft one after the other, the five perps bolted. "Freeze," we yelled, nearly in unison. Then the lights went out. We were in complete darkness with a five-foot head clearance and were the only thing between five panicked crooks and the one way up to the surface.

One of the items that we were required to purchase at the academy was a huge metal flashlight called a mag. Department authorized mags gave off a nice solid beam of light and needed a lot of batteries to do it. The steel handle full of D cells made mags as efficient for breaking heads as a nightstick and most cops used them as much for putting out people's lights as illuminating a room. We immediately put ours to both uses.

I lit up the twenty or so feet in front of me just in time to see one perp running past me. I swung and the flashlight's business end caught the guy squarely on the bridge of his nose. He went tumbling to the ground and my light flicked out. I jumped in the dark at where I saw him fall, landed on his leg, and managed to cuff him by feel. Later, I realized what I thought was sweat on my hands was blood from his face. Philly and Louie loudly struggled with other guys elsewhere in the dark. After all of us ran around in circles trying to catch and elude each other for a few minutes, Philly found his mag, got it on again and we rounded up all but one of the would-be metal thieves.

Louie and I had managed to corner the final guy, but he was hurt and panicked and refused to obey our instructions to put his fucking hands in the fucking air. We couldn't shoot him just for being too freaked out to listen. Louie dropped to one knee, lunged forward, and swung his nightstick onto the guy's legs. The sound was sickening. I dove in and caught the guy full in the chin with an uppercut as he tipped forward. It made no difference—Louie's nightstick had already stopped the guy cold. And vice versa. The guy was holding his legs and Louie was holding half of his nightstick in his hand. Louie's cocobolo wood baton was top of the line. Getting hit with one of those sticks is like being hit with a cast-iron frying pan. I thought I'd just done an excellent impression of George Foreman dropping Joe Frazier but Louie hit the guy so hard his nightstick cracked in two on the guy's shins as if it was a piece of china. The guy dove into my punch as he doubled over in agony.

With all five perps cuffed up, and a van on the way to get us, we pushed our prisoners up on our shoulders, pulled them through the shaft, led the ones that could walk to the side of the building lobby, dragged the others, and arranged them together on the floor. It wasn't until we were outside that we really looked at each other. Between the trip down and up, the chasing, the fighting, and the arrests, it looked like we'd gone deer hunting for a week in our uniforms. A couple of the perps even cracked up.

Back at the Command the guy Louie wiped out was sent to Coney Island Hospital to see what could be done with his shattered shin bones. Most of the Command turned out to congratulate us. An underground battle royale burglary didn't happen in PSA 1 every day. The three of us were put in for commendations and we each had to tell the story so many times to so many people in so many hearings and on so many forms that we made a small fortune in overtime. I'd kicked some ass, made a great collar, and got a medal and OT. Not bad.

As much as PSA 1 seemed like it was the edge of the world, it was still Brooklyn, and it was still a neighborhood. As I walked my patrols I always made a point to say hello to people, to stop and talk when I could, and let it roll off my back when people looked away or said nothing back. One winter afternoon not long after the underground showdown, an elderly black woman who I recognized from the neighborhood came up to Louie, Philly, and me. I'd made a point of greeting her, to no real effect, for the months that I'd been on Coney Island. She was pretty anxious as she started to talk. Unable to make up her mind about which of us to speak to directly, she chose to look over my shoulder.

"This old white man is not allowed to leave his apartment. He's being held prisoner in his own home," she explained. "A group of young boys are holding him there. They even walk the old white man to the bank on the first of the month and have him cash his Social Security check, and hand it over to them."

We asked her to run down the particulars as she knew them—the building address, apartment, how long she believed this had been going on, and how many guys were holding the man. She didn't know his name and refused to give her own.

After thanking her and comparing our notes we headed

to the apartment the woman had described. I held my ear to the door. I don't know what I was listening for. Finally, Philly knocked. If the old man or better yet some thug kid answered, we stood a chance of getting in and finding out if what the woman said was true. If not, we'd have to pass it up the investigative chain of command. Nothing. We huddled in the stairwell.

"Fuck, now what?" I asked. Louie checked his watch.

"Well it's almost end of tour. We'll have to give the info to the detectives."

"Like hell we will," I said. "We got this information ourselves, we'll come back tomorrow ourselves." Louie and Philly shook their heads.

"We got to give the squad the info," Louie said.

"C'mon, we don't even know if we'll be assigned to these projects tomorrow," Philly chimed in.

"I'll talk to whoever does the roll call tomorrow," I pleaded. "I'll try and get us here tomorrow." Philly and Louie remained silent.

"What if the old guy gets killed tonight? What if the lady who tipped us decides to call nine-one-one?" Louie finally said. "We'll all fuckin' hang, Mike."

He was right. It was a risk I'd take on my own, but there were three careers at stake. When we got back to the Command the three of us turned over our notes to the detectives working that night. We took pains to let them know we wanted to stay as involved as we could.

"Good work, guys," Detective Weiss said. "We'll see what happens with this thing."

"Yeah," added his partner Detective Shea, "if anything comes of it you guys will be involved I promise."

Two days later it was on the cover of the *Post* and the *Daily News*: HELD HOSTAGE IN HIS OWN HOME. Both papers carried the same shots of a poor old guy with a long white beard being helped to an ambulance by the detectives Shea and Weiss. This was more than a collar, it was an event. I later heard that the prison product scumbags who'd been leaching off the old guy's SSA checks were also sodomizing him. The papers weren't exaggerating for once—the old guy wasn't just released, he was rescued from a hell in his own apartment.

It was an arrest that I'd initiated simply by insisting on saying hello to an old woman who didn't trust cops. None of us received anything—not a pat on the back, not a thank-you, not a nod from the captain. Both Philly and Louie later came to me and said we should have tried it my way.

First week of April, opening day at home at Yankee Stadium. I'd set out on patrol solo on foot close to where we'd broken up the underground burglary. A skinny white guy in a greasy Members Only jacket walking across Mermaid Avenue caught my eye. His gait was sort of nervously cyclical—like he didn't really have full control of his body. As I wondered what his problem might be, he bent down and picked something up off the sidewalk. That really got me interested.

One of the corners of human psychology that the people who built housing projects didn't give much weight to is the principle of out of sight, out of mind. A certain portion of residents living on high floors of project buildings will take for granted that any available window is a garbage chute. Empty cans, sprung mousetraps, newspapers, TV dinner

trays, diapers, tampons, broken furniture—just about anything that people didn't want in their homes could come
sailing out the windows of the Coney Island projects at any
hour of the day or night. "Coney Island whitefish," slang for
a used condom, didn't derive from the condoms that wash
ashore on the beach, it came from the fact that used condoms tossed out of the windows of the projects along Mermaid Avenue bloated and burst in the sun just like their
namesake would if they were beached on hot pavement.

"Who in their right fucking mind would pick anything
up off the sidewalk on Mermaid Avenue?" I asked myself.
What the guy picked up was a bottle cap, and I knew from
the blacked and burnt ones littering project roofs alongside syringes and glassines that junkies used them to cook
up their heroin and make it shootable. Gotcha! Beelining
across the street, I grabbed the guy and shoved him up
against a car. He was light as a feather and put up no fight
whatsoever. Keys, change, a wallet with a few bucks—there
was nothing in his pockets that justified my eureka moment. But he had a chemical stink on him that I would come
to recognize down the line and croaked at me in a whiny
voice that would also become synonymous with heroin users. Sure as shit, I reached into the waistband of his pants
and came up with five little envelopes of white powder that
were moist with sweat on the sides that had touched the
guy's torso. I cuffed him up and keyed my radio.

"Unit one-five-four, have a car respond to Thirtieth and
Mermaid, holding one."

"RMP nine-five-five-eight responding, ETA about two
minutes." A few minutes later I had the guy in the backseat
of an RMP en route to my Command.

Drug collars came with extra paperwork. But I happily filled out the narcotic voucher for the five bags, the online booking sheet, and the complaint report with an almost giddy knowledge that I'd made a good collar using good old-fashioned street smarts. It was the beginning of my shift, too, so it wasn't like I was going to clear a bunch of OT just for doing my job right. The sections of the online booking and the complaint report marked "details" weren't really for anything epic. As I'd learned from Jack, I simply put the least amount of information necessary to get the point across. As a housing cop I was only really supposed to make arrests within the confines of NYCHA property. The first rule of housing collar paperwork was to keep the location as vague as possible so that the arrest wouldn't be recorded by a city cop precinct or get questioned by your superiors in housing. "Defendant found to be in possession of five bags of heroin . . ."—short, simple, and to the point. The desk officer signed off on my paperwork and me and my prisoner were transported to Brooklyn Central Booking. More signatures, more paperwork, and my bottle cap collector was lodged in a holding cell and I had a date with an assistant district attorney who would take over from me and prosecute the guy I had collared.

Brooklyn employed dozens of ADAs. Theirs was an assembly-line gig of interviews, depositions, hearings, and trials. ADAs sought the maximum penalty or a plea bargain leveraged to their advantage that made them look good in the eyes of their bosses. The first part of any criminal case they put together was an interview with the arresting officer. I sat and waited to be called by the ADA assigned to my arrest in a room full of other cops crammed onto a big smelly sofa, two old leather chairs, and a row of what appeared to be church pews. An old black-and-white TV played reruns of *The Honeymooners*. Three hours later I heard my name called. I grabbed my jacket and followed an overweight chain-smoking Irish ADA down a hall to an office the size of a broom closet.

The ADA pressed his ass into a small steel desk chair and coughed out an introduction.

"I'm ADA McBride," he said. "Take a seat and tell me what you got." I let him get up to speed by reading my paperwork before I started.

"Well, I was on the corner of Thirtieth and Mermaid and I saw a guy who looked like a junkie. He bent down and picked up a bottle cap." McBride shut my folder and looked at me sharply. "I had a feeling I knew what he was going to use the bottle cap for so I—" He yanked himself out of the chair and stood up.

"You had a 'feeling,' Officer?" He didn't wait for my answer. "We don't work on feelings, guesses, or assumptions here. This is the Brooklyn district attorney's office. You better not come in here and tell me you had a feeling, or a goddamn hunch, then decided you'd search this guy and throw out all his constitutional rights while you were at it!"

McBride went on for a while about the sanctity of his job, the law, and a half dozen other things. I didn't know how to answer. After a while I realized he wasn't looking for an answer. Finally he lit another cigarette, waddled around me, and headed back out to the hallway.

"I'll be right back, Officer. When I get back you should have a different perspective of how this collar went down." I was stunned. I was also pissed—pissed at myself for allowing this fat fuck to talk to me that way, pissed at Jack for not preparing me with the answers this guy wanted, and pissed even more because I'd used good judgment to make what I thought was a good arrest that now was in jeopardy of being thrown out because that intuition and common sense didn't line up with the inflexible letter of the law.

McBride's office walls were lined with plaques and certificates recognizing his successful convictions. These prosecutions, I thought, all involved arrests made by cops, and all involved working with those arresting cops and not yelling at them. McBride, like any other ADA, wanted to prosecute perps successfully. I was there not to tell my side of the story but to supply him with the right argument and right tools for him to do that. His self-righteous lecture and hasty exit were his way of telling a rookie cop to get his shit together and make himself useful.

When McBride came back to his office a few minutes later his cigarette was augmented with a cup of coffee, and he seemed much calmer.

"So, okay, now what happened here, Mike?" He took a puff.

"Well," I began, "I was walking on Thirtieth and Mermaid when this guy walks out of a building counting bags of dope." McBride smiled and nodded.

"Yeah? Go on. And what happened next?"

"Well, since the dope was in plain view, I walked up to him, took the dope right out of his hand, and placed him under arrest. I then called for backup and read him his rights while we waited."

"Congratulations, Mike. Very nice collar," ADA McBride replied, "very nice police work."

Juggling "behave-a yourself," "have fun," and "don't get caught," wasn't much different with a badge in Coney Island than it was with a bat in Canarsie.

Avenue D

Davey Blue Eyes is almost singlehandedly responsible for the consolidation of dope sales in lower Manhattan. If other people try to set up shop elsewhere, they either pay back to Davey, or suffer the consequences. As more snitches open up about Davey, I hear more about his keen interest in the other members of the greater New York narcotics rackets.

The name Miguel Lopez is rarely spoken above a whisper by those who know what it means. Lopez is the poster child for the new Colombian drug gangs that operated on the fringe of the city's drug trade in the seventies. The Colombians move into the criminal mainstream when cocaine surges in popularity and Nicky Barnes turns state's evidence and wipes out the remains of Frank Lucas's Harlem smack trade. Lopez's cocaine mini-empire is made possible by connections with Medellin Cartel kingpin Pablo Escobar. And his sovereignty is symbolized by his trademark—a small glass jar full of human molars and eyeteeth that his associates take from the mouths of the guys Lopez orders killed for transgressions and slights of any kind. Lopez flashes the jar like a badge, gently clicking the contents like a voodoo rattle.

Halloween 1985 in Douglaston, Queens. When one of his

street runners is discovered skimming, Lopez makes a call. The doorbell rings at a mid-block Cape. George Reyes and his wife Celia open the door. A punch bowl full of candy rests on an end table that's been moved into the hallway behind them.

"Trick or treat!" a half-dozen kids all shriek at once. There's a princess, a Batman, a vampire, a ghost, a Frankenstein, a mermaid, a Hulk, and a pirate. Behind the little kids stand three bigger, older kids. Two Batman masks and a Spider-man—just masks, their costumes are everyday work clothes and a jogging suit. Celia hands out the candy and the two big Batmans and Spider-man shove the kids into the entry-way. Celia falls backward onto the carpeting and five of the kids tumble over her. The Batmen grab the other three kids by the pants and wrangle them into the living room. Spider-man shuts the door and locks it. Some of the kids are scream-ing. Some think it's funny and laugh. Nobody's hurt yet. Celia scrambles to get up. She and George are very scared.

George turns and runs. There's a shotgun in the bedroom and a pistol in the kitchen. Spider-man walks a spray of bul-lets from a silenced nine-millimeter MAC-10 up George's spine and George spins and pitches forward into the hallway. Spider-man takes off his mask to see better and hands his gun to a Batman who herds the kids into the living room. All the furniture is covered in plastic. The television blares the news. The other Batman holds Celia's right arm behind her back at an awkward angle, with a revolver pressed to her forehead. The muzzle makes a red ringed dent on her skin. She isn't making a sound. Just shaking. Some of the kids are sobbing.

Spider-man comes out of the kitchen with a black-handled butcher's knife. George is still alive, spinal cord cut, legs useless, pulling himself down the hall. Spider-man grabs him by his slack ankles and drags him into the bedroom. He closes the door.

Celia starts to struggle as George disappears into the bedroom leaving a trail of blood and spit on the hallway runner. Batman hits her across the face with his pistol. She falls to her knees bleeding from her mouth and nose. The kids start to scream and the other Batman shoots out the television. The kids quiet.

Spider-man pulls George's body back out of the bedroom and the kids scream again. George's throat is slit and his tongue, impossibly long if you've only ever seen the part you lick and talk with, pulled through the gash. It's obscene. Blood is everywhere. Spider-man reaches into his jacket pocket and takes out a pair of pliers. He puts his foot on George's forehead, seizes a molar and adjusting for the salty slippery blood pooling in George's mouth, yanks as hard as he can, tearing out a full tooth, roots and all. Sweat drips from Spidey's nose. Tears run down the faces of the kids. Several of them put their faces on the wall and cover their eyes.

Spider-man motions to Batman. He fires the revolver. Celia's body jumps once and then she lays still on the carpet she vacuumed that morning. Spider-man sinks the knife into her throat and gives her a necktie. It's easier with women—no adam's apple. He rolls her lifeless head to one side and extracts a tooth from her as well. The three assassins leave the children alive. They'll never be able to describe the killers to the cops and probably never be able to watch Spider-man or Batman cartoons again. Anyway Lopez paid for two teeth, not ten.

The Batmans drag the bodies down the steps, over the sidewalk and into a waiting van. There are still groups of kids in costume going from house to house. The three men get into a Mercedes-Benz and slowly drive out of the neighborhood. The van vanishes in the direction of Long Island.

The message isn't lost on anyone Lopez deals with. But for Davey, it's a throwdown. A few weeks after the anonymous Halloween "gangland slaying" the papers described, Davey Blue Eyes decides to make Miguel Lopez his bitch. Lopez is selling in Manhattan, and Davey wants a piece. Through channels, Lopez tells Davey to go fuck himself. Davey sends his own trio to Roosevelt Avenue in Queens. They position themselves outside an after-hours joint run by one of Lopez's associates and gun the man down, leaving him to bleed out in front of his own bar. Lopez gets the message—have a sit-down with Davey Blue Eyes and settle the dispute.

A sit-down is arranged in the VIP section of an uptown nightclub. Lopez bribes the bouncers to disconnect the club's metal detector but Davey does the same thing and arrives with twice as many gunmen two hours earlier. No shots were fired, but a deal was cut. Lopez keeps the terms to himself. Nobody in his crew that was there ever mentions it again. It's left up to Davey to remind anyone working for Lopez who they answer to now. A couple of months later, Davey Blue Eyes is driving down Essex Street, when he sees a few of Lopez's crew leaving Castillo de Jagua burping garlic and cerveza Bavaria. Davey slows down, comes alongside, rolls down his window, and nods. Lopez's three gunmen make a point of ignoring him. Davey drives around the block and stops in front of them. He reaches his hand out the window and shows them Lopez's trademark jar of teeth. One of the three traquetos he's accosted is responsible for pulling at least a half dozen of them. Davey looks through the glass at the three men and shakes it. They hear the shake loud and clear and get the meaning even clearer—"You may work for Lopez, but he works for me now. Respect that or you'll be making this jar louder next time."

Seven

A cop can get shot, fall off a roof, crippled in a patrol car crash, or get beaten into a permanent coma with their own nightstick. I've known uniforms who had those things happen to them. But apathy can end a policeman's effective life just as completely as a bullet in the face. The next of kin of the cop killed on the job gets a lump sum check from the union, death benefit money from the city, a flag and a handshake from the mayor. A police officer who doesn't give a shit and stays on the job collects a bimonthly check himself.

From those first years in Coney Island through every posting in a two-decade career I've worked around a certain percentage of men and women clocking in, suiting up, and falling out after roll call only to spend each shift counting the seconds to their retirement. "Twenty and out"—that was the mantra for the beat cop who allowed himself to get stuck in a tar pit of fear and apathy. The only ambition these cops had was to get themselves into a precinct or specialized unit that allowed them to mark time for two decades, rubber stamp their way into some overtime and a promotion or two, and retire with a decent pension the second their contracted obligation to the people of the city of New York was up.

I was the opposite. Amid all the shrugging, gallows humor, and bullshit, I discovered in Coney that being a cop was a unique opportunity. First—the job allowed me to put bad guys in jail. It may not have been clear to me why I sat down and took the police exam after high school, but within a week of wearing a badge and a gun I was sure as shit glad that I did. People, especially people in the projects, needed help getting on with their lives when they were forced to live sandwiched between predatory scumbags. I felt obliged to help them out. Second—police work gave me what I'd looked for and found my whole life—fun, my kind of fun. I needed action, plain and simple. Running down and collaring up perps was simply the most fun I'd ever had.

Being a cop was the greatest thing in the world because helping out and a knock-around good time went hand in hand. The tension and risk that drove a lot of NYPD rank and file into an RMP with the windows rolled up or behind a desk until retirement was exactly what I craved. And unlike tear-assing around the MTA tracks, rolling pimps on Forty-second Street with my friends from Canarsie, or risking seven to ten years behind bars for jacking Joker Poker machines in Red Hook, I was doing the right thing. When I busted skells, I felt good *and* I was doing good. I was having "behave-a yourself" both ways. The irony was, as I learned on the street and in the courthouse, that if I worked by the rules, I wouldn't put anyone in jail or get any kicks.

The problem with Coney Island was that 99 percent of the workload was the kind of stuff that fed apathetic cops justification for showing up and doing nothing. Standing by while EMS techs carted off the sick and lonesome in aided cases, refereeing "he said, she said" arguments in domestic disputes, and other small-time, minimally adrenaline-inducing nickel-and-dime crime complaints wasn't for me. The only surefire way I found in uniform to feed my legal addiction to higher stakes police work was through drug busts.

After that first highly educational smack arrest on Mermaid Avenue and schooling at the hands of ADA McBride, I began asking and looking around PSA 1 for more of the same. But while I found a few decent narcotics collars, I also found that the drug business in Coney Island was small potatoes. A liquor store on Twenty-fifth and Mermaid that sold coke and dope along with MD 20/20 and Alizé yielded a few trips to Central Booking. Even on that handful of busts, I already had a better narcotic arrest and conviction average after a little over a year on the job than some cops managed for their whole career. As far as uniform NYPD beat cops were concerned, I had more collars than any of them would ever have until the rules changed in the nineties.

The housing police didn't have any rule forbidding uniform rank and file from making drug busts so I was under no obligation to observe drug dealers and junkies like they were endangered wildlife. If I saw a deal go down, I made a collar. If I could hide behind a car and sneak up on a junkie shooting or snorting a bag, I snatched him up. If I suspected drug activity, I was free to do whatever I thought had to be done. And I wasn't just able, I was willing. But the drug trade in the Coney Island projects couldn't hold a candle to what was going on a river away on the Lower East Side. It had been that way for years and in the making for centuries.

Young Charlie Lucky's entrepreneurial streak was something to behold. Even when working that "crumb" job clerking at the hat factory on the Lower East Side in his teens, he'd used his employer's shipping department (and hat boxes) to transport heroin to dealers and in turn customers on the East Side waterfront. The smack trade that Luciano helped get on its feet in the first quarter of the twentieth century had a future brighter than even Lucky could foresee, and the dope that he sold had its own pedigree dating back thousands of years. Growing poppies for opium rivals prostitution for the title of "world's oldest profession." The Mesopotamians were in the drug business more than three thousand years before Christ was born. Poppies thrived in the "cradle of civilization" climate and opium literally oozed out of them.

The good news was that opium could be good medicine. Whether losing a gangrenous leg to the saw, quelling the effects of dysentery, or giving a raving madman whose brain was ravaged by syphilis a little artificial serenity, most medical procedures went better with a ball of opium in the belly or a cloud of it in the lungs. The bad news, of course, was it was addictive as hell. Opium's narcotic effect romanced the human brain so suavely that what started out as doctor's orders could easily become the only thing that mattered. Eating or smoking the gooey black tar cast a euphoric spell and extended an addictive grip that spanned civilizations and held for centuries. Languages, customs, religions, political systems, and trade routes came and went, but opium stayed. Its manufacture was easy, its initial effects glorious, and its enslavement, though initially subtle, could be nearly unshakable.

If opium was just a medicinal blessing and a recreational curse, it might have gone away eventually. But what really put it over is that it was incredible business. The demand opium created in the brains of the people addicted to it was a conscience-free capitalist's dream come true, as long as he controlled the supply. The British not only traded and sold it in the Far East, they seized on it as insurance against uprisings when they helped themselves to what they could grab of China. An alternately stoned or jonesing populace couldn't really raise their axes together to throw off their shackles if they were occupied with scoring, dosing, and floating away.

Opium changed the map but morphine, a distillation of the active ingredient in opium discovered in the first years of the nineteenth century, changed medicine. The chemical process that created morphine became one of the procedural backbones of pharmaceutical pioneering. Morphine synthesis opened the door for a whole dynasty of chemical step-children, from caffeine to cocaine. The doctors and chemists who began prescribing morphine and putting it in various patent medicines and mixtures believed they had solved the problem of how to numb people's brains for good reasons without stringing them out and fucking up their lives. All the inventors of morphine really succeeded in doing was cranking up the potency and streamlining the whole process of getting wasted and hooked, especially after the invention of the hypodermic needle in 1824.

Alfred Nobel, the inventor of dynamite, and Hiram Maxim, the inventor of the machine gun, each believed that they had come up with an innovation so ruthlessly lethal that it would cause the world to see the error of humanity's addiction to conflict and stop waging war forever. In his inaugural address, Abraham Lincoln famously referenced "the better angels" of human nature. Like Nobel and Maxim, the scientists and doctors who kept trying to civilize opium just didn't count on what might be called "the bitter angels" that drove people to shoot each other, blow each other up, do dope to check out on life, and deal it to get rich. On the eve of a new century, an ambitious thirty-eight-year-old German chemist named Heinrich Dresser helped midwife a host of bitter angels. Dresser not only streamlined opium and morphine, he supercharged it and the illegal narcotics trade in the process.

Dresser was an accomplished second-generation scientist with a full professorship at Bonn University. An old school European clotheshorse with a taste for the finer things in life, Dresser was keenly aware that scientific discovery could go hand-and-in hand with financial opportunity. While four years in an academic ivory tower did a lot for Dresser's prestige, it did nothing for his bank account. He turned his back on academia and cut a research and development deal with Johann Friedrich Weskott and Friedrich Bayer—two aging businessmen and chemists who had been successful in the commercial dye-making business.

In much the same way that some companies sought to extend their corporate lives in the early 1990s by expanding into computers, Weskott and Bayer sought to diversify into the growing field of patent medicines. In exchange for ceding professional credit and patent rights for synthesizing new drugs, Dresser would steer Bayer's research and development division on the most commercial course possible. What Dresser got out of the deal was a tidy profit royalty for each successful drug his team worked up and he green-lit.

Like Lucky Luciano, Dresser knew his clientele and he knew his times. The leading causes of death in 1890s Europe were pneumonia and tuberculosis. How best to wipe out these diseases was still being debated, but Dresser understood that the main symptom of pneumonia and TB evoked uniform terror in layman and doctor alike. Both illnesses were characterized by a racking, hacking, phlegm-spouting cough. When anyone with TB or pneumonia coughed they shot an aerosol of infection into the public air. The contaminated phlegm they coughed up and carelessly spat onto the sidewalk got tracked into homes, schools, hospitals, and everywhere else on the soles of the shoes of the uninfected and the sick alike. In the minds of most of Dresser's contemporaries, particularly in big cities, a hacking cough was a potential gateway to the morgue and combating it was the foremost challenge to the 1890s medical establishment. Giving doctors a wonder elixir that would calm their patients hacking with ten times the strength of codeine, the current star in the opium-derivative stable, would make Dresser and the company bearing Bayer's name rich.

Also, like Charlie Lucky, Dresser understood the value of building on the groundwork of others. The scientific boom of synthesizing opium into morphine had quickly turned into a social bust. Morphine in various patent medicines and over-the-counter mixtures like laudanum became the mother's little helper of their era. Scores of housewives, professionals, and even kids began to beat a path to the family medicine chest when withdrawal threatened their fragile narcotic health. Conventional scientific wisdom of the day suggested that refining and strengthening opium's good side—ending pain—would somehow defeat its bad side—an addictive component that ruined people's lives.

In 1874, a British chemist named C. R. Alder Wright spent a few months tinkering with morphine in the hopes of finding a less addictive alternative. Toward that end, Wright—the future author of *The Threshold of Science*, a textbook that collected "simple and amusing experiments" for beginning scientists—conducted a simple, successful, and ultimately catastrophic experiment that wouldn't make it into his book. By boiling a quantity of morphine and a chemical agent over a stove for several hours, Wright got a saucepan full of an extremely potent opium derivative that cooked down and dried up into a fine, light-catching white powder.

After Wright sent the powdered result to a colleague for testing on animals, he received a description that anyone who's ever been around junkies will find all too familiar. Among the grocery list of effects that test dogs showed after being dosed, were, Wright's consultant wrote, "eyes being sensitive . . . pupils constrict . . . considerable salivation . . . slight tendency to vomiting . . . respiration was at first quickened, but subsequently reduced . . . the heart's action was diminished, and rendered irregular . . . marked want of coordinating power over the muscular movements . . . loss of power in the pelvis and hind limb." What the dogs couldn't tell their Dr. Feelgood was how high they were or how much they'd like some more once that first dose wore off.

More a researcher than a businessman, Wright took note of what he learned and moved on to those "simple and amusing" lab pursuits that would wind up in his book. A few decades later, at Dresser's urging, a Bayer staff chemist named Hoffman duplicated C. R. Wright's results. Measured purely for its cough suppressant abilities, the substance, diacetylmorphine, was substantially more effective than morphine or codeine. Test subjects with advanced respiratory problems reported that this new drug nearly wiped out their coughs (in a late seventies interview the Rolling Stones' Keith Richards said one of the upsides of smack addiction was that he never had another head or chest cold once he became a junkie). The test group also characterized their experiences as having an additional side effect of a powerful and very pleasant euphoria that brought with it a quality of *heroisch*—the feeling of being safe, emotionally cocooned, and impervious to pain and harm of any kind—in a word, heroic. Dresser dosed himself and agreed.

As a bonus, Dresser's new product could be marketed as a nonaddictive improvement on morphine, which now claimed some three hundred thousand addicts in the United States alone. Just as the original advocates of morphine became convinced that refining the pure opium experience would combat addiction, Dresser and his team persuaded themselves that their new cough mixture and pain medication, called heroin after its apparently irrelevant euphoric side effect, would quell the morphine epidemic, too.

In November 1898, Dresser presented Bayer's new drug to the Congress of German Naturalists and Physicians. Medication at the time was distributed primarily by physicians, so Dresser's pitch was the single most important step in Bayer's march to the marketplace. The Industrial Revolution was a boon for doctors and the pharmaceutical companies that supplied them. People never before had so many new ways to get sick and so many corresponding ways to treat their symptoms. The world's physicians looked to the group and their annual meetings as a forecast and update on what was new and noteworthy. Treatment with heroin would, Dresser told the medical congress, control coughing like never before and help well-to-do addicts and their well-compensated doctors end their morphine addictions with little withdrawal discomfort.

Dresser's presentation received thunderous applause and offers of support from the assembled members of the medical community. Bayer wasted no time shipping thousands of free samples with illustrated labels depicting a lion and a globe behind the brand name "Heroin" to doctors all over Europe and the United States. Company literature trumpeted their new invention as "preeminently adapted for the manufacture of cough elixirs, cough balsams, cough drops, cough lozenges, and cough medicines of any kind." The *Boston Medical and Surgical Journal* agreed, adding that heroin "possesses many advantages over morphine," particularly that, "it's not hypnotic, and there's no danger of acquiring a habit." Within eighteen months, Bayer was exporting over a ton of heroin to some twenty-three countries. The U.S. had a growing constituency of middle-class morphine addicts and doctors eager to believe the truly bizarre premise that a stronger version of the same thing would straighten them out. A pre-FDA America in which "the business of America is business" attitude applied to drugs, and middle-class consumers held a general obsession with spoon and bottle and magic bullet "cures," bit into heroin like a grizzly into an Eagle Scout.

Lucky Luciano wasn't averse to a little opium now and then himself and at a business level he knew a good, bad thing when he saw it. Dope wasn't just stronger than morphine; it was a hell of a lot easier to ship. In its basic powder form, junk was compact and light. It was also easy to resell at a markup. Cutting or stepping-on pure heroin with a benign and inexpensive powder of a similar consistency like milk sugar or baby laxative was a no muss, no fuss proposition. No wonder large quantities of the drug began to vanish from the labs making it and reappear for resale on the waterfront and tenements of the Lower East Side. With the right raw materials (opium, a couple of processing chemicals, and something to cook them in) heroin was a breeze to make as well. Bootleg heroin, the narcotic equivalent of bathtub gin, began to change hands on the black market alongside the bonded stuff.

The shine came off the crystalline new wonder drug pretty quickly. After their initial narcotic honeymoon ended, patients treated with heroin began to need higher and more frequent doses of the drug just to function. The "hypnotic" quality the Boston medical journal declared nonexistent wasn't just a risk, it was inevitable. By 1905, there were already over 180 clinical reports from American doctors confirming the dangers of continued heroin use. Nevertheless, the following year the American Medical Association approved heroin for prescription use. If higher doses were what the doctor ordered, then Bayer was only too happy to oblige. Whatever Bayer and physicians couldn't, and eventually weren't allowed to provide, the East Coast mob would gladly supplement for a price.

Police noted a sharp spike in crime and a disturbingly high incidence of perps who turned out to be heroin addicts, particularly in New York. The U.S. government responded by passing regulating laws on opium, morphine, and heroin in 1914. By 1924, heroin was for all intents and purposes illegal in the U.S. and Bayer was out of the smack business completely. But the genie was out of the bottle. American dealers like Three Fingers Brown and Lucky Luciano laid pipe for an international heroin conduit whose spigot was located in New York.

No matter what anyone may have said in *The Godfather,* nobody in the Mafia was able to resist milking a cash cow as lucrative as dope. The Luccheses reached out to the Corsican mob, the Genovese and Gambino families to the French and pre-Castro Cuba. The New York families didn't just sell dope on their hometown streets, they middle-manned it to organized crime outfits in Chicago, Kansas City, San Francisco, and elsewhere. Once Prohibition was repealed, the Mafia, rich from the spoils of the illegal liquor racket, foregrounded heroin as a central illegal commodity. Through the thirties and forties what began in America as a legal middle-class drugstore abuse became a criminal problem initially confined mostly to working-class whites. With organized crime's help, heroin was here to stay and New York remains its black-market American hometown today.

Dresser meanwhile grew wealthy and increasingly eccentric. His arrogance and habit of bringing a fat pet dachshund with him everywhere alienated his more straitlaced lab-coated colleagues. It didn't matter. The marketplace fallback that made Dresser rich enough to leave the pharmaceutical business behind and that kept Bayer afloat was another drug synthesized on Dresser's watch—ASA, or, as it became known commercially, aspirin. Set up in an academic research institute bearing his name, Dresser was beyond the pain of embarrassment. He may have been beyond pain of any kind. Rumors circulated that he was not only heroin's biggest champion but also a user himself. He died rich the same year that the United States pulled the plug of legal use and manufacture of his great discovery. The legacy he inadvertently left behind was Bayer aspirin and generations of fucked-up lives in the addict capital—New York City—and all over the world.

The memory of those dealers I'd seen selling heroin at the Avenue D projects on the way to the police academy was still fresh. Dope was where the action was and Alphabet City was where the dope was. As soon as I had enough time in, I put in a transfer to PSA 4 on the Lower East Side. Jack caught wind of it almost before the ink was dry on the forms.

"What's this I hear about you going to the City?" he asked me after roll call.

"Yeah, I'm transferring," I told him. There wasn't much more to be said and I already was feeling a little guilty.

"Well be careful down there," Jack offered. "There's a lot of dope, a lot of cash, and where there's cash there's dirty cops and where there's dirty cops, there's IA."

I shrugged my shoulders. "I'll be okay, Jack."

He gave me a weird smile for a second, and then walked away. I could tell he was disappointed—disappointed that I didn't see Coney Island as enough of a challenge or a home as he did and disappointed that whatever camaraderie he'd awakened between Philly, Louie, and me wouldn't be enough for us all to keep working together. We were a big success for him, and he was proud of us.

If I had any doubts about Alphabet City being where the action was, they didn't last long. I logged my first dope bust there before I even officially reported for duty. A few weeks before I was scheduled to start working I dropped by my new Command to check things out. After dumping some stuff in my locker, I decided to take a drive around my new beat. What I saw was shocking. Even though it was January and one of the coldest days so far that year, there were dope deals taking place on nearly every corner I passed. Junkies and dealers shivered together, exchanged dope and money, and parted company. A group of users followed one after the other into an abandoned building lobby being used as a "toilet" or a designated spot to shoot up indoors. Some nodded in front of liquor stores. Others stumbled out into the street from between parked cars. Seemingly immune to the cold and gravity, one guy stood on the corner of Avenue D and Fourth Street bent over nearly ninety degrees at the waist in a full nod without toppling over. As I turned the corner I saw him take a tiny step forward to sort of regain his balance, even though he was dead to the world. Predatory kids were just about licking their chops as they gathered in small groups and eyed potential victims among the visiting dope users who had to get in, cop, and get out without being robbed. It was worse than what I saw driving to the academy a few years before. But now I had a badge and a few years in so it just looked like there was a collar on every corner.

I knew that if I was really going to catch bad guys, I was going to have to bend the rules to do it. And if you're going to improvise, you need people around you that aren't married to the *Patrol Guide*, either. One of the guys I met at the academy was a kid named Gio from a Brooklyn neighborhood like mine. Growing up in a neighborhood with divided loyalties gave me a pretty accurate moral barometer and I recognized the same thing in him. Gio was clearly a knock-around guy and like me took a similar outlook when it came to doing things 100 percent by the book. Crooks always operate on the assumption that the ends justify the means. And I knew for myself and I suspected in Gio that we both had a similar philosophy when it came to our side of the law.

Gio had turned up in PSA 1 for a few weeks during part of his training. We'd worked together then and kept in touch after he was transferred to Alphabet City. When I told him I was making the move to his precinct, he set the wheels in motion at his command and arranged with his sergeant for the two of us to be in the same squad once I got there. Part of the deal he cut was an unofficial agreement that we'd work the roughest sector of what was already a really rough piece of criminal real estate.

After my driving tour of the LES, I met up with Gio and his partner Gene, who I'd be replacing once I started work for real.

"You guys looking to collar up?" I asked them, window to window with their marked RMP.

"Sure," Gio said, sizing me up. "Why not? If you can get us a collar, of course we'll take it." We didn't know each other's sense of humor yet and the way Gio said it, I felt like he thought he was calling my bluff. I wasn't bluffing.

"Cool," I said. "How about I go back outside and look and see who's dealing. I'll find somebody, make sure he's dirty and come back and get you guys. How's that?" Gio nodded.

"Okay." Gene shrugged and nodded, too.

I slipped my snubnose .38 deep down the small of my back, put handcuffs in my pocket, threw my badge under the front seat, got out of my car and headed for Avenue C and Fifth Street, just a few blocks away from where we had met up. Sure enough, right on the corner in front of me was a Hispanic guy standing around in the freezing cold, looking sort of pissed off and resigned to the fact that he wasn't going home anytime soon. It dawned on me suddenly that I'd never done this before. Sure I'd nailed junkies coming out of a liquor store front on Coney Island, and collared guys for possession, but I'd never bought drugs off anyone in my life, let alone pretended to in order to arrest them. What if he ignored me? What if he ran for it?

It turned out that I didn't have much to worry about. There wasn't much to it. The fucking guy started talking to me as I walked up to him.

"What you need, *papi*? H or coke? I got D and C, aw'right?" I felt like an idiot, or a Boy Scout. I wasn't sure what H or D was, or even if that was what he said. He had a squeaky mumble that was already familiar to me. While I searched for an answer he jerked his head at the corner behind me. I turned around. A regular uniform cop was stamping his feet against the cold.

"Fuck that cop," I told him. H was probably heroin and D stood for dope, but I wasn't positive and went with the sure thing, "Give me five bags of coke," I said. He nodded.

"Chill here, *papi*, I'll be right back." The second he was out of sight I hustled back to the block where I'd left Gio and his partner.

"G, I got you guys a seller," I told them. "He's wearing a short brown pleather jacket with a hooded sweatshirt underneath. He'll be on C and Fifth Street in five minutes." Gio smirked at me. He still thought I might be fucking with him.

"Okay," he said. "See you there in five."

When I arrived back at the dealer's corner he was there. I walked up to him and he grinned. The smile vanished as I yanked out my cuffs and lunged at him. Off balance, he was easy to spin around. I gave him a little help with a shove between the shoulder blades and he slammed into the side of a parked car. He struggled for a second. I smacked him in the head and he wised up and let me finish clicking the cuffs on him without a fight. Gio and Gene pulled up in their marked RMP right on cue.

"Here you go," I told them as I handed the guy over. Gio searched the dealer and came up with the five bags of coke I'd asked for. As Gene shepherded the guy into the backseat of their patrol car Gio looked at me for a second in silence.

"You cool with this?" I asked him.

"Yeah, sure this is cool," he said. He didn't sound so sure.

"You know what to tell the DA when you go to Central Booking, right?" I asked in a lowered voice.

"No, tell me," Gio answered even quieter.

"It's simple. Just tell the ADA you saw this guy with the dope counting them out like a goddamn blackjack dealer, okay?"

"That's it?" Gio asked.

"Fuck yeah, that's it. Just charge him with the possession, not the sale, and everyone will be happy about the whole thing. It'll be an easy misdemeanor collar for you and Gene."

"Okay, yeah, good idea." Gio and I shook hands. He seemed more relaxed. "See ya in a few weeks," Gio said. "Thanks for the collar. Don't forget, I got the locker right next to mine for you. Don't let anyone in the Command tell you it's taken, okay?"

I nodded at Gene and waved good-bye to the perp.

As I drove back to Canarsie, I wondered if what I had just done was entrapment. If it was, so what? I really didn't give a fuck. He was a drug dealer, so screw him. It felt good to put a guy like that in cuffs and in a cruiser on the way to Central Booking. I figured Gio would make the collar stick and thought of McBride and his plaques. All Gio had to do was keep his story simple and stick to it. It was his first time but not his last and it was probably going to get easier to do each time.

C

Avenue D

Felix Pardo is a high roller moving big quantities of dope to Brooklyn, New Jersey, and Queens. He doesn't sell to anyone on the D so he's not directly my problem. I'm curious about him, though. I know a lot about Felix from our snitches. Supposedly he's been dealing with Chinese gangs his whole life. His parents are from the Dominican Republic and barely speak English but Felix is fluent in Cantonese, English, and Spanish. He's supposed to be an okay guy for what he is. Someone points him out to me and I'm surprised how innocent and ordinary he looks. He's not dressed in flash clothes or rings, doing a macho gangsta prison yard walk, or driving some eye-grabbing jeep. If it weren't for the nearly six-foot blond Puerto Rican girl covered in jewelry holding his hand he would have looked like a kid in grad school. Word on the street is that for some reason the big guys on Third and D hate Felix. Davey Blue Eyes himself has supposedly taken a particular dislike to Felix. So have Davey's sometime allies and assassins from Cherry Street, the Navarro brothers. There isn't much rhyme or reason for the animosity, but in their world there doesn't have to be.

One night Felix comes out of a Pathmark on Pike Street along with his cousin, an accounting student at City College.

His cousin doesn't notice a customized Mertz with black tinted windows that glides into gear as they cross the parking lot, but Felix makes it instantly. The car draws close and Felix shoves his cousin and tells him to run like hell. They drop the Heinekens they just bought and take off like shots. Felix knows the terrain and heads down an alley that looks left over from the nineteenth century and is too narrow and uneven for the Mercedes to get through. His cousin follows him. But when they get to the far end the car is already there. A rear door opens and they see Davey Blue Eyes pointing two nine millimeter pistols at their balls. "Get in," Davey says to Felix. The two cousins look at the guns and each other, Felix gets into the Mertz, and the door slams. A moment later Davey's window rolls down. "A hundred thousand tomorrow," Davey says to Felix's cousin. "A hundred thousand or his mother never sees him again. Right here, tomorrow six a.m." The cousin waits until the car drives off, runs to a payphone and passes the message on to Señora Pardo. Before she's hung up the phone she's rummaging in the back of her closets for the dozen shoeboxes of cash Felix stashed there. She hangs up the phone and starts counting out bills.

The following morning Davey's Mertz pulls up and Felix's mother is there at the curb watching. A rear window slides down just far enough to accommodate the shoebox Felix's cousin has under his arm. The cousin pushes the box through, the window goes back up, and the Pardos wait while somebody inside counts. A short while later the door opens, Felix tumbles out onto the street and the car roars away. Even from fifty feet away Felix's mother can see that her son spent a lot of the previous ten hours having the shit kicked out of him. She fights back the urge to scream at Felix's bruised and bloodied face. It's better after his cousin helps him up. At least he's alive, no sense in attracting attention.

Eight

Brooklynites have had such a love–hate relationship with Manhattan that we even refer to it as "the City," as if we lived on the prairie. No amount of Brooklyn pride could change the fact that Manhattan had two dubious distinctions over the rest of New York. One—rents were higher. Two—compared to Brooklyn, Queens, Staten Island, and even the Bronx, in the eighties, the heroin trade on the Lower East Side was off the hook. Everything else about the neighborhood was, too.

I saw a fifties science-fiction movie on TV once when I was a kid. In the movie a lost civilization builds a miles-wide underground machine allowing everyone on their planet to instantly transform thoughts into flesh-and-blood reality. When astronauts from Earth arrive on the planet the civilization that made the machine has destroyed itself and been extinct for centuries. What the masterminds that built the thing hadn't factored in is that a lot of the most powerful stuff going on in people's heads should really just stay between their ears. "Monsters from the id," the Earth scientist who discovers and activates the machine cries out before he's ripped to pieces by a gargoyle that materializes from his own secret, crazy places. That's kind of the way the Lower East Side felt to me sometimes. The neighborhood itself was a mechanism that allowed people to act on and realize impulses that anywhere else they'd keep in check.

A guy's girlfriend fucks his two best friends (or says she did) and the guy grabs a baseball bat and beats both his friends' heads in on the sidewalk. Between rounds of Bud tallboys and bathtub speed in an abandoned Puerto Rican social club, a group of cowboy artists transforms the vacant lot next door into a "sculpture garden" train wreck of metal, paint, and stone work reaching three stories into the sky. A couple on a city-run methadone maintenance program go into business for themselves by holding their daily prescribed and dispensed dose of liquid methadone in their cheeks until they get around the corner from the clinic on Avenue B and spit it into strangers' mouths in exchange for cash they then take and go score real smack on Third Street. Outer borough rock-and-rollers blow off church, shul, or cartoons to march around a dance floor throwing punches, taking intentional headers off the stage, and pass each other back and forth like a manic version of the Jets and Sharks carrying Tony away at the end of *West Side Story* to the sound of jackhammering punk bands at weekend hardcore "matinees." For a pretty wide variety of natives and transplants, Lower East Side life seemed to be about taking what was inside and making it happen on the outside no matter what the consequence or cause.

"The criminal, the mentally ill, the socially rejected, and those who have given up the attempt to cope with life," is how one academic described the so-called urban jungle. "Single men, pathological families, people in hiding from themselves or society, and individuals who provide the most disreputable of illegal-but-demanded services to the rest of the community." Sounds familiar. Every person has the capacity to unravel and every neighborhood harbors misfits alongside the well adjusted. Saint or psycho, the trials of life can light anyone's fuse. Something about the Lower East Side just shortened some people's wicks.

For more than a century the neighborhood had been the end of the line in Manhattan. Like Canarsie, a lot of the Lower East Side was once swamp and marshland. Until it was drained and filled, Manhattan's southeastern edge going south from Fourteenth Street leached into a fast-moving tidal channel that narrowed enough between the Brooklyn and Manhattan shorelines to earn the designation the East River. Most of the neighborhood had no subway service. The double L barely glanced off the Lower East Side's northern border, the IRT and BMT lines skirted its Western edge at Astor Place and Broadway, and the F, J, and M trains snaked underneath it en route to Brooklyn and Queens with barely a handful of stops between them serving the streets above.

Generations of people arrived in the neighborhood hauling a generous allotment of cultural and psychological baggage that they would unpack on the neighborhood's streets and inside tenements, factory buildings, and storefronts. For a while in the early twentieth century, the area around Tompkins Square Park had the largest German-American population in the U.S. But almost overnight the Germans were burned out of the Lower East Side melting pot when a ferry boat called the *General Slocum* caught fire while hosting a church-sponsored field trip in the summer of 1904.

The parents of a generation of Lower East Side German-American kids watched helplessly from the shore as their community's future burned to death and drowned in the East River. All that remains of Little Germany is an old church building on Seventh Street, a few architectural hints along Avenue B, and a monument to the *Slocum*'s thousand-plus mostly underage dead within the *spielplatz* the kids had once played in—Tompkins Square Park.

Ukrainian and Polish families that came in the late nineteenth and early twentieth centuries were still there when I began working in the neighborhood. If they owned buildings they rented apartments and storefronts that could've been had for peanuts just a few years before to NYU kids for exponentially increasing monthly ransoms. There was some kind of Eastern European lunch counter on almost every block. Stanley's on Avenue A, Christine's on First Avenue, and Kiev on Second Avenue are all gone, but you can still get kasha varnishkes (a mix of steamed buckwheat and bow-tie noodles that is as savory and filling as spaghetti and red sauce) with your morning eggs instead of home fries at Veselka on Ninth Street. East Tenth Street still hosts a genuine Russian bath almost directly across the street from Lucky Luciano's old family apartment, complete with steam rooms, a rock-lined "Russian room" sauna, and a changing area equipped with cots to sleep off a ritual beating from a masseur and any vodka consumed before or during a visit.

The Eastern European Jews that once filled the apartments and stores below Houston had mostly moved on by the time I arrived, but synagogues and *schvitzes* remained along with Bernstein's Kosher Chinese Food on Essex Street, Katz's Deli (not Kosher and a dining mecca for three states' worth of local law enforcement the way doughnut shops were in L.A.) on Ludlow, and the B&H Dairy Lunch farther uptown near St. Mark's Place.

The corner of First Avenue and Tenth Street retained traces of the even littler Little Italy that nurtured Charlie Lucky. John's Restaurant where Joe the Boss's hit squad settled a score and shot a couple locals in the bargain was (and is) still there same as DeRobertis pastry shop. Lanza's Restaurant down the block from DeRobertis on First Avenue was reportedly a social club for made guys, and until it was finally opened under entirely new management for real in the nineties, tourists and new arrivals were firmly but politely directed back out to the sidewalk when they wandered into Lanza's in search of a meal. Across the avenue Rosemarie's Pizza was so unselfconsciously old school that in August the management posted a sign saying they were closed for a week's vacation, and a mix of employees and regular customers would hang out in front of the storefront in folding chairs until the week was up.

The sidewalks of the Lower East Side have been decorated with gallons of mob rivalry blood. The neighborhood also spawned Thomas Rocco Barbella, better known as Rocky Graziano, one of the greatest boxers who ever lived. Not to be outdone, the Lower East Side's Jewish community produced Barney Ross, a guy who held fight titles in three different weight classes, singlehandedly fought off two dozen Japanese soldiers at Guadalcanal, and beat heroin addiction when he got home from the war.

They used to say that California must have been on a slant away from the rest of the country because all the nuts rolled there. But Alphaville had been East Coast visionary central for more than a hundred years. Nikola Tesla, Ethel and Julius Rosenberg, Allen Ginsberg, Charlie Parker, Emma Goldman, and Alexander Trosky all passed through or lived there at one point or another in their lives. The neighborhood offered a soapbox or a hideout. The genuinely creative, the genuinely clueless, and the genuinely nuts came from everywhere to reinvent themselves in a place that bore no resemblance to wherever it was that they came from.

The Hells Angels motorcycle club bought into the block on East Third Street between Second and First Avenue in the late sixties. New recruits earned the bottom rocker on their colors by standing guard over their brothers' machines all night in any weather across the street from a mural immortalizing Angel badass "Big Lenny" Giordano throwing a punch like Popeye the Sailor and the wisdom, "When in Doubt, Knock It Out." A hippie surge in the sixties brought a more delicate pseudonym for the area around Tompkins Square Park—"the East Village." Sterling Morrison from the Velvet Underground, a group that gestated in a Ludlow Street loft, remarked years later that the best thing about San Francisco's Summer of Love in 1967, was that the hype surrounding it lured most of the parasitic hippie creep element of Lower East Side counterculture out to the West Coast for a season.

The neighborhood was like some dry-docked coral reef constantly growing over the wreckage of immigrant armadas or individual adventurers who had run aground there, settled in, then either been wiped out like the Germans or picked up stakes and sailed on to fairer shores in the outer boroughs and suburbs. Every block was built on layers representing generations, strata of society, traditions, beliefs, ambitions, delusions, compulsions, desires, and everything else.

Each Lower East Side block was a crazy quilt of buildings and storefronts rented, owned, operated, and frequented by different members of an almost absurdly diverse community. Art galleries held openings alongside synagogues honoring the sabbath. Puerto Rican cuchifritos (maybe the single most thorough exploration of deep-frying ever conducted) places shared blocks with vegan restaurants. Polish bars served college kids on dates alongside old-timers who'd been drinking since breakfast. Both ended up shooting pool and singing along to the same Johnny Cash songs by closing time. A block south of a Turkish-run newsstand serving the best egg creams and iced coffee on the planet, and around the corner from an old-time Italian funeral parlor, a Korean-owned dry cleaner on Avenue A turned a side business renting VHS tapes into a chain of video stores that became world famous.

The sheer volume and variety of humanity encouraged a kind of myopia rather than connection. It was entirely possible for people in the Lower East Side to go their entire lives totally unaware of someone living the same number of years on the other side of a six-inch-thick wall of wood, drywall, and plaster. Unless you found some kind of key that opened the doors separating neighbor from unaware neighbor, it was hard to see the connections that bound people in the neighborhood together.

During the mid–late eighties, the unavoidable fact was that heroin connected nearly everyone in Alphaville to someone else, whether they saw it or not. Smack was like an X-ray flashing through every apartment, every business, every life in that teeming patchwork neighborhood. It rippled out from the Avenue D projects like a shockwave. Junkies and non-junkies ran a gauntlet of lowlife rip-off artists that began at the foot of the buildings. Loose gangs of neighborhood kids were only too happy to risk juvenile detention for the pleasure of cracking open a head and taking drug money or milk money for a kid's breakfast. Vomit, steaming in the summer and frozen solid in the winter, decorated sidewalks, park benches, and stoops whenever a new shipment of dope was strong enough to cause even seasoned addicts to empty their stomachs after snorting or booting it up.

The door to any apartment with anything of value in it had to have at least two deadbolts on it. Every window was barred. There was a locksmith on almost every block. Some residents put axle grease on their windowsills and littered them with broken glass so that skinny, single-minded, and totally desperate junkies would think twice about Spider-manning onto an air conditioner or scaling an air shaft to their window. Lower East Side bar and restaurant bathrooms were guarded like bank tills. Proprietors installed buzzers on toilet doors as a kind of velvet rope system to keep junkies from inadvertently graffiti-ing a stall with their blood while shooting up or with their puke afterward. If a junkie managed to get into a men's room, sharp-eyed bartenders would snap off the appropriate breaker and plunge the addict into darkness. One bar on Second Street and Avenue A installed blue lightbulbs in its rest rooms. A glowing harvest moon reflected in the toilet bowl water when you pissed and if you tried to shoot up your blue veins were nearly indistinguishable from the rest of your arm in the murky light.

"This is Ed Koch, your mayor. You know the Sanitation De-partment cannot sweep this street if you don't move your ille-gally parked car. Please get it outta here!"

When Ed Koch shook my hand at the NYPD commence-ment ceremony in Madison Square Garden in 1983, I was surprised, as people often were, by how tall he was. I wasn't surprised at what a smooth operator he was. At the time Koch was heading for his third term and was famous for asking crowds "How'm I doing?" The taped message about moving your car blasting from a select group of street sweepers dubbed the "Ed Koch talking brooms" was more the mayor's real style. Koch had the politician's gift for one-way communication down to a science. In any public dia-logue Koch paid close attention to people agreeing with him and closer attention to the sound of his own voice dismiss-ing anybody that didn't. Either way he came away from any encounter truthfully claiming to have fulfilled his mayoral duty by dialoguing with the voters. No matter how contro-versial or problematic the exchange, Koch was always "do-ing" just fine.

Homesteaders and activists on the Lower East Side hated Koch for being the de facto auctioneer at a decade-long sell-ing out of a neighborhood that nobody had given a shit about for years. But you can't blame Koch for wanting to see the city get back up on its feet financially by putting new price tags on old buildings. Anyone assuming the mayor's office at the time would've done the same thing Koch did. They just might not have looked so happy about it. The sev-enties had been a fiscal disaster for the city and a political disaster for the politicians who oversaw it. Among the sou-venirs of economic hardship on hand when Koch took office were hundreds of derelict residential buildings and empty lots all over the Lower East Side left in the city's care when they were abandoned, foreclosed on, or seized for unpaid taxes.

Real estate, like narcotics, is a great opportunity for middle men. In the late seventies housing speculators gambled that it was worth risking the relatively cheap purchase price of city-administered properties in the Lower East Side (particularly around Tompkins Square Park) in the hopes that they would become more valuable. They guessed right and a lot got rich. The city was only too happy to offload buildings and lots for cheap so that they could become tax-revenue generating, neighborhood-transforming, commercially viable apartments, storefronts, co-ops, and condos. Agencies created years before to help small-time real estate owners and buyers now mobilized to remove legal and financial roadblocks for big-time speculators and the developers that followed.

Most of the neighborhood's residential tenants were protected by rent control and rent stabilization laws that had been on the books for decades. Old-time businesses didn't have the law on their side and new owners and old landlords alike began exterminating old stores and restaurants by hitting commercial tenants with absurdly high rent increases when leases came up. Mom-and-pop shops were shuttered overnight as new and often short-lived galleries, boutiques, and bars took their places.

The Lower East Side's separate, undiscovered vibe began to evaporate. By the late eighties the hippie dream of a fringe community utopia was already impossible. When it comes to real estate dollars, you really can't fight City Hall.

Not in New York. Manhattan had only so many square miles and apartments, and in the eighties, a lot of financially set new arrivals were willing and eager to trade some safety and yuppie amenities for the thrill of buying into a place that was pretty much the capital of cool.

The writing was literally on the wall—"Not for Sale," "Speculators Go Away," "Rent Is Torture"—but the reality had been looming since the mid-eighties. When developers finished erecting the Zeckendorf Towers at 1 Irving Place in 1986, the immediate fallout from this luxury housing high-rise complex just beyond the northwestern limits of the Lower East Side was that it forced some West Village residents to buy watches. The Zeckendorf's pyramid shaped top floors cut off an entire neighborhood's view of the massive two-story ConEd clock tower. But the real shadow from the three-tower complex reached east and south across Tompkins Square Park, to a building called the Christodora House on Avenue B.

For more than half a century the Christodora House was the only non-project high-rise on the Lower East Side. It went up in the late twenties as part of the same American settlement house movement that earned Lillian Wald a housing project named in her honor. The idea was for volunteers to mix and mingle and work with recent immigrants and the poor in the Christodora's meeting rooms, classrooms, music studios, dormitories, and medical facilities. Rental properties in the top floors of the building were supposed to pay for the upkeep and supplies of the charity work and public facilities downstairs. It didn't work. After World War II, the building was vacated, condemned, and purchased by the city.

The Christodora lay vacant and, outside of various legal and illegal underground activities, unused for twenty years until city cops from the Ninth Precinct raided the lower floors, cleared out the people they found in there and welded the Christodora's doors shut in 1969. After five bidless years, the city sold the building at auction in 1975 for about one and a half million dollars less than they'd paid in 1948. The speculator that bought the Christodora flipped it (without doing any work anywhere on it) in 1985 for about twenty times what he had paid for it.

Even though it was a complete wreck on the inside, the Christodora was still a high-rise on the outside, and therefore a strong anchor with which to stabilize new development in the area. The Zeckendorf Towers had already driven the last nail in the coffin of a mini-tenderloin area of SROs, porno theaters, seventy-five-cent mug bars, a pool hall, and a boxing gym around Fourteenth Street and Third Avenue that had been a sort of scaled down Forty-second Street for years. Scenes with the child prostitute character and her pimp in *Taxi Driver* were shot just a few blocks from where the Zeckendorf went up ten years later. Once the Christodora was renovated and reopened, it would help sanitize Avenue B the same way the Zeckendorf started the clock on the area surrounding it. Despite what some of the big mouths protesting gentrification in Tompkins Square Park may have said, it wasn't a nefarious conspiracy. It was a simple fact of the free market. "Private reinvestment improved housing conditions, stemmed deterioration, and strengthened neighborhood commercial areas," an eighties city-funded study concluded. More development money converting cheap local real estate into expensive local real estate would smooth the rougher curbside edges of the Lower East Side.

In response to charges that he was selling out longtime low- and middle-income residents, Ed Koch, whose own mansion on the Upper East Side was a job perk paid for by the taxpayers, simply offered, "If people can't afford to live in a neighborhood, they shouldn't be there." Those that didn't have the skyrocketing price of local fair market rent or a mortgage would be, in the words of one Lower East Side would-be Donald Trump, "pushed east to the river and given life preservers."

The frustration for developers looking to send old guard immigrants and bohos swimming to Brooklyn was a series of high-rise obstacles along Avenue D—the end of the neighborhood alphabet and the last residential avenue before your feet got wet. Protestors, activists, and homesteaders may have been a pain in the city's ass, but sanitizing and upgrading the Lower East Side was severely handicapped by the Avenue D projects and the drug sales going on inside of them, not by shouting slogans and staging the occasional riot in Tompkins Square Park.

Soon after New Year's 1984, Ed Koch and the NYPD reassigned a couple hundred uniform and plainclothes city cops to the Lower East Side in a heavily publicized program called Operation Pressure Point. Citing "complaints from the community" the department instructed Pressure Point cops from the Ninth and Seventh precincts to arrest drug dealers and users. By the summer of 1986 there were more than twenty thousand arrests logged by Pressure Point cops. But only five hundred of those ever went to jail. Pressure Point was toothless. Uniform city cops were denied that neighborhood power to transform impulse into reality when it came to dope arrests. And just like everyone else, they were scared shitless of going into the projects. High-visibility, low-yield PR moves like Pressure Point were mostly a thorn in the side of decent law-abiding people that lived on the D and the visiting junkies and hell-raisers with little genuine connection to the area. Under Pressure Point, drug sales barely slowed but if you double-parked or drank a beer out of a bag on the street, look out.

I read once about a boomtown in Alaska that was accidentally built over a polar bear migratory breeding ground. Along with a nearly endless winter, the people that lived there had to contend with bears coming in their windows, raiding their kitchens, eating their pets, attacking them on the street, you name it. Their home-town was also the two-ton marauding mammal capital of the world. Census surveys in the eighties showed that the Wald and Riis houses on Avenue D were more densely populated per square foot than the most overcrowded cities in Asia. The estimated twenty-five thousand residents of the nearly fifty project buildings throughout the Lower East Side were mostly hardworking, low-income families of Puerto Rican descent. As if life wasn't already hard enough for the people who lived in the Wald and Riis houses, they weren't just trying to live while sitting on top of each other, they were going about making a life in the center of Smacktown, USA.

In our first year on patrol in Alphaville, Gio and I saw mothers and fathers fighting through hallways crowded with junkies like they were in a zombie movie. We watched kids on their way to school kicking used hypodermic needles in front of them like cans. Mothers breast-fed infants on park benches a few feet from nodding dopers somehow still standing though nearly comatose and bent sharply over at the waist. They waited on city-run food lines on the same block as rows of junkies lining up to buy smack before lunch. They paid for milk with food stamps in the same bodegas where junkies sold their food stamps to pay for a fix. Arrogant and violent young kids earned a million dollars a year moving heroin while hardworking fathers grew old making barely enough to keep their families fed and healthy.

Along with rising rents, high crime, and high expectations, new arrivals and old-timers alike all faced a potential complication in their lives. Scores of people came to the Lower East Side on the pretext of running away from a life that didn't suit them to a life lived on their own terms, only to wind up strung out, fucked up, and on their way to an early grave. If the Lower East Side of the eighties had a motto, it might have been "Come for the Neighborhood, Stay for the Drugs."

For me the crazy snow globe of the Lower East Side wasn't based around Tompkins Square Park, the Christodora House, Cooper Union to the west, St. Mark's Place, or any of the other parts of the neighborhood that were buzz words or hangouts then and are sought after real estate or tourist destinations now. My Lower East Side was the ground zero for a heroin epidemic that gripped the neighborhood—the Avenue D projects and the smack flowing out of them. When I officially began working in PSA 4, the housing projects of the Lower East Side, Gio and I were assigned to Sector D, an area that included several different parts of the neighborhood and that was big enough that we patrolled it in a squad car. The roughest part of Sector David was a strip of city-run residential real estate along Avenue D—the same area that had pissed me off so much during that drive to the academy a few years before. As far as cops were concerned Alphabet City's street dealers only worried about two things: the first was buy-and-bust operations staged by the Manhattan South Narcotics Division. The second was the Housing PD. I found out later that Manhattan South Narcotics didn't actually like sending undercover officers into the Lower East Side projects. Their guys often were robbed of their buy money on the way in just like the visiting junkies. And housing? Well, I was itching to test the waters on that one. Gio and I were looking for action, and we soon realized that if we hung out around the Wald and Riis houses on Avenue D, we'd find it.

Avenue D

Davey Blue Eyes maintains a highly lucrative balance between hands-on and hands-off operations that keeps the cash rolling in while keeping Davey himself unknown to anyone below his top tier of main dealers and the neighbors he grew up with. Territorial challenges from outside the neighborhood like the Colombians from Queens are the only things guaranteed to get him to use his own gun. When a new Harlem dope crew begins selling and diverting customers who have been coming downtown to score, Davey takes a personal and direct interest in keeping the playing field pitched his way.

A quick look through a chop shop in Long Island City yields an unregistered Dodge Astro van stolen off the streets of Yonkers. A wad of cash later, Davey drives the van into a Chinatown auto body shop for a rendezvous with the Alvarez brothers—main dealers on the D with a car service front on Attorney Street and a way with a cutting torch, a wrench, and a jack. Over the next week they execute a punch list of modifications Davey writes out on a paper napkin at a Cuban-Chinese lunch counter on Canal Street. The Judas Priest mural on the outside of the van gets a coat of rust brown primer. The interior, wheel wells, fenders, and doors are bulked up with steel armor plate,

stock windshield and windows are replaced with tinted bulletproof glass, and the undercarriage is fortified with special
shocks to deal with the new weight and to prevent betraying the
movements of anyone inside. A periscope goes in along with a
heating, ventilation, police scanner, and electrical system that
run independently of the engine while the van is parked for long
periods of time.

Late one Saturday night a pair of Davey's Harlem competitors and two heavily armed associates emerge from the 1018
Club on the site of the old Roxy. Inside the club Mike Tyson
holds court alongside porn stars and coke dealers. Outside the
club the two dealers, both drunk and high and fresh from getting blown for a taste by two girls they invited into the VIP
lounge, goof on a transvestite prostitute on the corner and
head over to another hype night spot a block away. Neither
they nor their two bodyguards take any notice of a van parked
at the end of a block of warehouses.

Inside the van Davey watches his targets draw closer like a
duck hunter in a blind. "Shit's on," he whispers to the five men
with him.

He phoned each member of his crew the day before telling
them to get some rest because they were going to party in his
new van and surprise some homeboys on Eighteenth Street tonight. One by one they appeared on designated corners to be
picked up. Some are already wearing their flak vests and guns,
others had them in gym bags and put them on after getting
in the van. Once they parked outside 1018, they pass joints
and sip from forties, waiting for the two dead-meat uptown
pendejos to arrive. The velvet rope crowd parts for celebs and
anyone else the doormen know. Davey's Harlem quarries go
inside around midnight backed by two bodyguards. It's nearly

4:00 a.m. now and they're walking right up to the van and into a world of hurt.

As the Harlem foursome turns the corner, Davey's crew rolls back the van's side door like a Huey helicopter in Nam and opens fire with nines and .357 revolvers. The dealers and their entourage reflexively and uselessly cover their heads and faces with their hands and are cut down mid stride. At the first shot bystanders storm the velvet rope then crawl under cars and try to hide behind lampposts like kids playing hide-and-seek when they discover the club's doors are locked shut.

Just as the van is about to pull out and disappear down Tenth Avenue, a passing blue-and-white surprises Davey and his gang and blocks them in. While the officers on scene survey the carnage and yell into their radio for backup, Davey and his crew ditch out the back door of the van and escape on foot to a second car they have stashed nearby. Investigating detectives give the van a once-over and immediately call the bomb squad. Among the beer empties, chip bags, handguns, and ammo boxes inside is a crate of grenades Davey's crew is forced to leave behind.

It's the first time any of Davey's operations come under direct police scrutiny. The Colombian confrontation is a write-off. But the 1018 hit is a fuck-up. When Big Arthur Washington comes out of jail a few months later, Davey decides to let Arthur do as he pleases for a while and hang a face on the Lower East Side dope rackets other than Davey's own.

Nine

When it came to crime, if New York was a melting pot, then the Lower East Side was a microwave. Neighborhood tenements had nurtured Lucky Luciano, Bugsy Siegel, and Meyer Lansky and provided a boot camp, hunting ground, and hideout for the full range of the worst of human behavior. So much so that it also became a proving ground and testing range for reformers. As far back as 1854, various private concerns had experimented with building or renovating model housing blocks for "improving the conditions of the poor." Inspired by more sustained government-funded efforts in Europe, Mayor La Guardia spearheaded the first totally publicly paid for, constructed, and maintained housing block in the country in 1934. Even at the height of Roosevelt's New Deal it took some doing. La Guardia first set his lawyers on Vincent Astor, the "boy millionaire" who had inherited a fortune after his old man went down with the *Titanic*. Once a court ruling halted haggling over a piece of real estate Astor owned on the Lower East Side, La Guardia oversaw the assembling of a poker hand of federal grants and state funds that paid for the mixed demolition and gutting (the Feds would only pay for "renovations" not new constructions) of a two-dozen tenement block on Astor's former parcel bordered by Avenue A, First Avenue, and Second and Third streets on the Lower East Side. In 1936, the First Houses were born.

An assembled crowd on a freezing cold December day in 1935 stamped their feet, blew on their hands, and watched La Guardia dedicate the First Houses. Unlike the towering projects that would become the NYCHA's norm after World War II, the First Houses were modest four-story buildings offering qualified residents (couples with kids had to be married and at least one parent had to have a job) comparatively spacious apartments with oak floors surrounding a shady tree-filled quad for about six bucks a month per room.

The apartments filled quickly, mostly with middle-income Italians and Jews. So did the massive collection of new addresses in Stuyvesant Town and Peter Cooper Village north of Fourteenth Street. Privately funded by the Metropolitan Life Insurance Company, this maze of apartment buildings set on grassy cul-de-sacs established a comfortable, primarily middle-class lid on the boiling-over Lower East Side below Fourteenth Street. To the south lay Knickerbocker Village, another privately cofinanced development that like the Met Life complex quietly enforced segregationist rental policies that NYCHA and the First Houses didn't maintain.

The First Houses were the NYCHA's first child—well planned for, welcomed into the world, doted on, and given every break their deep-pocketed city and New Deal federal government "parents" could afford. But among those watching La Guardia cut the ribbon in 1935 was a guy with a housing plan for the city all his own. The residential buildings that were born from his ambition were more like the NYCHA's pointy-headed step-children.

Robert Moses had unsuccessfully tried to take over the city's public housing initiative for years but La Guardia stopped him cold each time. Finally after World War II, under ex-cop Mayor Bill O'Dwyer, a few years short of bailing out of office just ahead of a police corruption scandal, Moses was named construction coordinator for the city and putting up public housing fell under his control at last.

Post-war Manhattan was filling up, and Moses had an idea of how to stretch the remaining real estate a little further. If he couldn't get rid of the poor altogether, Moses could at least push them off to the side. Using landfill, some of it rubble from the London Blitz brought to the U.S. as ballast in British freighters, Moses filled in the swampy eastern edge of the Lower East Side to extend it into the East River. Three massive construction projects went up on this virgin territory. One was the FDR Drive, a north–south highway that would allow cars coming to and from Jersey, upstate, and the outer boroughs to bypass the neighborhood altogether. Another was a strip of park between the highway and the water beyond connected to the neighborhood itself by bridges and walkways over six lanes of traffic. The third was a series of gigantic apartment towers that would eventually run from the edge of Stuy Town down to Knickerbocker Village.

A 1946 editorial in the *New York Times* took note of the foundations being laid (after some delay) on this new strip of designated low-income buildings. After Stuyvesant Town and Peter Cooper, these new towers would be the next steps, the *Times* said, toward "a Lower East Side we may view with pride instead of shame." Once the federal government passed legislation to underwrite urban renewal programs in various American cities Moses had the financial muscle and legal mandate to fulfill his ambition to "tear down every building in the slums and put up new ones on less land, then bring the people back." But the *Times* and the city planners, bankers, and politicians failed to appreciate the difference between the modest layout of the First Houses, the segregated middle-class enclaves of Stuy Town and Knickerbocker Village, and the gigantic instant ghettos named after Jacob Riis and Lillian Wald, founder of the Visiting Nurse Service of New York and the pioneering infant health initiative at the Henry Street Settlement, that Moses oversaw.

The Wald and Riis houses hosted the same population surge and ebb as their sister buildings in Coney Island and the other Title I urban renewal buildings that came after. The garment and textile industry below Houston Street tanked during the fifties—a victim of the unregulated low-cost labor that made overseas factories irresistible to clothing manufacturers. The GI Bill and a cheap construction boom made owning a house possible for a new generation of Americans. Middle-class and working-class Lower East Siders alike were moving out to the suburbs as fast as they could pack. The people that arrived to fill the Riis, Wald, and other new Lower East Side projects and to join the relocated former residents of areas cleared out under Title I all over the city were mostly Puerto Ricans, who moved north to the U.S. after World War II.

Lucky Luciano had weathered World War II with a win on points. An ambitious Manhattan DA named Thomas Dewey had managed to put Lucky Luciano behind bars indefinitely on a trumped-up prostitution charge in 1936. The Feds had enough legitimate evidence to lock Luciano away on a narcotics rap at the time but Dewey's instinct for PR told him that portraying Luciano as a pimp would play better in the papers. Lucky continued to run the Five Families crime commission he'd chartered soon after Maranzano's funeral while waiting out a half-century jail sentence. Meanwhile, Western Europe was about to explode and the Mafia and the U.S. State Department were both on Mussolini's shit list. Luciano kept tabs on the Five Families and waited for the Feds to sign up for visiting hours at Dannemora.

Once war broke out with the Axis powers, the U.S. government wasted no time reaching out. Luciano controlled the docks at home and had strong ties to the rabidly antifascist (and after the war, anticommunist) Cosa Nostra back home in Sicily. On the promise of a reduced sentence, Luciano made sure the New York waterfront stayed safe (or that his guys stopped spreading sabotage rumors and starting suspicious fires for the worried home defense forces to obsess on) and that General Patton could roll his tanks up through Sicily in record time.

After VE Day, Luciano was released and deported back to Sicily for his troubles. Back on the island that spawned him, Lucky built a heroin network worthy of the New World order and that took full advantage of his cordial relationship with the CIA. American Cold War spooks utilized Sicilian Mafia contacts all over Europe to keep tabs on communist governments and activities and disrupt labor organizations. In return, Luciano was permitted a free hand in finding new paths to the drug markets in his former adopted country.

The Sicilian Mafia established a powerful and efficient manufacture and export system that processed and moved opium, morphine, and heroin from the Middle East to Marseille and Sicily to Cuba to the U.S. But by the late fifties the U.S. mob had suffered some tough breaks. Narcotics sales and possession had been legally reclassified as federal crimes in 1951 and 1956 and bad breaks with congressional investigations and some lucky busts by various local law enforcement agencies had put an unwelcome spotlight on organized crime. Meyer Lansky's beloved Cuba would soon be out of the picture courtesy of Castro's takeover.

Heroin was too lucrative to give up on. In October 1957, a contingent of New York mobsters met with their Sicilian counterparts in a series of dinners and meetings in Palermo. Over local shellfish, wine, fruit, and espresso, U.S. and native Mafia, including Luciano hashed out a plan that would create stronger ties between the two halves of an organization divided by an ocean and, increasingly, by custom. At Lucky's urging, the assembled racketeers also pledged to ramp up dope manufacture in Europe and actively concentrate heroin business in the poorest American neighborhoods. Urban renewal and slum clearance provided a new map for their sales regions.

By the early sixties urban planners and politicians were calling out the ideas and practices behind urban renewal for what they were—bullshit. Jamming poor people into huge towers cut off from everything that made city life worthwhile made no sense. Moses's development juggernaut had created a half-assed urban dystopia that was only livable in the mind of a rich guy who would never have to occupy the buildings he created. Instead of the diverse, stimulating, chaotic shuffling deck of people and backgrounds, businesses, schools, jobs, and recreational opportunities that defined the rest of the neighborhood, the people of the Lower East Side projects were consigned to a high-rise holding area that cut them off even more from the city they lived in than the language barriers and prejudices they already had to contend with. Buildings like the Wald and Riis houses had been built as way stations for new Americans en route to that better life that everyone came here for. Instead they became as hard to escape in their way as Alcatraz.

At the same time a flood of dope from Europe, some smuggled directly into New York, some imported up through Miami, was taking its toll. NYCHA's holdings were well on their way to some 180,000 units and crime was growing right along with the acreage. New buildings like many of the ones I patrolled in Coney Island were now designed like fortresses with graffiti- and vandalism-resistant-tiled common spaces, caged lighting, and heavy steel fixtures that made them resemble slaughter houses more than vertical neighborhoods. By the seventies, with the city teetering on bankruptcy and the old system of rental qualification long scrapped, the Lower East Side public high-rises like Wald and Riis were battlegrounds.

The rise of the DEA and big busts like the Pizza Connection case at home, and political moves abroad, cracked and dented the old Mafia heroin pipelines. New avenues opened from Southeast Asia pioneered by Matthew Madonna, Frank Lucas, and Nicky Barnes. Mexican and South American suppliers and dealers entered the picture. The floodgates opened and heroin poured into the U.S. in greater quantities than ever before. As always, the mouth of the faucet was New York City.

When negotiations began between the British and the mainland Chinese on the return of Hong Kong to Chinese rule, Hong Kong's crime cartels didn't waste any time wondering about the outcome. A steady new stream of immigration from Hong Kong to Chinatown in the early eighties brought with it cheap and strong smack. Gangster or not, an emigrating Hong Kong resident could finance their new life in America by agreeing to bring a package of heroin with them, and hundreds did before the People's Republic pulled the plug on Hong Kong drug sales. A Chinatown-based wholesaler could literally walk a couple kilos of dope to the Avenue D projects. Supply and demand rose equally, and Harlem and the Bronx, once the centers of U.S. heroin dealing, were soon eclipsed by Avenue D.

People tend to recall the eighties as the crack era. But rock cocaine couldn't hold a candle to the new Chinese heroin coming into New York and getting sold on Avenue D at the height of crack media hysteria. The price point on a bag of smack made dealers a lot more money a lot more quickly than selling jumbos of rock. Chinese white heroin was so strong and pure that it was incredibly versatile. You could, if your customers weren't too picky, step on it any number of times and still have them coming back for more. Both crack and heroin were virulently addictive, but cultivating a crack habit was like throwing yourself in a bonfire, while getting strung out on dope was more like slowly roasting yourself to death. Crackheads got to the can't hide it, can't hold a job, can't keep a relationship level much faster than junkies. The honeymoon period with smack was more work-friendly, and dope addicts didn't destroy their lives and families and therefore their buying power anywhere near as quickly as crackheads. That made them much better customers.

One of Robert Moses's final brainstorms before stepping down in 1968 was a proposed superhighway interchange that would divert multilane freeway car traffic directly through Washington Square Park. Moses's dream of an L.A. cloverleaf in the middle of Greenwich Village didn't pan out. But an accidental part of his legacy was that the Riis, Wald, and other NYCHA developments on the Lower East Side—convenient to the FDR, bridges, and tunnels—were the new heroin crossroads of the world.

The average white-bread cop saw the Lower East Side as some kind of jungle where amoral human animals preyed on each other and got what they deserved. To these guys the violent crime that threatened to gut the area was the residents' fault, somehow. My new partner and I felt differently. You didn't need to be a criminologist to see what the root cause was of all the lawbreaking and accompanying misery in and round Riis, Wald, and the other Lower East Side projects. Like the puke, blood, burglaries, and almost everything else that sucked for every Alphabet City dweller, the problem was dope.

In our first years on the job in PSA 4, the majority of the collars we made and the complaints we responded to could nearly all be traced back to or involved a bag of dope and a hand either buying or selling it. Assaults were usually junkie on junkie. Robberies were usually junkie versus someone who looked like they might be able to bankroll a fix, or kids looking to separate a visiting addict from his or her buy money. Homicides were evidence of a big-fish dope dealer like Davey Blue Eyes cleaning house—either exterminating competition or pruning his own workforce of a snitch or a thief in their midst. We didn't see the project dwellers caught in the middle of this chaos as mopes or scumbags. It was too easy to paint everyone with a single brush. We saw most of the people on our beat as individuals simply trying to get by under very difficult conditions. We didn't see their neighborhood as an irredeemable ghetto that needed to be walled up or nuked. We saw it as salvageable. We liked it there.

Gio and I both grew up a few miles from each other in Brooklyn. We knew a lot of the same people and shared a similar take on the Lower East Side that separated us from most of the cops we suited up alongside those first couple years in Alphaville. We had complementary attitudes about the things that mattered—the job, girls, the bad guys, and what we needed to do to get the most out of a shift in PSA 4. Most important, we both just loved the neighborhood—the crazy energy, the one goddamned thing after another adventure of it, the people we saw every day and took the time to get to know, from the drug dealers and skells, to the families and the sexy Puerto Rican girls who would flag us down to flirt.

We worked around the clock. Like Coney Island, shift rotation was either 8:00 A.M. to 4:00 P.M., 4:00 P.M. to midnight, or midnight to 8:00 A.M. But unlike Coney Island, we almost always worked together and with each other. Each tour had its own pros and cons. Day tours were great if you wanted your evenings to yourself, but they could become an unending series of radio runs responding to aided cases, which were tense, depressing, and almost never yielded a collar. I learned to appreciate what a hell being an EMS tech was working days. Sick, hurt, dying, and crazy people are never easy to deal with and some day tours Gio and I would literally go from one aided case to the next—chest pains in a twenty-five-year-old crackhead who looks sixty that turn into a fatal coronary before he's even in the ambulance; a supposedly broken hip that turns out to be a bruise and a pinched nerve from passing out on top of an empty whiskey bottle; a baby that's been dead for hours but whose mother still clings to it.

I enjoyed four to midnight the most. There always seemed to be something boiling up on the street for us to get in on, and the sheer volume of work meant we could pick and choose what to do and where to go. Between four and twelve the dispatchers at Central spat out jobs at a machine-gun pace. During these shifts we cultivated the cop's art of listening to the radio with an ear for our call numbers amid the dozen or more listed in rapid succession, and for what might be an interesting call to respond to. Whether you were talking up a girl, listening to a ball game or fast asleep, you needed to respond when your number came up. Cops who couldn't develop that kind of variable focus didn't last very long on patrol.

The downside of four to midnight was that between all that radio traffic, surprise inspections from supervisors, and dealing with paperwork, we really only had about three hours in which to find a collar. The best shifts often ended early—we'd make an arrest during the first few hours we were on duty and then spend the rest of the time on the clock processing it. The worst involved babysitting a corpse or securing a DOA's apartment until the medical examiner arrived or parking our butts outside of a hospital room where an injured perp was getting treatment.

After midnight was the fucking Twilight Zone. As anyone who lives in New York can tell you, a lot of the City that Never Sleeps really does kill the lights and hit the sack from the witching hour on. Not in Alphabet City. Late nights in the summer months the air itself seemed to sweat and everyone moved in either slow or fast motion. The girls out at that hour all go-go danced down the sidewalk, each to a different song. In the winter it was like a ghost town, but with ghosts sprinting out of sight as you turned a corner or huddling together over a trash can fire. It didn't matter what the weather was—we always had a full late-night plate of fights in the street, muggings, EDPs (emotionally disturbed persons), shots fired, and the true classic of the wee hours, the domestic dispute.

Hot or cold, everyone we dealt with in the midnight to eight shift was high. Booze, junk, coke, crack, angel dust, or a cocktail of two or more. If they were already sad, whatever was in them at that hour made them sadder. If they were already set to start some shit, it made their fuse shorter. Nobody thought straight. Most of the people we went to see in the middle of the night had already made pretty questionable choices. We always had to keep our wits and our senses of humor about us. Some nights it was such an unending fucked-up kaleidoscope of weirdness that you had to laugh.

"Available RMP to respond to one eighteen Avenue D apartment one-X, ten fifty-two family dispute." It was about two in the morning on a night that had already been a snoozer when Central broke the first patch of silence we'd had in a while. Gio grabbed the radio.

"RMP nine-two seven-seven on the way, K." Somewhere along the way "K" had replaced "ten-four" or "roger wilco" as standard NYPD radio jargon.

Nothing escalates faster than a family dispute—usually couples having it out. The phrase "you always hurt the one you love" might have been written by a housing cop. I was driving and I hit the siren and floored it through the intersection.

"I hope it's a good one," Gio said.

"Yeah. Too slow tonight," I replied. We'd already become connoisseurs of the family fracas. They broke up the monotony of a dull night like this one and were usually good as some kind of guerilla theater. Also, we were almost guaranteed a collar. What people rarely realized when they called the cops about a neighbor arguing, was that we were expected to arrest someone. The department had too many bad PR experiences where cops arrived on scene, talked everybody down and left only to be recalled when one of the people involved had managed to really hurt or kill another one after all. If we responded, we arrested someone. I stopped our car on the sidewalk in front of the address and we sprinted into the lobby. Ground floor apartment. Thanks, Central.

As we neared the door to apartment 1X we both turned down our radios and listened to hear whether the show we were about to referee was rated PG or R. The yelling and screaming was loud enough that I was surprised we hadn't heard it on the sidewalk. One, two, three voices. Fuck. Gio and I looked at each other—an unspoken "on your marks . . ."—and I rapped loudly on the door. No one answered. I knocked again, this time with my nightstick and kept knocking until I heard the lock turn on the other side of the door.

"Who?" a female voice yelled from inside.

"Police officers. You'll have to open up," I said, turning my head to listen for anything else I might want to know before we met face-to-face. The door opened. The woman who answered was three hundred pounds if she was an ounce. None of it was clothing. She smelled like someone had marinated her in rum. A cigarette in the corner of her mouth traced an oval in the air as she slurred, "Who call you? Who? We don't need you! Get outta *mi casa*! Go away!"

"Look, someone called. What's going on here?" I stood up straight, leaned on the door, and spoke in my best "police business" voice. She was wasted and rattled and unconsciously she stepped back far enough that we pushed our way inside. The apartment stank of booze, cigarettes, and sweat. The plastic covers on a couch near the door had gone yellow from old tobacco smoke. Gio caught my eye as a male voice whined from the next room.

"*Por favor, por favor,* come back here. In here, in the bedroom!" I grabbed the fat naked lady's hand by the wrist and brought her into the back room with us. Inside an even fatter and far hairier body lay handcuffed to the bed. Turns out this show was going to be rated X.

"Look, look what she did to me," the guy whined. "She said we were gonna have some fun like this but she leave me here and she fuckin' with her old lady." As if on cue the fat lady started screaming at the guy in thousand-mile-an-hour Spanglish, lunged for him, and swung her arms wildly at his helpless body. I tried to hold her back, but with physics on her side she broke free and belly-flopped on the poor guy. The impact sounded like dropping a thanksgiving turkey in a kiddie pool of Jell-O.

"Lady, cut it out!" I wrenched her arm back behind her. "Sit down on the floor!"

Gio looked over my shoulder, eyes bugged, as a third hefty package emerged from the bathroom wearing a pink bikini bottom that nearly vanished into her rolls of flab. For a second I pictured Don King.

"I can't find them! I'm sorry, but I had to call the police," she screeched. "I can't find the damn keys!"

"Okay," I said to all three, "any more naked overweight people gonna pop out of anywhere, or is the clown car empty?"

It took some patience and a lot of repetition, but eventually we got the three of them calmed down. Gio decided not to let it die.

"Okay now, what's the deal here?" he asked loudly, rubbing his hands together. "Who was fucking who, and when's the next party?" The three started in again like he'd flipped a switch. I had to hide my face so they wouldn't see me laughing. The joke wound up being on Gio. Lady Don King had found her keys finally. Neither responding officer had any intention of touching three hundred pound Moby Romeo so we coached the girls through the process of unlocking him. They were both too wasted to get the tiny key in the lock, however. The bed and the guy on it took up almost the whole room and there was no way they could get to his cuffs without crawling around on top of him. It looked like we might get stuck there all night. It was my night to drive and Gio's night for paperwork and we both understood that unlocking fatso was on the paperwork side of the necessary humiliations of law enforcement. Gio drew the disgusting duty of slithering over the guy to unlock him.

"There's a little handhold down there below his waist, if you can't get leverage," I told him. Watching him crawl up the guy redefined dirty work.

When we walked out of 118 Avenue D we were still laughing. Gio thumbed the radio and gave Central our disposition. We hadn't made an arrest and needed to go on the board as having settled the matter to our satisfaction.

"Central, RMP nine-two seven-seven."

"Go ninety two seventy-seven."

"Central be advised that dispute at one eighteen Avenue D is condition corrected. If you get any more jobs there tonight, don't send patrol units, send pizza."

"I don't know what that means, unit," the dispatcher said trying to stifle a laugh, "but copy."

Avenue D

Thanks to the van hit, Davey goes on DEA's and NYPD's radar around the same time we learn about him through Big Arthur Washington's rampage. One afternoon the Feds get lucky and put together a six-vehicle surveillance that tracks Davey's black Mercedes from Avenue D into Queens. On the Fifty-ninth Street Bridge Davey makes the surveillance team and uses a new weapon he's recently acquired to cut them loose—a cell phone. Davey makes two calls and a little while later he's flanked by a Jeep and a town car. On cue the Jeep and town car block two lanes of traffic, Davey runs a red light, floors it and is gone. At least at first.

The DEA team radio each other, comb the immediate area but can't find a trace of Davey's car and in the process lose the other two vehicles. The team breaks up and the DEA agents all take the long way back to Midtown still hoping to catch Davey by accident along the way. Davey hasn't vanished completely. He spots one of the DEA tails going by and decides to do a role reversal. After a few blocks the young agent driving the car Davey spotted realizes he's being followed. He then realizes the car following him is Davey's. He gets on his radio and sends a mayday out to the other five cars, but they're scattered all over

Queens and can't get to him. Davey's on the agent's bumper now. The young guy looks into his rearview and turns around but can only see tinted windshield. The Jeep and the town car join him. Davey cranks up his stereo and the vibrations travel bumper to bumper. The agent has his gun out on the seat next to him. Suddenly he spots the light fixture of a police precinct. The agent floors it, and nearly wipes out a cop standing on the precinct steps when he screeches to a halt and runs inside, gun in hand. In a moment he's back out again with two uniforms in tow. Davey's gone. So are the Jeep and the town car. All that's left of them is black paint on a government bumper.

Ten

Movies and TV make it look like cop partners automatically complement each other and get along just fine. *Dragnet, Adam 12, Starsky & Hutch, T.J. Hooker, Miami Vice* are built around a couple of cops who seem to be able to spend eighty hours a week in each other's company without showing any stress or strain. The truth is that kind of chemistry between two beat cops and even detectives working together is rare—as rare as a marriage with the same unity of purpose and lack of friction. The two of you are side-by-side for eight hours or more a day, five days a week, either sweating your asses off or freezing your balls off. No matter how steady a shitstorm a given day on the job presents, you can't take each other for granted and can't take petty bullshit out on each other or blame your partner for anything that can't be talked out or fixed down the line. When you start getting into that bad roommate headspace on duty, you're asking to either burn out fast on doing actual police work, or worse, get both of you hurt bad or jammed up with the bosses.

No cop, I don't care who he or she is, can operate all out, every day on a beat like the one Gio and I shared in Alphaville. It's just like any other gig—good days follow bad days. One shift one of us would maybe feel the burn, want to go home on time and get laid, not feel like taking a call that would put him waist deep in human misery while the other would be spoiling for a collar, a fight, overtime, and a weird story to laugh about later. We took turns driving and being the recorder—the partner in charge of the small mountain of paperwork every uniform shift produced. One tour we would relax, take radio calls, and let the drug collars wait, another shift we would go to war with the dealers and junkies on the D and spend half a day extra in processing and booking. Gio and I had solid intuition about which of us was up for what on most days. It made the job livable and it made it doable. Neither of us would ever have gotten as far as we did without the other.

We read each other's mood within the first twenty minutes of a shift, picked up on each other's cues all day or night and arrived at every radio call showing a united front. Neither of us was ever surprised or caught off guard by the other one's reaction to the crazy shit we'd find. It was important in some situations not to verbally communicate in front of a suspect. If they sensed confusion, they could get brave and try to hurt you, or scared and try to run. Correctly reading a look from your partner could mean the difference between facing a knife, chasing a skell down twenty flights of stairs, or just cuffing the fuck and frog-marching him to the elevator. I always knew when Gio was going to go for his cuffs during a family dispute. I don't think he ever misread me when we tackled a pair of junkies at the same time. We never got in each other's way in a beef and always laughed off the stuff that was just too absurd for words.

As the months in uniform wore on, the voyeuristic appeal of Avenue D after dark wore off and I began to prefer day tours. They were less fun and risky than midnight to eight, but a lot more educational. The important thing with the eight to four shift was to get out early, before someone found some bullshit aided case call for us to respond to, and hustle a collar from those A.M. junkies that I'd seen the first time I came through the neighborhood. They were easy to spot. In this mostly Hispanic neighborhood, the morning junkie was usually a white guy in a wrinkled suit, or a construction worker trying his best to walk, talk, and look like he wasn't compelled to be where he was by a four-hundred-dollar-a-day monkey on his back. These guys and girls were the eighties' Willy Lomans. They lied to their spouses, children, coworkers, and anyone else they had to in order to keep the dope going through them. They were a sad and sorry bunch of motherfuckers.

The script rarely varied. We'd pull up alongside one of these mopes in our marked car. With all the suburban entitlement they could muster, they'd pretend not to see us, or look down the street for whatever it was we must really be looking for. It was sad. We'd creep along next to them driving as slow as the car would let us, and watch their eyes land on everything except us. Eventually, they'd stop and look around as if they were suddenly lost. That wrenching change from single-minded search for dope to lost lamb in the big city was a hard one to pull off. They'd look up at the tall buildings, squint at street signs, and study their watch as if they were late to catch a train. That was our cue.

"You all right?" one of us would ask. "You look lost."

"I'm waiting for a friend," was the usual response.

"Oh, and he's late, huh? Where were you gonna meet your friend?" By this time the junkie is sweating. We're just not going to go away. Sorry.

"Here," they'd say.

"Here? No address, just 'here'? What's your friend's name? Where does he live?"

The next answer was the end of act one. No matter what they said, our answer was the same: "Give us your dope or you're going to jail. Now."

"Dope, no, I swear to God, Officers, on my wife and kids that I'm just here waiting for somebody." If a guy broke our balls about "why aren't you out catching real crooks" or any of that bullshit (you'd be amazed at how many junkie lawyers shopped in the Lower East Side) we would give him a hard time back. A few threats about charging with intent to sell usually shut them up. If not, or if they bolted, there were other solutions we had tried and tested. Most guys caved quickly, and admitted that, yeah, they partied a little and yeah, they had bought a little dope, sure, we could have it, and hey, were we serious about *not* taking them to jail? Well, um, no.

We were rookies and we needed collars. One bag of dope or a ten-bag bundle, college professor or crackhead, we needed an arrest to boost our stats, earn us more freedoms, and let us use most of the rest of the shift pumping a perp for information while we processed them.

"RMP nine-eight oh-seven, has one under from Third and D, Central." That was our wake-up call to the dispatcher. Other units would still be drinking their coffee and eating their doughnuts when we were out kicking ass and taking names.

I loved getting up and out early and bringing some ass-hole in on a dope charge. The early birds came in handy. They were usually an easy collar that didn't get sick in the backseat, smell bad, or whine all through the booking process like the more hardcore addicts we'd grab. They were also easy to get information from. Gio and I were both genuinely curious about how the dope business worked. Our assembly line approach to creating collars didn't put a dent in the dope business that was fucking up the neighborhood. So rather than just nailing a guy, calling it in, and heading for the valley of vouchering and paperwork, we began to grab them and question them.

Junkies can be like children. Like a baby grabbing for the tit, they have an infantile need that trumps every other part of their consciousness. It's all about avoiding pain. If answering our questions meant shortening or eliminating the pain of going through withdrawal in Central Booking and a cell in the Tombs, they would tell us just about anything. Our sidewalk burlesque show became truth or dare. Where'd you cop? The corner? What corner? What's the dealer's name? What's his dope called? What does he look like? Has he been there long? Is he part of a crew? Who turned you on to him? How often do you cop? How long have you been coming here to do it? Where else have you copped? What corner? What's that guy's name? What's his dope called? You get the picture.

When one of them dummied up and refused to answer or got wise with us, we'd smack him in the head or across the mouth, just like the nuns at Catholic school. It was an antiquated method, but it was time-tested and it worked. We learned where dope was being peddled, and we became familiar with junkies and the guys that sold to them. Now when we drove down Avenue D past all the spots, we had names and descriptions we could fit on each corner dealer, and the brand of dope they'd be pushing.

The high-functioning addicts were especially helpful. They all acted like they didn't belong there and were only too happy to rat out anyone they could in the hopes that we'd let them go or even sometimes let them keep their dope. In time we began to do both. That same black-and-white, right-and-wrong mentality I found so unrealistic at the academy didn't last long when it came to dealing with the dope scene on the LES. We didn't set out to, but we were, out of sheer curiosity and disgust, compiling a dossier—an unofficial fact sheet that would eventually lead us to the one guy running the whole sick show—and that information came at a price.

It was a high-wire act—ballsy as hell for rookies. On the plus side our arrest activity, the means by which the department weighed out worthiness for promotion, and the stats for our Command were phenomenal. We were making drug collars, good ones, in uniform which was practically unheard of in those days. No one in uniform anywhere else in Housing PD, or NYPD, was vouchering hundred bag packages of dope like we were, let alone the other guys in our Command.

On the minus side, we were using those early morning drug collars to avoid aided cases and the other workaday aspects of being a housing cop that didn't agree with us, and a lot of our arrests were based on common sense observation that would never have held up in court if we detailed each story as it really happened. As I'd learned in Coney

Island, "We saw a guy who looked like a junkie, searched him and discovered that he was a junkie and had dope on him," didn't cut it in the courthouse, so we didn't pitch it that way in our paperwork or our interviews with ADAs. The punch-line was the same either way—a junkie or a dealer got taken off the street—all we needed to do was streamline the setup sometimes to make it work. It was arrogant at best and drifting across the line into rogue cop territory at worst.

Our new hobby of grilling the skells we busted to try to make sense of the 24-7 heroin bazaar going on around us, wasn't exactly protocol. What we were up to was task force stuff, not uniform rookie cop stuff. We were young and loved what we were doing and had the confidence of a two-man team that played well together and the free rein of a precinct skipper who appreciated how good our arrest spike looked on the paperwork accounting he was obliged to pass upstairs. If we looked into the future, it wasn't very far. A promotion to plainclothes was as likely as a disciplinary hearing. In the meantime we got our kicks and our collars the way we liked and tried not to do anything we'd really lose sleep over.

The post-Knapp paperwork ordeal of making a narcotics arrest was its own trial by bureaucracy. I swear the laborious process of vouchering evidence and processing drug collars in the eighties was one of the major contributors to New York's street heroin nightmare. Even cops that could get away with arresting dealers and junkies like us in housing usually couldn't be bothered because of the necessary administrative follow-through. When you made any kind of arrest, you had to deal with your Command's desk officer.

The desk officer (D/O), usually a sergeant or a lieutenant, was most often a cop who'd taken the apathy route. If doing nothing while wearing a badge was your idea of a good time, then being a desk sergeant was a slice of heaven.

The majority of desk sergeants were careerists who worked the civil service side of police work, seeking a safe spot in the supervisory ranks without ever actually making any collars. Typically, a desk sergeant or lieutenant was someone who gravitated toward hiding out in the back of a precinct house studying the *Patrol Guide*. After roll call all that most desk officers had to do was read the paper, not choke on their coffee, and shift their weight enough to avoid hemorrhoids until their watch was over. Repeat five times a week for two decades and collect a full pension.

What ruined most desk officers' day were go-getter uniform cops like Philly and Louie back in Coney Island and me and Gio in Alphabet City coming in with actual arrests. Procedure dictated that every salient detail about the collar and the condition and disposition of the prisoner be recorded in the precinct's log—place of arrest, charge, priors, the perp's apparent health while in custody, time spent within the Command, time out to Central Booking, the whole deal. As A/O (arresting officer) I had to search the prisoner in front of the D/O, inventory anything I found, and then count out the perp's money to the penny. It wasn't fun for anyone, but it was torture when the desk officer couldn't be bothered and thought he could teach you a lesson about interrupting them while they were reading about Miss July's hobbies and turn-ons, or Rickey Henderson's hammy and picturing themselves chipping golf balls in Boca. Imagine your worst junior high vice principal, DMV, or bank teller experience and multiply it by a hundred. The precinct bosses could make what's already a lousy procedure feel like a root canal.

In narcotics arrests, the A/O had to transport the prisoner from the Housing PD Command to the local NYPD precinct (generally the Sixtieth in Coney Island and the Seventh on Pitt Street in Alphabet City) to inventory and put away ("voucher" in honor of the combination envelope and form used) the narcotic evidence found on the prisoner. So, having bid a clipped but polite good-bye to my own pain-in-the-ass D/O at the Housing Command, I now stepped into round two with an even bigger pain in the ass—a D/O who wasn't even my boss. Regular city cop NYPD desk sergeants and lieutenants genuinely disliked the interruption just like mine did. They also bitterly resented the fact that it was coming from a cop from another division and Command and that the arrest involved the extra unfamiliar paperwork of a drug bust that the D/O's own men weren't even permitted to do.

Adding to the fun was the department's laborious procedure for putting confiscated drugs into evidence. I had to count out, individually label, and initial every bag of dope I found on my prisoner (1 of 100, 2 of 100, 3 of 100, and so on). This wasn't such a big deal in Coney Island where the pickings were small, but in Alphabet City, even before I made plainclothes, I would sometimes bring in perps holding three or four hundred bags of dope. Having counted and numbered each bag, I then had to put them in a clasped manila envelope, seal it, and sign the fold. If I missed a bag, or the numbers didn't match up, I was in for a hard time from a captain or an inspector and ran the risk of receiving a

Command discipline. Command discipline punishment could range anywhere from a warning to having precious vacation days taken away. If a problem with vouchering happened too many times, or enough bags of dope were brought into question, Internal Affairs got called in. An IAB investigation could result in charges and specs filed, a departmental trial, up to thirty vacation days taken away, or possibly even getting fired from the job. No wonder so few cops bothered making drug busts.

Once after we made plainclothes, Gio and I busted an Avenue D small-timer named Fats. We followed procedure, took him first to our Command then to the Seventh Precinct, and vouchered the two dozen bags he had on him as evidence. An hour later we get a call from the Seventh Precinct. Fats was found with another bundle of dope on him inside the Seventh's lockup. We missed ten bags? There was no fucking way. Gio and I went back and leaned on him.

"What the fuck, Fats? I checked you out top to bottom," I told him out of earshot of the Seventh's glaring desk sergeant. "Where did you get this dope?" Fats whined and wheedled and eventually admitted the truth. He was owed some dope from another dealer who was also in the cells with him. The cop that busted this other dealer had missed a bunch of dope when he searched him. Fats got his dope back, and got me jammed up in the process. I didn't want to rat out the other dealer's arresting officer, but I also didn't want to take a hit. I gave Fats an ultimatum—tell the desk sergeant you found that dope in the corner of the cell, or stay off of Avenue D until further notice. I dodged the complaint and Fats got another count added to his online booking sheet.

Another time I finished tagging and bagging four hundred glassines of smack only to find that the adhesive on my voucher envelope didn't stick. I took the envelope to a big industrial sink in the Seventh's basement to moisten the glue and accidentally dropped a few bags down the drain. I had no choice but to go back out on the avenue and grab enough dope off some junkie to replace what had washed down the drain, match the numbers of the new dope with what was missing from the envelope, and then get the fucking envelope sealed at last. Again, not a peep from the Command or IAB.

"Weather is the best policeman." I used to hear Jack Genova say that about once a week during my rookie years on Coney Island, and I'd heard him say it in my head about once an hour since coming on the job this morning. Gio and I had drawn an eight-to-four shift, but the rain had been coming down so heavily since before dawn that there was literally nothing for us to do. We were rained out like a ball game. It was my turn behind the wheel again, but the torrent pelting our windshield was like movie rain—thick and continuous as if it were man-made—and I didn't want to spend any more time driving against it than I had to. We'd spent what seemed like hours parked on the corner of Houston and D. A *cuchifritos* sign flashed through the torrent outside. Inside the car we were both lost in our own thoughts. The rain pounding on the roof and windows was like white noise. Anyway, we'd both pretty much run out of things to say for the day. The radio would occasionally bark out a job, but none of them was for us. I'd take the dullest, most unnecessary aided case or the biggest pain in the ass emotionally disturbed person over this. Then:

"Available unit, ten fifty-four, aided case, possible EDP up on the roof of ten Avenue D, possible jumper. Units to respond?"

We were only fifty yards from the building. I jammed the car into drive. Gio was already on the radio.

"Nine-five seven-seven, K, we're ten eighty-four at the scene."

It was a U-turn to the address Central gave. As we screeched to a stop I sensed something drop to the sidewalk next to us. We could make out a loud, dull thud through the rolled-up windows. We got out fast and were instantly soaked. A male body lay twisted on the sidewalk. The guy's arms were exposed. Even in the driving rain I could see that they were ulcerated and had the collapsed patches, scarring, and withered contours of someone who'd given up on everything but shooting dope. Blood, lymph, and God knows what else was pouring out of the back of his shattered head and washed away in the downpour. Chunks of brain bobbed into the sewer backup that had filled every gutter in the neighborhood since breakfast. Eventually they'd flow out into the rivers. We needed a minute to take this all in. The rain didn't matter anymore.

Whether he fell or jumped didn't matter either. What seemed important somehow was his body language. The guy had hit Avenue D so hard, less than a body length from our car that his hips were twisted nearly a hundred and eighty degrees and both legs were bent completely backward. We moved closer and an EMS van pulled up on the sidewalk next to us. One of the techs knelt, swore, lifted the dead guy's head and made an effort to fit some of the brains that hadn't been washed away back into his skull. I gave the EMTs a break and helped lift the corpse into the back of their truck. He was wet and heavy, his eyes open and life-less like a casualty in a war comic.

I moved my head around a little to see if I could look into them like he was still alive, but you can never find yourself in a dead guy's eyes. As I studied his face he stopped being a body and became a person for one final moment. He looked familiar. I knew him, or used to know him. He was nameless to me, but I'd seen him around—a member of the walking dead so far gone that there was no point in even arresting him. There was nothing a guy this bad off could tell you that you couldn't see from across the street as he searched the ground outside and between the project buildings for dis-carded bags of dope hoping to get one last little taste the same way bums smoked the final quarter-inch of tobacco left on a cigarette butt.

What he was telling me now was a sad, sad story of a guy so bad off he'd just as soon die as live. I watched the EMS van pull away. Neither Gio nor I were in a hurry to get back in our car. Somehow standing there in the rain like idiots felt better than trying to act normal and radioing Central from inside the RMP. I looked down the avenue. The weather had stayed so bad for so many hours that we weren't the only ones ignoring it. A dope hot spot on Third Street was doing a light business. People walked and ran along the sidewalk oblivious to the blood and brains mixed in the puddles, unaware that another fucked-up life had reached the end of the line and added an instantly forgotten layer of human landfill to the Lower East Side.

Avenue D

School Boy lives in Alphabet City but his reputation spreads throughout the New York drug underworld. He looks like a schoolboy—younger than his age, well groomed, dressed like he was going to take communion with a school backpack over one shoulder. His look and easygoing, low-key style enables him to walk up to just about anyone and have a gun out and firing before they can do anything about it. School Boy may look like a kid who's lost his dog, but he's a hitman who's killed dozens for Davey and others who can afford his price to clear human obstacles from their path.

We get so many inquiries from detectives all over the city about School Boy that it's become routine. We want to catch him, but he knows us just like we know him. School Boy doesn't kid himself. He knows we won't need an excuse to toss him when we see him, so he learns when we work and only packs heat in his schoolbag when we're off the clock. It sucks for us because we can't catch him with a gun, but it really sucks for him. A lot of the people he's killed have friends and a lot of those friends want School Boy dead. The hours he spends unarmed have to be giving him a lot to think about.

After nearly a year of grabbing guys fitting the description

*of another killer named Sammy Molina, Gio and I finally col-
lar Sammy and hand him off to our detectives. With Sammy
in custody and arraigned for two homicides, the detectives ask
us to round up one of Sammy's homicide witnesses at Fifth
Street and the FDR Drive as a favor. It's the end of our shift but
we're happy to do it. We're even happier when we pass Macatumba, Londie, and School Boy sitting on a car hood together
on Third and D. School Boy turns green when he sees us.
"Motherfucker!" I say to Gio, "School's dirty!" I swing back
around and he's off, running like hell down the D, backpack
in hand.*

*"Op Eight in pursuit Avenue D and Fourth," Gio says into
the radio. School Boy hauls ass right past us, books down
Fourth Street and tosses the pack as he goes. He thinks we
won't follow him against traffic. He's wrong. I floor it, forcing
a cab up onto the curb, pull up in front of School Boy and we're
out. Gio runs back for the backpack and I chase School Boy a
half a block before dropping him and slapping him around in
the middle of the street. I cuff him and drag his sorry ass back
to the car. He whines the whole way about running because he
had dope on him and that he doesn't know what backpack I'm
talking about. Bullshit.*

*But Gio can't find the backpack. Several uniform cars pull
up. The guys in them join the search. They can't find the backpack. Without that bag, we don't have enough to hold School.
We drive over to Houston and D with School Boy cuffed in the
backseat to give the uniforms time to find the bag. But after
fifteen minutes of searching, still no backpack. I'm about to
cut School loose and literally have the key in his cuffs, when
the radio squawks. "You guys lose something?" the uniform on
the other end says. We drive back to the scene with School Boy,*

and the uniform is standing there holding up a backpack. A passing car had parked on it and it rolled up inside a wheel well. School's gun is inside. The cuffs stay on. School Boy curses us out the whole way back to the Command.

Months later, he's singing a different tune. The night before he goes on trial for the gun we find in his bag, the Navarro brothers from Cherry Street up the ante in a war they're having with the Third and D crew. With Davey Blue Eyes's approval, they pull up in a van next to a car with Macatumba and Londie from Third Street in it and open fire. Londie's killed instantly and Macatumba barely makes it out alive. If he didn't have to be in court, School Boy would've been in the car with them. During the trial, quiet, polite, and dressed as always like a schoolboy, he pauses at the prosecution's table where we're conferring with the ADA and calmly thanks us for saving his life.

Eleven

PSA 4 Command was a tight collection of rooms on the ground floor of the Vladeck Houses on Grand Street. Roll call took place in a dusty basement classroom space with a half dozen chairs, a blackboard in the center, and a TV set on a rolling cart off to one side. I stood through roll call as I had for nearly two years waiting for the squad sergeant to dole out the evening's assignments. The sergeant was detailing some memo from on high that I'd unconsciously tuned out. There was an old shoeshine machine in the back of the room and I found myself wondering how it got there and when the last time was that anyone had actually used it.

For some reason when the sergeant awkwardly delivered the observation ". . . see you new guys need to know—some of you old guys, too—you need to remember that when you *work* on this job, you can go places," he got my full attention. For a moment, like everyone else in the room except the sergeant, I had no fucking idea what he was talking about. It was like waking up in a hotel room and forgetting where you were and why you were there. "Gio, Mike, c'mon up here." By the time the words were out of his mouth I remembered. The two of us stood up, dodged nightsticks,

.38s, and knees, and awkwardly made our way to the front of a squad full of eyes. I shuffled into place doubly embarrassed at being in front of the class and caught off guard by this presentation.

Sarge cleared his throat and announced, "Guys, I want everyone to know that tonight will be the last night Gio and Mike will be working with us. They've been reassigned to the Operation Eight unit." The room erupted with a mixture of genuine and sarcastic applause. I didn't care either way. PSA 4 was no different than any other housing Command or city cop precinct—there were some good guys in our uniform squad and there were a few four-star assholes, and the full range of police eagerness, apathy, arrogance, commitment, and incompetence in between.

Sarge stuck his arm out and shook Gio's hand and then mine before we took our places back in the roll call line we'd come from. His palm was as dry as paper. "See," Sarge said again, "if you *work* on this job, you can go places." After we were seated, he finished with the assignments for the evening. The last patrol squad shift either of us ever worked in uniform was a relatively uneventful tour in Sector David.

In the mid-eighties New York was still years away from the police hiring bonanza that began under Mayor Dinkins and eventually climaxed with Rudy Giuliani's famous cleanup. But the FORD TO CITY: DROP DEAD days of the seventies when laid-off cops picketed One Police Plaza and even rioted, were already a thing of the past. Reagan was in the White House and federal purse strings loosened for every pre-9/11 politician's favorite vote-getter—The War on Drugs. Each NYPD and housing Command had its own plainclothes squad. PSA 4 was such a hot zone that it had two. The federal government picked up the tab for the second one—Operation 8. Washington's money bankrolled overtime costs for a squad sergeant and four-man crew whose beat was narrowed to eight specific projects within PSA 4 and for RMP 9864—a brand-new unmarked Chrysler to tour them with. Op 8 cops answered to the PSA 4 Command captain, who in turn answered to the department. His bosses answered to the Feds who'd earmarked the money.

It was all about crime statistics—complaints, arrests, and convictions detailed in graphs, spreadsheets and lists. PSA 4 and the Lower East Side were throwing off the curve big time and Op 8 was put in place to bring those stats under control. The way to do that was to arrest drug offenders. So the center ring of the Op 8 circus were the buildings Gio and I had been specializing in for the last two years—the Wald and Riis houses. If we were working there anyway, why not do it in plainclothes? We lobbied heavily and hard for our spots on the Op 8 roster. As luck would have it, two Op 8 vets made detective at the same time and would shortly be moving on. After a few weeks of the six of us working together, we would be the new meat replacing them when they collected gold shields and headed upstairs.

Making drug collars on the Lower East Side could feel like you were emptying the ocean with a soup ladle. You grab a junkie or a dealer, arrest, process, and arraign him on Friday and on Monday he'd be back on the same corner. The situation in Alphaville was out of hand enough, and the system fucked up enough, that if you wanted to stay in the game you needed something to believe in or get behind. Gio and I just loved the action and the neighborhood. We connected with the electrical jolt of running down perps and taking risks and fed on the energy that radiated from every shadow we crossed and character we met on our beat. Our new colleagues connected with something else—each other.

The five guys we joined at Op 8 were some of the best cops I would ever work with. Sergeant Andrews, Tony Mastro, Jerry Able, Frankie Nieves, and Pete Donnelly were all razor-sharp vets with incredible street smarts and instincts. They logged some of the biggest drug weight and dollar arrests in the city. "I know you guys know how to collar up and had a good thing going on patrol," Sergeant Andrews told us on our first day at Op 8, "but this is a whole other world." He studied our expressions for a second then continued. "You liked being on patrol, but you're going to love being in my squad with these guys. It's a real family here. Not like on patrol. We're a family, and we look out for each other. One hand washes the other, and both hands wash the face. Any questions?"

"No," Gio and I answered in unison.

"Okay then, Mike I want you to work with Frankie until he goes into the bureau. Gio, I want you to partner up with Tony for a few weeks. It's not that I don't trust you guys, it's that you need to learn the ropes from people who know. You're about to learn from the best. Okay?"

Frankie Nieves was a thin Puerto Rican guy from Brooklyn with shoulder-length, jet-black hair and a poker face for every occasion. Frankie looked enough like a Hollywood Indian that the dealers and dopers on the avenue called him "Indio." Frankie wasn't a month away from a gold shield because he was stupid. But he wasn't about to pass on what he knew until he was sure that I would fit in with the squad and use what he'd learned the hard way as well as he did. It took a few days but he thawed once he had a chance to feel me out.

The first discovery I made in plainclothes was just how different the neighborhood was when you weren't wearing a police uniform. Everyone changes how they act when they're around a uniform cop. Most people just didn't realize it. When Frankie and I walked into a bodega, no one pretended not to look at us, like they would've if we'd been in blue. Being in plainclothes was almost like being a ghost. Dressed in jeans and sneakers, I could walk right past guys I'd busted mere days before without them so much as batting an eyelash.

Sure some people in the neighborhood recognized Frankie, and it wouldn't be long before they would recognize me and Gio, but it always took a moment and sometimes a moment was all we needed. It was so much easier to catch people off guard when you weren't in uniform. In plainclothes I could stand at a bus station and act like I was waiting for the M21 like anyone else while scoping out dealers in their spots. Lookouts and steerers no longer shouted "Five-O" or *"agua"* ("water"—the ocean, like police uniforms and cars, is blue after all) to let the block know that a cop was nearby when I turned the corner.

It was important to dress as low key and naturally as possible in plainclothes. Some of the guys in the Seventh and Ninth precincts' plainclothes squads never really got that message. Stuffed into skin-tight bike pants with a long-tailed button-down shirt to cover the gun and badge on their belt, and a bulletproof vest peeking through their shirt collar, they looked so absurdly out of place that they might as well have been wearing their dress uniforms.

The most vital pieces of gear for any plainclothes cop were the same anywhere in the city. When Frankie made an arrest he put on two things—his shield, which hung around his neck like a medallion on a chain, and a colored bandanna. Every cop in every roll call everywhere in the city was told what the color for the day was. A plainclothes cop had a bandanna for each color in the daily rotation in his locker. If he knew what was good for him, he'd sooner forget his gun than forget what the color for a given tour was or leave his headband behind. That bandanna was the only way a uniform cop arriving on the scene of an arrest could tell a good guy from a bad guy. In a city full of new and nervous cops, a lot of them suburban kids from Long Island or upstate, a guy who played and looked his part as well as Frankie did ran a genuine risk of getting gunned down by one of his own.

"I know the headband looks stupid as shit," Frankie said the first time we made a bust together, "but I don't want some new jack white kid rookie shooting me in the back."

Frankie wasn't a cowboy and he gave a lot of thought to his place in the crazy fish bowl of life in the projects. His movements were slow and deliberate, and the points he made were always on target. Frankie had cultivated an eagle eye for street drug traffic, the ebb and flow of buyers and sellers, and the mechanics of a smack sale. Official Op 8 procedure involved spending hours at observation points within and near the projects tracking dealers and buyers. When an Op 8 cop saw a deal go down he would radio descriptions to other members of the squad who would then grab the buyer out of sight of the dealer. If the arrest was good, we'd then work our way back in, bust the dealer by description, and make a case based on what we saw and what we got off the perps we arrested—drugs, confessions, or information.

Rock stars and rich kids bought their drugs in apartments, hotel rooms, cars, and the bathrooms of bars. Everybody else had to score in the projects. Truth is, just about all the smack in New York came through PSA 4 no matter where it was going. If he's jonesing badly enough, a junkie will go anywhere to buy and shoot up a bag of smack. But generally, though, your average addict didn't like going inside a building to cop. Since the Avenue D projects had been written off by nearly everyone outside of Op 8, they didn't have to. Dealers were free to cater to their clientele and make sales on the sidewalk. Staging street corner drug deals let junkies get in, score, and get out, and reassured dealers that their customers wouldn't hang around nodding out or OD'ing and that their guys could see trouble coming before it got there.

What it meant for us was that we could observe everything about a drug deal. The first lesson of Op 8 was to get to know the observation spots used for studying dealer and junkie traffic. Nobody gets into the drug business to get up early and there were always down times where Frankie and I could slip into a maintenance office, unrented apartment, or neighboring rooftop without being seen by anyone we were there to look at.

Gio and I had made enough collars to recognize how the game worked on a uniform cop level. Huddled alongside Frankie watching dope and money changing hands from an unused office he had the keys to in back of a heavy dope spot in the Wald Houses at 30 Avenue D, parked across the street from 50 Avenue D or 950 East Fourth Walk, or in an empty project one-bedroom full of paint cans across from a three-story building at Third and D that was like smack sale Grand Central, was a master class.

Once we settled in, Frankie would look out through the painted metal mesh that covered most ground-floor windows and start calling the plays like Tim McCarver.

"Okay," he'd say, "that guy is steering, that one is getting ready to re-up for them when they're done, and that one is selling." He sketched out verbal profiles of customers. "He's here to buy weight," Frankie would say about a guy crossing the avenue toward a dealer. "I've seen him before. Probably Jersey, probably good for a package." A deal, some point-to-point radio conversation between us and our colleagues waiting for the buyer's description in the unmarked car a couple blocks away, two cops, and one pair of cuffs later, Frankie's assessment would turn out to be on the nose. In less than a month Professor Nieves's Smack 101 got me straighter on the ways and words of dope dealing than I would've taught myself in five more years on uniform patrol.

Smack wasn't sold at street level by weight as much as by unit. And the basic unit of measurement in a dope deal was, in those days, a ten-dollar glassine (a kind of wax paper envelope) of dope. Ten bags makes a hundred-dollar bundle held together with a rubber band. Junkies whose tolerance had gone up far enough and who hadn't emptied their pockets and those of everyone who cared about them would sometimes buy a bundle a day. A package was ten bundles—a hundred bags of dope—and would set you back a thousand bucks. Packages were wrapped tight enough to be about fist size.

Since they were a solid felony bust and a potential gold-mine for anyone who successfully beat a dealer for one, packages usually only came out one at a time to be broken down and sold as bags. Because of the risk of getting busted or ripped off, the corner dealers rarely held more than a couple of bundles at once. Guys called runners kept their dealers supplied or "re-upped." The big stashes were hidden in apartments upstairs, and runners would carry salable material by the bundle or package to and from the stash to the corner dealer they worked for as needed.

"Hot 103," "Thriller," "Mr. T," "Polo," "Red Line," "Body Bag," "Elegante,"—the steerers were the guys who called out the brand name of a dealer's smack like carnival barkers.

"Yo, get your Hot One-Oh-Three here. Got that kick-ass shit, yo! Kick-ass D!—pass me by, you won't get high!" When a steerer got a buyer's attention, he'd answer whatever questions the junkie might have and walk the customer to their dealer's spot. It was always a major selling point if a brand was known to be so good that it had killed a customer or put someone in the hospital with an OD.

Ever since a bunch of South Asian businessmen opened up a row of different Indian restaurants on East Sixth street in the late sixties, the joke went that there was one enormous kitchen underneath the block serving all of them. When it came to brand-conscious junk buyers, the joke was on the customer. Despite the individual sales pitches and names, most of the dope sold out of the Avenue D projects came from the same shipments. Any variation was a matter of how much it had been stepped on by the main dealers who broke it up into bags. The brands were merely salesmanship for the crews and customers but they were also a reliable way for us to ID and track individual dealers.

The last guy in the chain was the lookout. Like the name said, he was there to scan the sidewalks and streets for cops, stickup kids coming to rob a spot, pissed-off competitors, unsatisfied customers, and the inevitable crazies that might fuck up commerce and bring unwanted attention. A half-naked guy covered in his own blood staggering down the street with a needle bobbing in his arm in the middle of winter could slow sales as much as a blue-and-white parked at the curb. Good lookouts were hard to come by. The number of guys Op 8 sent to Central Booking attests to that. But the good ones did exist—ambitious kids who didn't get so high or drunk that they couldn't concentrate, guys whose game was to make themselves so useful and familiar with the gig that they would become dealers themselves and make some big money.

If he had good material, guys working for him who weren't idiots, and he kept from getting busted or shot, a street corner dealer would normally earn between five hundred and a thousand dollars a day. The runner was paid by the trip like any other messenger. Most made about two hundred dollars a shift, depending on the number of runs he made. The lookout was good for another two hundred or so a day, and the steerer usually banked between forty and fifty dollars for his troubles.

Corner dealers and the crews they worked with all answered to another guy—a main dealer who stayed off the street except to make periodic checks on his guys. These main dealers usually had multiple dope-selling spots, each with their own corner dealer, runner, steerer, and lookout. Depending on how many spots the main dealer ran, if the weather and material were good, everyone stayed out of jail, and his guys weren't stupid, brave, or fucked up enough to rip him off, a main dealer stood to make between ten and thirty thousand dollars a day.

Most of the corner dealers, steerers, and runners grew up and lived in the projects. Everybody likes a short commute. They felt safe, knew where to hide from cops and rip-offs, and could realistically expect their friends, family, and neighbors to mind their own business and shut the fuck up about what went on in the street. The main dealers made enough money that they drove in from apartments and houses they bought or rented outside of the neighborhood. These main guys were the ones that I wanted to know better. Who were they? What would it take to bring them down and put them away? As it would turn out I was already on my way to having both of those answers.

Growing up in Canarsie, where both *omerta* (the Cosa Nostra code) and the "blue wall of silence" (how cops sometimes described their approach to curious outsiders) were the rule, had given me an exaggerated idea of the lengths that people would go to keep secrets. What I discovered on the Lower East Side was if it weren't for informants, no one would ever go to jail. Everybody on the wrong side of the law, and I mean everybody, has a price. Drug dealers, junkies, and most other crooks will rat out each other and incriminate themselves at the drop of a hat. Either you were so scared that the person you ratted out was going to hurt you that you kept silent about something you knew or you weren't and you didn't. There were a lot more people in Alphaville scared of going to jail, and a lot who got enough of a bump out of being paid for what they said that few people in the projects thought twice about fingering a neighbor, brother, coconspirator, or even themselves.

Criminal justice may be founded on all kinds of high-minded principles of fairness and the needs of the community, but when it comes to drug dealing, justice depends on informants. On the Lower East Side law and order boiled down to this: cops pay off snitches, turn bad guys to their advantage by going easy on them, and play them against each other once they have their confidence. Passing harsh drug laws makes politicians look and feel good, at the same time that it gives prosecutors a big, heavy stick to wield in discussions with perps and their lawyers. DAs and prosecutors waive or reduce charges and sentences and make other arrangements on behalf of the accused criminals who will play ball with them and lead them to a better conviction of someone bigger and badder. The cold hard truth is that the people drug dealers need to fear the most are other drug dealers.

Gio and I had created our own brand of "discretionary procedure" while we were on uniform patrol. We weren't systematic about it, but when we wanted to learn something about who was dealing or buying in the neighborhood, we weren't above letting a guy go if we appreciated his honesty with us, or threatening or touching up someone dirty who we were sure could show us someone dirtier. We never took money or drugs or any of that kind of renegade shit for our own gain or comfort. Never. But toward the end of our time in uniform patrol, we did start shaping cases and situations in order to get collars and gain insight into what the fuck was making the Lower East Side New York's heroin headquarters.

An Internal Affairs investigator could probably make a good case for us losing our badges over some of the leeway we already gaveth and tooketh away. Within another year at Op 8, looking over our shoulders for IAB would become part of the way Gio and I worked. When I first started in plainclothes, I wasn't sure where Frankie stood in the gray area between legal departmental procedure and what it actually took to get narcotics offenders off the street. Initially working with Frankie sometimes felt a little like visiting with an older relative and having to remember not to swear. I didn't want to volunteer any information or war stories that might make him wonder about Gio or me.

One day I was seated alongside Frankie in the Op 8 RMP driving down Avenue D, when he pointed at a twitchy young Hispanic kid on the sidewalk and told me to pull over.

"Fuck me, there he is!"

The guy Frankie pointed at looked like he was going to rabbit at first but when he caught sight of Frankie he just bowed his head dejectedly. He seemed relieved. Frankie made a show of turning out the guy's pockets and shoving him around a little before calmly telling him to meet us on the roof of 484 East Houston in ten minutes. "Ah, but *mira*, Indio, I got to go to the clinic, you know?"

"It'll wait, Ponte," Frankie said. "I've been looking for you all week. Don't make us come looking for you again."

Ten minutes later we were fifteen stories above the Wald Houses looking down on slowed traffic jamming up the FDR when Ponte came out the roof door.

"Who's this?" Ponte asked Frankie.

"His name's Mike," Frankie replied. His manner was more macho than I'd ever seen before and he suddenly had a strong Hispanic accent. "He's new but he's gonna be here for a while. You better come across with something good, and make friends with him. You do not want him on your bad side." I played along and stood there in stony silence looking at Ponte like he was a roach.

"Yo, I gots something good, Indio, believe me," Ponte said. "Over in the FDR park dealing going on like fuckin' mad crazy. The guy running the material over is a little black dude named Little Punk. He's running Red Line on his bike over the overpass right there on Houston and the Drive."

"Where?" Frankie asked.

"Yo, like right there!" Ponte said and pointed down into the trees along the riverbank. "Like right now! You can't miss his ass today, he's wearing a purple hoodie, and he's on a bike. One thing though," Ponte cautioned, "you got to make sure you catch him going into the park. That's when he'll be carrying the shit. When he's going in. He's got nothing when he's coming back out again."

Frankie nodded, reached into his pocket, and gave Ponte a twenty-dollar bill. I'd seen him pull out the same fifty- or sixty-dollar fold of cash at lunch and knew for a fact that it was his own money. That's when I knew I could relax a little around Frankie Nieves.

According to the rules, police informants have to be fingerprinted and registered with the department. Their prints went through the FBI fingerprint file and their paperwork had to be signed and approved by the brass. Under almost no circumstances could a registered informant be on parole or probation. That disqualified about 99.9 percent of potentially useful snitches anywhere in the five boroughs. A guy like Ponte was for sure an addict and without question on parole, or eluding an outstanding warrant for some stupid shit. He didn't have a chance in hell of qualifying for registered informant status. Even if he could, in order to get paid, you and your informant had to fill out stacks of forms, which in turn needed to be processed and approved by about a half-dozen pencil pushers in the department.

Like the Knapp ban on uniform drug collars, registered informant red tape was meant to slow down corruption. It may have, but it slowed down useful intelligence gathering as well. The drug dealing landscape was constantly shifting. Who knew if Little Punk would be riding dope over the Houston Street exit ramp tomorrow? And Ponte needed his money now. Guys like him were always between fixes. Twenty bucks went a long way when your informant might get sick without his bag of dope.

Ponte's hand steadied as he slipped the twenty into his hip pocket.

"This better work out," Frankie said. Ponte gave the thumbs-up.

"Red Line, you watch. At least a package, papa." He doubled the thumbs-up and smiled at me. I watched him run off to the roof stairs and wondered where and what he was going to cop. Probably not Red Line at Little Punk's East River Park spot. Frankie turned to me, his poker face and even voice both back in place.

"So let's go get us a collar."

On our way out Frankie radioed the other guys in Op 8 and told them we'd be performing a watch on the off-ramp on Houston and the Drive that Ponte told us about from our RMP. He also arranged to have two guys watch the overpass at Sixth Street that ran between the Wald Houses and the park just in case.

"Guys like Ponte are good but they're still junkies and sometimes they only get half the story right," he explained.

When we'd been in place about half an hour, Frankie broke a lengthy silence.

"These things sometimes take patience," he said. I nodded. Some tours with Frankie were an undeclared contest to see who could say the least. But, sure as shit, a second later Tony's voice came over the radio.

"Heading your way, male black with purple hooded sweat jacket on a bike. He's looking back and forth. Be careful, for sure he's your runner." Frankie and I bolted from the car, hustled up to the overpass, leapt over a guard rail, and crouched down out of sight of anyone coming up after us. Cars climbed up from the FDR, slowed at a stop sign in front of us, and turned onto Houston Street or went down the on ramp into the three-lane jam up below us. A dark-skinned Hispanic kid no older than eighteen rolled up on a BMX snapping his head from side to side inside a purple hoodie just like Tony said. I grabbed him and he yanked backward over the rear wheel of his bike like a guy in a western getting shot off a horse. Frankie and I both fell on top of him. The kid's bike bounced to the pavement on its side and he fought like a bastard. All three of us were amped on adrenaline and it wasn't as easy to get him cuffed as I thought. A station wagon honked at us as we dragged him over to the side of the roadway. Once we had the kid down we tossed him. Eureka. There were two hundred bags on the son of a bitch and each one was stamped Red Line. Everyone had a price, and everyone could be bought, sold, and caught. Little

Punk was worth twenty bucks to Ponte. Two bags in Ponte's arm netted us two hundred bags vouchered into evidence and taken off the street.

Avenue D

Evening shift and not much action. Gio and me hear about a shake-up at one of the dope spots at Third Street and conduct surveillance from an unrented apartment in the Wald Houses on the D that the building's manager gave me the keys to at the end of the summer. It's a good vantage point and the manager is a good guy, so the inspection and small amount of painting the apartment needs to get listed available in the NYCHA system isn't getting done. There's not much to see tonight, or at least nothing we hadn't seen before that will help us unlock the higher mechanics of the street dope trade. I'm feeling restless. We both are.

Back out in the RMP, I watch a blond chick in five-inch heels and a white leather mini totter out to a fancy pimped out Cadillac on the curb. NYCHA and the heroin trade are both equal opportunity, but most foot traffic on the D in the eighties is Hispanic. We nearly always stop and watch Caucasians and blacks we don't already know to see what brings them to our little corner of the world: 99.99 percent of the time it's the same thing.

You don't have to be a street genius to realize what this broad is all about. By the time she arrives at the Caddy, we're there, flashing tin. The car, a total throwback seventies Super

Fly–style Caddy looks familiar to me, but I don't dwell on it at first. When he powers down his window and smiles at our badges, the driver, a rail-thin overdressed black dude, looks even more familiar than the car.

"Evening, ma'am. Sir. Police officers," Gio says in his best Joe Friday impersonation. "Help you with something?" I kick one of the fenders with my shoe to gauge just how fucked up everybody is. The guy snaps his eyes back at me but keeps his face pointed at Gio. The woman just sort of sways instead of jumping. What was obvious half a block away is depressingly clear up close. She's a prostitute and a user with the double dead-eyed gaze of someone who's surrendered way more of themselves than they can ever get back. She has on long opera-type gloves but they don't quite cover an abscess and a small tangle of track marks on one arm. The guy in the car is clearly her pimp. I suddenly realize why the car looks so familiar. Holy shit. Small fucking world . . . I start to laugh.

"Cat, right?" I say to the guy. He's the Forty-second Street pimp who shot up Richie Gascon's car on Eighth Avenue when we were in high school. It's so far from what Gio expects to hear that he breaks character with a "what the fuck?" look at me. The pimp is stunned. I know his name but he has no idea why or how to play it. Is this good news or is he fucked?

It's like old home week all of a sudden. A few days before I see another familiar face on the D. This one's from Canarsie. I know him as Taco. His kid brother is my age and was in some of my high school classes. It's one of those perfect "Autumn in New York" type days and for once I'm not caring about who's selling and what's going down. But Taco's clearly there to cop and it looks like he's making to score from a guy we've used a lot for information. Worst of all, Taco calls me "Rambo," a nick-

name nobody in Canarsie was gonna learn if I had anything to do about it, and starts whispering shit to me about who's selling, and hints that he's earned a few bags from me for sharing. It's fucking surreal. The longest conversation I ever have with a guy whose brother sat next to me in algebra and it's about trading fucking dope for information? No explanation, no apology, no "Hey, don't tell no one in the old neighborhood but I've had some hard luck," nothing. He's a rat and I'm THE MAN? Nah, he's Taco and I'm Mike and we're both a long fucking way from Canarsie. I blow him off and two hours later I see him licking his finger, sticking it into empty glassines from the gutter then back into his mouth.

Now this scumbag from the past, Cat. He's got his act a little better together.

"Yeah, yo Officers, my lady friend and I were just leaving," he says pointing uptown with an upraised pinkie with an inch-long lacquered nail on the tip. I don't remember that from the last time I saw him. He's got both hands flat on the dash. It's like a dog rolling over on his back in submission. He wants us to know he's not going to pull anything out of his pockets or turn the motor on in a hurry.

"Yeah? You and your lady friend mind stepping to the curb?" Gio replies. Cat looks at me.

"Yo, listen," the pimp hisses, his voice dropping into a conspiratorial whisper, *"can you give us a break, man?"*

"Why should we do that, Cat?" I ask, frankly enjoying fucking with the guy by using his name. He'll never remember who I am in a thousand years. Cat looks at me with awkwardly theatrical confidence. He's gotta be high on blow.

"I know Rambo, man. Fastback and Rambo! We know those dudes!"

What? This just got even weirder. I recognized him and know his street name and now he's throwing around my and Gio's nicknames like we're his ticket out.

Enough. "Get the fuck out of here," *I tell him.* "Seriously, just get the fuck out of here. We see either of you anywhere in the projects again, we're gonna tell your friends Fastback and Rambo how much you pissed us off." *I say the names like I never heard them before.*

The girl wobbles around the back of the car and gets in. Cat the pimp thanks us and they drive off. Gio looks at me like I've grown a second head.

"Feel like telling me what the fuck that was all about?" he asks. "You and 'Cat' go way back?"

"Bro, you're not going to believe me."

"Try me," he says and walks back to the RMP. It's probably the first time Gio's ever seen me let a potential toss and bust slide and for sure the first skell I don't ask about Davey Blue Eyes since White Boy Ronnie let the name slip. I steal one last look at the Caddy's taillights heading back to Times Square and laugh again. Cat gets a pass. For old time's sake. First Taco from Canarsie, now this. Small fucking world.

Twelve

After a month working with Frankie, word came down that his and Pete's paperwork were done, their promotions were finalized and they were on their way to the Housing Detective Bureau at week's end. The last night we worked together I asked Frankie a question that had started to bother me.

"How'd you not get personally involved with this shit?" I asked him. "I mean you're here all the fucking time, you watch these dealers fuck up so many lives. It's almost like a personal insult, isn't it? How do you keep your head on straight and not let it get to you?"

"It's a job, Mike. Just a job. Don't ever take it too seriously or personally. You're not here to clean up the world. If you make a good collar great, if one gets away that's okay, too. You just can't let the job and the bad guys and the baby mamas and the strung-out junkies get to you. Do your job, get promoted, and get the fuck out of the LES." As he continued, I realized he'd had something he'd wanted to tell me. "This place isn't worth you losing your job for, you get me? You try too hard to help these people and you'll be the one going to jail for doing something shady. Do things by the book and you'll be all right. If not, you'll have Internal Affairs after you. You can worry about the perps, yeah. They're assholes but they're not to be underestimated. But worry about yourself. If you take this thing personally, you'll do something that the department can't ignore and they will hang you out to dry just as quick as the fucking dealers would push you into traffic. You don't need that bullshit."

The short time I worked with Frankie the farthest I saw him cross the line was laying out some pocket money for information. Everything else was by the book. Maybe I already had my answer. Playing by the rules was the way that cops like Frankie and the other Op 8 guys kept their distance from the job. As good as they were, and as many great arrests as they'd make, guys like Frankie didn't really care. They couldn't. They didn't trust themselves to keep from getting into quicksand by outthinking both the bad guys and the brass. I wasn't sure I could ever work the way they did. I wasn't sure I wanted to.

With Frankie and Pete gone, Sergeant Andrews reassigned Gio and me to work with the other two Op 8 vets. Jerry Able was a tough-as-nails Irish guy who grew up on the last Irish block in Dominican-dominated Washington Heights. Jerry's old neighborhood had one of the worst crime rates in the city and the Lower East Side held few surprises for him.

My new partner Tony was close to thirty years old and came from a family of cops. He'd had a skin condition since he was a kid in Brooklyn. His face was always beet red and flakes of dead skin fell from his face and collected in his lap, on his shirt, and everywhere he went. I think he'd been getting shit about his face for most of his life. Some of the perps called him *"langosta"* or "lobster," which made him crazy.

Tony was an excellent cop who did everything meticulously and was great at taking notes and paperwork. He also had an infectiously retarded sense of humor. I don't think we ever sat down for a meal without him telling the waitress, "Gimme a turtle soup and make it snappy." You had to be there. Despite his skin flaking all over me, and a tendency toward nervous twitches, and flashes of bad temper, I really enjoyed working with Tony. No matter how out there or twitchy he would get, he was always up for it when things got hairy.

Sergeant Andrews's description of Op 8 as a family was truer than I first realized. Some days when me or one of the other guys started unpacking baggage of one kind or another it was like a bad breakfast table scene. One particularly muggy night the four of us had spent an entire shift patrolling PSA 4 together. I sat behind the wheel of RMP 9864 heading back to the Command. One of the perks of our company car was that it had FM radio. Mick Jagger and the Rolling Stones were singing "Gimme Shelter" on CBS FM when Tony interrupted.

"Hey, Mike," Tony said, "why don't we go over to the Seventh and gas up before we head back so tomorrow when I go to court I won't have to stop." The gauge had dipped below the quarter-tank hash mark. I could tell Gio was in a shitty mood. He'd been waiting to pop off at Tony for hours.

"Let's not and say we fuckin' did," Gio snarled.

"Why the hell not? I always leave the fuckin' car with at least a half tank of gas. You want me to start the fucking day tomorrow with the reserve light on?"

"God for-fuckin'-bid you left it full just one time, though. Right?" Gio turned to me for some kind of confirmation. He was right but he was more intent on making the most of this petty bullshit than scoring a useful point. I wasn't having any of it.

"Leave me out of this, ladies," I said as firmly as I could get away with. Jerry made a show of looking out the window like he was alone. Tony's red face was flushing a deep plum in the rearview mirror. He began to scratch at it hard.

"What the fuck's wrong with you anyway," Tony yelped at Gio, "all night you're acting like you're on the fucking rag." The two of them went at it like Jan and Marcia and I made the left to gas up at the Seventh Precinct. Suddenly the other radio drowned out the Stones.

"Central, man shot, St. James and Madison! Perps are in a white Maxima they just got on the overpass to get on the Drive northbound." The cop calling it in was out of breath. Horns honked in the background. Tony and Gio fell silent. I made a hard right across two lanes of traffic and headed for the FDR Drive.

"Get on the Drive, we'll stop traffic, they'll run right into us!" Tony yelled. He and Jerry unrolled their windows and leaned out to wave back traffic we needed to cut off. Gio put the cherry-red dash flasher up and I flipped the lights and sirens on. We powered into and ahead of a stiff eastbound traffic flow and screeched onto the Drive northbound at Houston Street. I floored it for twenty yards then jammed on the brakes, and jerked the wheel. We skidded to a perfect angled stop across both northbound lanes, blocking any traffic coming up the Drive in our direction, and initiating a hail of horn blasts. All four doors opened simultaneously. Gio and Jerry already had their guns drawn. Tony and I pulled ours within a step of hitting the pavement. The horns stopped. We worked our way from car to car, down the growing column of stilled traffic. I'd been mainlining pure adrenaline since the call came in.

"Over here! They're over here!" Tony yelled. His gun was fixed on a trio of hoods in do-rags peering out from the windshield of a white Maxima. Jerry, Gio, and I were in the car and on them in seconds. We yanked them out and slammed them on hot highway tar. This was why I became a cop. I was on the line between under control and out of control and loving every second of it. Tony holstered his gun. "I got it, got the gun!" He held up a shiny nickel-plated .357 he'd found under a seat. With my knee on the back of my perp, I looked over at Gio. He'd just finished cuffing up his mutt and he smiled and flashed Tony the thumbs-up. The gas crisis was forgotten. We were family—temperamental but good in a fight. Jerry keyed up the radio and announced in a "listen up everyone else" voice, "Central be advised, Op Eight has three under for that shooting over by St. James."

Op 8 was by design an observation operation, not an undercover investigation unit. We were supposed to observe and arrest, and the other guys in Op 8 left it at that. A lot of cops act like they'll catch something or get hustled somehow if they give their collar a lot of attention. Freezing out a perp once you've gotten his or her statement is classic cop behavior. During our time in uniform Gio and I had learned so much from our little backseat, sidewalk, and interrogation room Q&A sessions with the perps and victims we met, that it seemed like a waste not to continue the same work in soft clothes. I liked to listen and we really did want to learn how the dope business worked so that we could take it down. Just like in uniform, Gio and I asked questions, remembered what we were told, and made whatever we learned of value from the merry-go-round of bad guys that we spotted, tossed, collared, questioned, and either busted or let go, worth their while.

Pete and Frankie had worked a few rats. Jerry and Tony gathered some info from their guys and handled a few snitches of their own. Gio and I took cultivating informants into new territory. No information was too insignificant. Nobody willing to share something we might find useful was turned away, or had to leave the street corner, stairwell, rooftop, or interview room empty-handed. By doling out twenties, giving back the odd stray bag or two of dope, turning a blind eye for a few hours while a street dealer made quota before shutting him down and most important, just by listening, Gio and I soon had so many friendlies on our hands that we struggled to keep them straight. Before long we were having to split our rats up between us and moved them in and out of lobbies, stairways, and roof landings so fast hoping they wouldn't bump into each other.

Every few years some anthropologist announces that there's a defining quality about human beings that ought to replace the Latin adjective in the scientific name for the human species *Homo erectus,* "upright man." The argument is that there are any number of other qualities that better describe what separates us from other apes than the fact that we walk standing up. If my time on the Lower East Side is any reliable indication, human beings should really be called *Homo penintentiarius*—"confessing man." Within a year of getting into Op 8, the desire to tell us something seemed to be the unifying personal quality of everyone my partner and I collared, helped, or met. Every guy and girl who ratted out his or her boss or boyfriend, sister, spotter, neighbor, or competitor, had one thing in common—they each thought they were the only one with enough balls to talk to us. Pretty soon, in addition to quizzing the dealers and junkies we tossed and collars we made, people we'd never even seen before began coming up to us with stuff they thought we should know. We didn't have to go fishing— the fish just jumped into the boat.

It was a unique situation. On one hand the people we came in contact with weren't used to being heard, certainly not by cops. My partner and I had taken the time and gone to the trouble to learn how things worked as best we could, and the locals who knew the score appreciated that. We saw and understood what both legit residents and the scumbags did. At the same time, our constant presence on the street and the stories filtering back about how we were only too happy to tune a guy up for fucking with us, or add or subtract details of an arrest if it made our case better made the perps we quizzed afraid of us and the straight-arrow civilians who came calling positive we'd take action. If you were a bad guy we were sure as hell going to treat you like one, so why not be nice and tell us something good? If you were a good guy and had a problem we could fix, we would listen and we would try. If you were in-between, well, take a seat. I'll be with you in a minute.

Our informants, "friends," and fan club in the ant farm world we worked were a hustler's version of the United Nations. Out-of-towners, familiar faces, total strangers, Puerto Rican, Italian, Dominican, Irish, Chinese, Orthodox Jews, American blacks, African blacks, Caribbean blacks, you name it. Short, tall, fat, skinny, college-educated, high school dropouts, neighborhood storeowners, women, children, users, hookers, preachers, the whole range of urban life—anyone that was down on the Lower East Side up to no good or trying to sidestep the bad guys came to us for a break or a pass or friendship or some kind of combination of the three.

Part of Jerry and Tony's work style was to drive more than walk. RMP 9864 was a nice car and they were tired of the streets. That was fine by me. I liked to walk. Who drives in Manhattan, if they don't have to? You miss what's going on when you go around the city with the windows rolled up. And I didn't want to miss a thing. Walking around the projects gave us presence and visibility. It allowed us to familiarize ourselves with the people in the neighborhood. It also allowed the people in the neighborhood to familiarize themselves with us. And to rename us.

One hot summer day about two months into our time at Op 8 Gio and I were hanging out near the spot on Fourth Street and D. Gio jerked his thumb at two scowling black dudes walking tall and tough away from the avenue. I'd seen them coming in before and was already pretty sure then that they were small-time Jersey dealers up from Camden or Newark to score a couple packages to sell back home. Color lines cut sharply on Avenue D. We knew just about every African-American, Asian, and Caucasian badass among the Puerto Rican and Dominican majority by sight and by name. These were fresh faces.

If these guys bought a package they could nearly double their money. Any markup was worth it to their home turf junkie constituency. The convenience of having everything ready to go in ten-buck decks was worth a drive from as far away as Ohio for some guys. Out-of-towners were easy for us to make and, since they usually bought at least a few packages, were prized busts. We didn't need to discuss it. Gio grabbed one of the guys, tugging him to the side and shoving him to a car hood. My guy decided to run. He sure as hell knew how.

Tall and thin, he bolted back to the avenue like an Olympic sprinter. I gave chase, thinking that I might lose him as his stride opened up, until he headed toward the back of 30 Avenue D. I knew I had him on geography now. Weaving between parked cars slowed him down. The low chain-link fence in back of the building would slow him even more—enough for me to get my hands on him. I got to him as he was trying to hurdle a long wooden bench. When I yanked him down to terra firma, I discovered that he could fight almost as well as he could run. The guy had a foot on me both in height and reach, and the two of us stood there, legs akimbo trading punches like prize fighters in a painting behind a bar. We were both in tank tops and it was so hot out that some of our punches just sort of slipped off each other's hides. As I ducked an overhand right, I realized then that I was simply fighting for a collar but this guy was fighting for his freedom and his life.

Watching other people work has always been one of New Yorkers' favorite pastimes. The crowd that gathered to see me and the kid from Camden pound the fuck out of each other began to cheer like fans at a rap concert. "Go, Rambo, go, Rambo, go!" Rambo? I'd been growing and trimming a beard since the day we went to plainclothes. I guess there was more than a passing similarity. "Lower East Side," "LES," "Alphabet City," "The D," "Loisaida,"

"East Village,"—the neighborhood itself had nearly a half-dozen nicknames. Pretty much everyone I met that lived there had some other handle they went by, too. Now I had mine. I landed an uppercut in the kid's left eye socket. He was reeling, but I wasn't about to let my audience down. I beat him down, kicked him, and beat him again. The lesson was clear. Call me what you like, but know that you will not run from me. If you do, you'll get what this prick is getting and more. Do not raise a fucking hand to me. Before you try it, remember how this guy looked when I finally cuffed him and called in the collar. Rambo, huh? Okay, now you know me. But I know you, motherfuckers. Tell your neighbor Davey Colas. Remember the movie? "I'm coming to get you."

"There he goes again." A few weeks after going a few rounds with the Jersey bulk buyer, Jerry, Tony, Gio, and I were sitting in the RMP across the street from a dope spot on Fifth Street doing pretty lively business. All four of us were focused on one customer, or would-be customer, doing a bust-shy series of walk-bys before going in to score. Of all the backgrounds I'd seen represented in the junkies scoring in PSA 4, this was a first. The guy walking nervously back and forth in front of the spot we were watching was a meter maid, excuse me, a "traffic enforcement officer." "Maid" in this case was way off base. He was six foot five if he was an inch, with a uniform cap perched on a high forehead above eyes locked on the dealers. When he finally made us, he went through the exaggerated motions of writing a parking summons and sticking it under the wiper of a delivery van just north of us on the avenue and vanished around the corner. Suave.

"He'll be back," Jerry said.

Jerry and Gio reparked 9864 farther off the avenue, and Tony and I grabbed a corner dealer to ask him what gives.

"Fucking pain in the ass, Rambo," the dealer said. "Been here since noon. Nobody on the D gonna hook the motherfucker up, though, because he looks like a cop. He's an undercover, right?"

"Why the hell would anyone go undercover as a fucking meter maid?" I asked him. "Go ahead and hook him up, bro."

The dealer scowled. "Why, so you can bust me? Again? Fuck that shit . . ."

"No, so I can bust him, stupid," I said, leaning in to make my point. "Listen, if I wanted to bust you, you'd be in Central Booking already eating a day-old bologna sandwich. You think I don't know how long you been out here selling? You think I don't know you're selling for Animal? Meter maid's out here since noon but you're out here since eight this morning." He smiled, gave a little "you got me" palms-out gesture, and shook his head. "It's either you or meter maid over there," I told him. "Serve him and make him my collar, or be a wiseass and make yourself my collar. Either way, my man, I'm going through the system tonight with one of you motherfuckers."

"Aw'right. So how you wanna do this?" he said.

"Easy. Once he cops his dope, take your hat off. We'll be watching. I'll bust him for the buy, not you for the sale. Just don't give the signal till he's dirty. Got me?"

He got me. The meter maid returned a short time later. He looked around but didn't see the RMP where we'd backed into a space behind some Dumpsters. He walked right up to the corner guy I just briefed. Our guy talked with him, their hands touched a couple times, and a moment later, the hat was off.

The meter maid headed up the avenue a lot quicker than he came down it. I realized why when he got to the corner of Sixth and D and stepped onto an M14 bus heading north. In three-quarters of a mile the bus hangs a left on Fourteenth Street and heads out of PSA 4. The son of a bitch timed it perfectly so the bus would arrive, he'd get on, and the bus would pull out as the light changed.

I ran back to the car. Instead of pulling the bus over and making a big deal out of busting one asshole, Jerry drove us farther up the avenue, passing the bus along the way. Tony and I got out at a bus stop at Twelfth and D just as the bus arrived on the corner. We got on and there he was sitting in the center rear seat, smirking like he had his book and pen out as a meter went red. We walked to the back. He was clenching one hand.

"Open it up, man," Tony said.

"C'mon, let's see what you got," I added. The guy just shook his head like a bratty kid. He made a show of trying to get up a couple of times but I just kept shoving him back down into his seat by the top of his head. He was huge, a city worker, and everyone on the bus was watching to see how this played out. Neither Tony or me wanted to throw him the beating he increasingly deserved, but neither of us was enjoying looking like idiots, either.

Finally the big jerk slowly opened his hand for us and the rest of the bus to see like he was doing a magic trick. It was empty. A lady near the front actually gasped. To an untrained eye this probably was starting to look like two white cops in street clothes hassling a black uniform city employee in front of a busload of law-abiding citizens for no clear reason. But even though the meter guy played to the crowd he wasn't winning them over. Everybody that has ever been ticketed hates meter maids. Finally I let him get up and I cuffed him. The pantomime stopped when the cuffs came out, but his loud "somebody do something" protests ended when Tony found a half-dozen dope bags where the guy had apparently tossed them when we got on the bus. A passenger sitting a few seats from him nodded to me after frowning at the dope and at the meter maid. In essence she was saying she saw him make the toss.

The bus stopped, we hustled meter guy off, and got him into the car. On the way back to the Command Jerry handed me the radio mike. People think cops get a break from traffic enforcement. It isn't true. We get ticketed just as much as anyone else and all four of us wanted to milk this bust for all it was worth. "Central be advised," I said with a grin. "Op Eight has one meter maid in full uniform under and to PSA Four for possession of heroin."

The radio goes wild. "Way to go, Op Eight! Great job!" Even the dispatcher congratulated us. The channel didn't clear for a full minute. As we pulled up at the Command, nearly a dozen different cars from various precincts greeted us with sirens and horns beeping, lights flashing, and cheering and applause over their radios and grill loudspeakers.

The guy was big. It was a struggle getting him off the bus and into the car and it was a struggle getting him out before walking him into the Command. He'd ridden in the backseat with his cap in his lap but out on the sidewalk Tony put the guy's cap back in place. "There," Tony told him. "You were out of uniform, Officer."

When the meter maid's union rep arrived to go with him through processing, he told us the guy was supposed to be in Midtown writing summonses until six.

The varying attitudes cops have about their job will always isolate risk-takers from the rest of the rank and file. Cops who don't give a shit think you make them look bad, cops who are scared think you might get them hurt, and cops who think that the job owes them promotions and raises just for getting to work on time, resent that you leave them so far behind in arrest statistics, citations, and all the other bureaucratic thumbs-ups the department gives to officers who actually get off their asses. Even excellent cops like Tony and Jerry had their limits. They were great guys and I always knew they would have my back, but exotic arrests like the meter maid bust were what they lived for, not the idea of bringing down the entire Avenue D smack business and putting Davey Blue Eyes behind bars. Maybe it was the age difference. Tony and Jerry had maybe five or six years on us, but they were cop years and hard ones. They were ready to move on and that sometimes made it feel like there was a generation gap a mile wide between us. Seeing their buddies promoted to detective had reenergized Tony and Jerry, but the way that Gio and I liked to work made them seem cautious and conservative by comparison.

If I knew someone was selling, or had bought, I'd grab them. Simple as that. If there was a building open nearby, I'd take them inside and search them. If there wasn't time,

I'd toss them out there right on the sidewalk. If I knew you were dirty, I was going to prove it, and later in court I was going to make it stick. It didn't matter how. Tony never called me out directly on anything, but I could tell some of the things I was willing to do to make a small collar big or an iffy collar a good one were more risk than he was comfortable taking.

"You have to see it," Tony once said. "You just can't know someone is dirt, it's not worth it. I don't work like that." The closer he got to a gold shield and a pay raise, the more he stuck to the book.

"No problem," I told him. I respected Tony and appreciated all that I'd learned from him and from Frankie. Getting the guys in the squad in trouble with IAB was as unthinkable as letting them get shot by a perp. But I wanted to be let off the leash and Gio did, too. I got such a kick out of working my way that the book was always an afterthought.

After about two weeks, Sergeant Andrews sat us all down.

"All right guys," he said, lighting a little Clint Eastwood cigar, "I'm gonna make some moves here. I think everyone is gonna be happy and go out and produce for me. Tony, you and Jerry will work together." Tony and Jerry did their best to look surprised. "So, of course, Mike and Gio you two guys are gonna go back to being partners."

With the squad now pared down to two sets of cops, we got into the Op 8 routine the way it had been designed. At least a few shifts a week, Sergeant Andrews would go out on patrol with one team riding along in the Chrysler our uncle Sam bought us. "Who's looking?" was the first question at the start of a shift. It was an observe or catch proposition and we took turns either tracking perps for the guys catching or doing the collars and the processing ourselves. Gio and I preferred to do the collars. We liked getting in there and getting on the bad guys directly. Tony and Jerry were fresh from seeing their partners promoted and would rather observe. There were less risks in watching. With Gio and I back together as a team everybody got what they wanted. We could do our thing without fear of fucking up anyone's careers but our own. Jerry and Tony were free to work their way. The big winner was the captain. Between the old school slow-and-steady approach our ex-partners had perfected and the anything-goes style that Gio and I were now free to explore, crime numbers in PSA 4 began to change.

Making the bosses look good was the best job insurance you could have in the police department. Reprimands and cautions from the sergeant on up became mere hand waves as long as we were making the Command's stats strong. Collars bought us freedom. Op 8 was an anticrime squad, not just an antinarcotics squad. When word came down from One Police Plaza, aka the Puzzle Palace, that the bean counters saw specific types of violent crime on the rise, we were supposed to do something about it. The column with complaints of specific crimes needed to have a column of corresponding arrests alongside it. Captain Cataldi tells Sergeant Andrews that HQ is on him about robbery stats in the PSA 4 projects? Not enough robbery arrests to go with the complaints? Gio and I were only too happy to oblige. Who were we to not try and help out the cap?

Cap made sure that word filtered out to all the cops in his Command that robbery arrests would be the priority until the numbers got better. So I made robbery arrests my priority. If I saw two junkies get into a fight over a bag of dope, I'd separate them, and tell one, "Yo, so this prick robbed your money, right? Before you answer, let me just remind you that if you say he didn't, you're both going to jail." Making that threat on a Friday when the manpower bottleneck on weekends meant that anyone collared on a Friday would not see daylight or a fix until Monday usually got results.

"Yeah, Officer, this motherfucker robbed my ass," m'man would chime in.

"Central," Gio would say into his radio, "be advised, we have one under for robbery." Between the junkie-on-junkie beefs, guys getting burned on dope deals (the old "give me your money and wait here" act never went out of style), and the other drug-related petty annoyances throughout the neighborhood that could be rewritten to fit the new priority at One PP, we were bringing in one, two, sometimes three robbery collars every couple of weeks.

It took balls. It was a little complicated and definitely risky, but our request-a-thon worked for as long as it needed to. Within a few months redirecting some of our arrest traffic into robbery collars brought the columns enough into balance that the captain could relax. Like nearly everyone else in the police department, he was only too happy to turn a blind eye if it meant his impossible job could get easier.

Gio and I must have locked up about a hundred perps in the first couple of months of getting partnered again in plainclothes. Our bread and butter remained drug busts. At first we just nailed the corner dealers, their buyers, and the runners who carried material to the spots the way that the other Op 8 guys had been doing before we got there. Soon we were locking up the steerers and lookouts, too. The charge we came up with for lookouts was loitering for the purpose of engaging in narcotics. They rarely stayed in jail long, but it interrupted a street dealer's workday nevertheless. Busting steerers took a little research.

"If the guy brings a buyer to the dealer, isn't he also selling?" I was playing twenty questions with a sympathetic ADA in a tiny shared office downtown at 80 Center Street. People always crap on lawyers, but the Manhattan DA's office was a lot more gung-ho about fighting crime than some police precincts I knew. "I mean he's standing there advertising the dope to prospective buyers. Isn't that a sale? Doesn't the mere offer of a controlled substance constitute a sale?"

"Well, yeah, offering a drug is considered an attempt at a sale by definition in the New York State penal law," the ADA said. "Fuck 'em. You're right. Arrest 'em and let's charge them and see what happens."

Court days were like playing hooky for some cops, but I took the DA's part of the job and my testimony seriously. At the very least I needed to keep my story straight when swearing under oath to things that may or may not have been entirely true. Trial testimony against the Avenue D dealers and junkies was a blinking contest between me and the defense attorney. It was like a three-sided chess game where all the players were cheating in some way and knew it. The defense attorney knew his client was guilty, the ADA knew I'd given him everything I had in order to make his case, and I knew what the jury needed to hear when I took the stand. Everyone involved, with the possible exception of the jury, knows that the truth lies somewhere between what a cop says and what a perp did. It's all a big twisted system that often leaves good cops wondering if they should stretch the truth, ignore the facts, or out and out lie to convict some scumbag criminal. I never wondered. I never got stage fright or clammed up on the stand. I always knew the answer, always had it ready and I never lost a case.

Part of the appeal of being a steerer or a lookout was the belief that if you didn't carry drugs or do hand-to-hand sales you weren't likely to be arrested. Now everybody in a corner sale crew had equal chance of going to jail whether they were dealing, muling resupply, steering, or keeping an eye on the block. Op 8 was now closing down multiple spots and fucking up whole operations—Davey Blue Eyes's operations. If we couldn't charge Davey, we sure as hell could make his life harder.

As always, it was a matter of cash. The big shots like Davey had to keep their crews happy. But instead of making bail for a dealer or a runner that got popped with a package on him, Davey now had to regularly dig into his wallet and come across with bail money for an entire Third and D crew from the steerers on up. The guys that worked for him were taking more risk and wanted more money to compensate for it. Davey liked things smooth and clean and we almost singlehandedly were making his business rough and messy.

By doggedly working a single area within Op 8 instead of bouncing around from project to project like the rest of the squad, we were making a difference and I was sure we were fucking up Davey Blue Eyes's life. We also were making a name for ourselves. The Riis and Wald houses were a world we had penetrated. We walked, rode, watched, busted, and hung out around the same people every working day and night. We liked a lot of the people we met down there. Some

of them liked us. Either way everybody began to know us—
Davey Blue Eyes who remained out of sight, the dealers who
worked for him, their crews, the junkies who looked away
when we came around, the old guys we cracked jokes with,
and the pretty Spanish girls who flirted with us, confided in
us, and invited us into their apartments.

After enjoying that initial period of anonymity with
Frankie when I first transferred to plainclothes, I knew
when I was known and could see when I'd been made. One
afternoon Gio and I got to stare into our own faces.

DON'T MESS WITH RAMBO AND FASTBACK!

There we were, part of the downtown cartoon mirror
world looking down on ourselves from a graffiti mural. It
was around Easter and the moment had kind of a weird vibe
left over from a Hispanic church procession that had just
passed made up of a guy dressed as Jesus hauling a cross
with very realistic discomfort behind a van crawling down
the avenue blasting Spanish language hymns and prayers
and a parade of priests and parishioners singing and praying along behind.

"What the fuck . . . ?"

A local artist had taken it upon himself to "immortalize"
us in acrylic and brick. There we were, our names bigger
than life, clearly recognizable staring down from a wall on
East Second Street. We weren't undercover on the Lower
East Side, we were everywhere! As weird as it was to see, I
liked it—Fastback and Rambo in front of an angry Bengal
tiger. The paint looked fresh. It couldn't have been up for
very long. I wondered if Davey Blue Eyes had seen it yet.

D

Thirteen

I stood in position in the hall of 950 East Fourth Walk and watched a pair of Drug Enforcement Agency agents tug on gloves, pick up a metal battering ram by its handles, and approach the door of a ground-floor apartment. I'd seen firefighters make short work of the same metal doors more than a few times. These guys looked like they knew what they were doing and my money was on them, not the door. The cop in charge, DEA Special Agent Carl Ruiz gave the guys with the ram a hand signal.

"DEA! Open up!" Ruiz shouted and the ram swung into the door. It fell in on the third hit, top forward. Ruiz and his men were inside almost before the door settled to the ground. Gio and I were on hand as backup making sure that no one entered or left the building during the DEA's raid. They were there serving a warrant in a NYCHA building and common sense dictated if they were going to have a knock-down, drag-out in Wald Houses, Housing PD needed to be standing by.

A few minutes later the same agents marched out, stepping over the battering ram where it had been dropped, with the particular distracted slump of cops who'd cranked up the adrenaline and charged into an apartment blind only to emerge empty-handed. Ruiz caught my eye at the doorway.

"He wasn't there, the prick," he said with a sigh. A maintenance guy from NYCHA walked into the middle of the handful of milling Feds and housing cops to size up the door-rehanging job.

"You'll get him," I replied. As Ruiz, Gio, and I walked out to the sidewalk together, Ruiz stuffed a hand into his windbreaker pocket and showed me a mug shot of the guy he didn't get.

"You guys know him?" I looked at the picture and nodded.

"Sure, Little Loco. He doesn't do anything on the avenue here, but I know he has material." I pointed east toward the Brooklyn waterfront. "I think his spots are over in Williamsburg. Thinks he's some kind of player."

"Haven't seen him for a while, but he's around for sure," Gio added.

Ruiz smiled. "Any idea what he's driving these days?"

"Last time I seen him he had that hooked-up BMW, right?" Gio said. I nodded back. "Sort of blue-gray."

"Fuck," Ruiz said. "So, how do you guys know him?"

"We kind of know everyone down here," I said.

"If you guys see him would you grab him for me? He's my whole case. He was the main target." Gio and I both nodded.

"No problem, happy to collar that little douche bag," Gio said. Ruiz handed each of us his card. I stuck mine in my pocket. Gio tossed his into the gutter. We both watched Ruiz drive off. I'd been thinking a lot lately about DEA. They were on the avenue all the time now and generally I liked the way that they got things done. Guys like Ruiz weren't dicks, ran clean operations, asked questions, took suggestions, and were always good about giving credit where it was due. This had been a hurried job, but usually when they set up an arrest or search in the buildings they worked closely with Op 8 and were always grateful for the additional info Gio and I usually had for them.

"He seems like somebody we could work with, you know?" I was kind of testing the waters.

"I dunno," Gio replied. "He'll call up next time he needs a tour guide down here, I guess."

If the Feds needed a tour, we were the guys to give it. It was now over two years since I began working in Op 8 and we'd been doing our thing on the avenue for long enough that it seemed like there wasn't a single veil left to lift in PSA 4. What had seemed alien and hostile and fucked up then was as much like the back of my hand as Canarsie was in the seventies. The cast and the set were always the same, it was just a different story each day.

Supposedly, *Sesame Street* was at one point going to be called "1, 2, 3, Avenue B," before that was scratched in favor of the title that's now a household name. The sidewalk sets of the show itself resemble high-stoop brownstone Harlem more than the tenement and housing project LES, but something about the mixture of real and outlandish live-action cartoon puppet people populating the studio-bound sidewalk evokes the streets Gio and I worked in Operation 8.

Every spring, sure as the first crocuses peeking up through the dirt in the trash strewn common areas around the Riis Houses, and the first new generation of summer flies buzzing around garbage on the street, an animated neighborhood character would make the scene. During the winter it was easy enough to spot this enormous, lumbering white dude with the particular swinging walk of someone whose girth was overtaxing his skeleton and whose pasty skin and glazed eyes were those of a guy whose immune system had declared war on his liver. When the weather got better he toddled through the neighborhood in Bermuda shorts—his huge, dimpled, ash-colored thighs rolling up and down like taffy pistons. There was no mistaking him— Rockets Redglare.

Old-time animators called the exaggerated motions in old cartoons "squash and stretch." Rockets Redglare was the living, breathing 3-D embodiment of that principle. With his undulating walk, squeaky "I ate alum" voice, outsize glasses, and beatific toothless smirk, he turned every sidewalk he went down into a panel from some kind of bizarro world Bazooka Joe bubble gum comic come to life.

Rockets was a kid from Little Italy born to a junkie mom and a wiseguy dad. His mom was murdered by an abusive boyfriend who filled in at home once dad was sent back to the old country handcuffed to a Cunard Line gunwale by the Feds. This lineage left Rockets with a dual legacy. On the one hand he had the entitlement of a precocious abused kid that had been passed from aunt to grandma to aunt throughout his childhood. "The women in my family treated me like a Mandarin prince," Rockets used to say when holding court in the East Village bars he worked like an old-time ward heeler campaigning for drinks and drug money instead of votes. He also had the blood and brain chemistry of a baby who had been unsuccessfully detoxed in the womb and was already addicted to narcotics before the doctor who delivered him in Bellevue's OB ward gave him the other kind of smack with a rubber-gloved hand.

A combination of overgrown cherub charm, vicious wit, and nearly superhuman and totally unapologetic appetite for drugs and alcohol gave Rockets a weird charisma that he exploited to the hilt. Even casually telling a wide-eyed NYU coed in a local bar that she looked "like the kind of chick who could satisfy a whole motorcycle gang," earned him a kiss on the cheek instead of a faceful of mace. It was as if he'd found the exact middle ground between degenerate clown and degenerate ringmaster. When he was younger he was big, smart, and reassuring enough that band, club, and bar managers hired him as a roadie, doorman, bouncer, and titty bar MC. What his bosses often found out the hard way was that in those days Rockets was also the man to see when you needed to score or wanted to get into a sold-out show on the other side of the door he was guarding.

While working as a bouncer at the trendy Red Bar on First Avenue in the eighties, Rockets's practiced response to one coked-up patron smashing a bottle on another's head was to separate the two parties, hail a cab for each, send the bleeder to Cabrini Emergency and the hitter to another bar before anyone who'd been nicked by stray glass or sprayed with blood made it to a payphone and called the Ninth Precinct. Rockets was part of Warhol darling artist Jean-Michel Basquiat's entourage until Basquiat was killed by a speedball in 1988. When Sid Vicious's girlfriend Nancy Spungen was stabbed to death in the Chelsea Hotel, Rockets was there, too. Some say he was the source for the dope that Sid used to join Nancy via OD. Others say Rockets did Nancy in himself. None of this kept the tabloids from dubbing him both Sid's and Basquiat's "bodyguard." Rockets stayed coy on the topic until the day he died.

Just about everyone who knew or recognized Rockets from the streets of Alphaville experienced the same late-eighties moment of shock while at the movies. Either at the St. Mark's theater on Second Avenue (home of the weirdest double-feature pairings in the city) or at the tiny syringe-strewn single-screen theater on Grand and Essex there he would be—*that guy*—Rockets, on screen forty feet high bitching about sushi alongside Madonna, hassling Tom Hanks, and sending a hate letter straight to Eric Bogosian's heart. It turns out that the St. Mark's Place cabaret shows Rockets hosted and performed in the early eighties, along with two moonlighting firemen and a bartender who worked at Vazac's on B and Seventh, caught the eye of casting agents. Rockets, the bartender, Mark Boone, Jr., and one of the firemen, Steve Buscemi, began appearing in art films, TV, and Hollywood blockbusters in the mid-eighties.

Fame of a kind brought Rockets perks of a kind. The teeth he'd lost to the bad, good life were replaced courtesy of a Hollywood paycheck during a year spent as a fish out of water in L.A. But the neighborhood and his mother's chemical legacy wouldn't let him go. Maybe it was the other way around. No matter how much he worked in front of the camera Rockets never gave up a side career hitting up friends and acquaintances for money, squashing and stretching down the streets of the Lower East Side and alternately getting strung out on and dried out from booze and drugs.

Old friends, bartenders, and starstruck college kids alike were happy to spot him a twenty and buy him drinks in exchange for stories about his fucked-up childhood in and out of rehab and reform school and the crazy life and off-the-wall career he'd managed to make of it. So what if he'd copped a prison rape story from a book he read or nodded out before the punchline of a joke? He was good enough company, as long as you didn't mind lightening your wallet a little and didn't have to help him up off the ground. As his health faded and body ballooned, the movie limelight dimmed and sentimental tavern owners, doting bartenders, and famous friends were all he had left.

Eventually, years after I had left Alphaville behind, one of Rockets's patron bartenders, a guy named Luis who'd come up to the Lower East Side from New Orleans for the punk rock and stayed for the drugs before cleaning himself up, inherited a little family money and decided to make a film on the subject of Rockets himself. The picture, *Rockets Redglare!*, featured the title character reading from his unpublished memoir *User's Manual* and was littered with off-the-wall testimonials from his less self-destructive Lower East Side luminary friends. The film became the talk of the 2003 Sundance Film Festival. Unfortunately, Rockets's overtaxed body had thrown in the towel two years earlier, and he only attended in spirit. And, like Nancy Spungen, Sid Vicious, and Jean-Michel Basquiat, Luis joined Rockets soon after their film hit big in Utah via a motorcycle wreck upstate.

Reagan Youth was a rock-and-roll band formed by Forest Hills high school buddies that earned a loyal following with high-energy, ritually combative shows, and simple but smart and catchy songs that were like infectious anti-establishment nursery rhymes. On stage, a kid born David

Rubinstein and renamed Dave Insurgent lovingly mocked the ritual riot antics of the crowds at Great Gildersleeves, A7, and CBGB's eighties hardcore all-ages Sunday matinee bills.

But the sharper and more of the moment a rock band is, the shorter its lifespan is likely to be. Even the Beatles only lasted ten years. Reagan Youth pulled the plug when their satirical namesake left office in 1990. But what really lit the fuse for the band's bust-up was Dave's heroin habit. After years of chipping, the son of Holocaust survivors was not only shooting up, he was dealing.

He wasn't the only one in the household doing it. Rubinstein hooked up with a girl named Tiffany from Metairie, Louisiana, who was also on the punk scene, also strung out on dope, and went from exotic dancing to curb service prostitution to support both her and Dave's habit. Neither of them had much luck pursuing their respective livelihoods. Dave was so unreliable that a group of dealers he'd burned bought him a beat down with a baseball bat for nonpayment. The doctors who opened up Dave's skull and removed some of his brain to prevent a potentially fatal hemorrhage guessed that if his head wasn't covered in thick matted dreadlocks, he would've been DOA. Dave was in a coma for days. When he woke up he had a prominent scar bisecting his forehead, and a quarter second or so reality hiccup caused by a lobotomy that probably saved his life.

One day in June 1993, Dave watched his wife climb into a Mazda pickup with a guy she reassured her husband was a freak but a regular. She told Dave that she would be back in a half hour and that when she returned she'd have dope for both of them. The next time her husband saw her she was on a morgue slab.

A few days later in the hours before dawn, two state troopers cruising the Southern State Parkway on Long Island hit their lights to pull the same pickup over for a missing rear license plate. The driver hit the gas and barreled down an off-ramp. Five cars eventually joined a ninety-mile-an-hour chase. Mario Andretti couldn't maintain control of a small pickup truck at that speed for very long and after misjudging a turn the Mazda plowed into a light pole in Mineola. The driver was unhurt. When the troopers tossed him they found an X-Acto knife in his pocket and a smear of Noxzema on his mustache that made it look like he was drinking greasy milk. When they tossed the truck they found Tiffany's rotting corpse under a blue plastic tarp in back.

The cold cream on his face was a trick the driver, Joel Rifkin, picked up from the movie *Silence of the Lambs*. The corpse in the back was inspired more by an Alfred Hitchcock picture called *Frenzy*. Tiffany was the last of seventeen prostitutes Rifkin had picked up, raped, and strangled since the late eighties. Detectives picked over the ID cards, clothing, jewelry, and other souvenirs Rifkin collected from his previous victims inside the house he shared with his adoptive mother. Around the same time, widowed, strung-out, and brain-damaged Dave received word that his own father had accidentally run over and killed his mother in a parking lot in Queens. Shortly after he cooked up and shot up enough heroin to make his heart both stop aching and stop beating.

The Alphaville heroin trade and unchecked human greed ravaged the neighborhood like a man-made plague. But to make things even worse, doing narcotics and having anonymous sex played a key part in spreading an actual medical epidemic through the streets. No amount of police intervention was going to stop it, and everyone was at risk. In 1980, rumors began to spread around the West Village piers and in male-only bathhouses of a flulike illness so specific about who it made sick that it was initially called "gay pneumonia." By the time I began patrolling Alphaville it had a name, AIDS. What little people seemed to be sure of was that AIDS was an incurable and pretty much fatal virus transmitted from person to person, straight or gay, either by fucking or by sharing a needle or doing anything else that brought infected blood or semen in contact with a noninfected blood. The PSA 4 projects were populated with people that fucked just as much as anyone else did and probably shot up heroin more than anywhere else in the world. If you were screwing around on the Lower East Side in the eighties, you were inevitably within a person or two of a needle and, therefore, one unprotected fuck away from chronic and, in those days, usually terminal illness. Gay, straight, young, old, junkie, or clean, AIDS cut a swath through the Avenue D projects that might have been the saddest and most fucked-up thing I saw while I was there.

If AIDS hadn't been an illness that evoked societal hangups, maybe the people in charge might have taken it on as the epidemic it was right from the start. It became an issue instead of a disease. President Reagan didn't even say the word "AIDS" in public until 1987, and by then thousands of New Yorkers were infected. The New York City Health Department's first move had been to close gay bathhouses. When someone pointed out that it wasn't just a gay disease and that there were lots of straight sex clubs around, the city closed them, too. That still didn't address the health risk to IV drug users sharing needles and anyone who they fucked. The city went back and forth about whether or not the Health Department should exchange clean needles for used ones for years. A charter needle exchange program finally began in the end of 1988.

Cops working narcotics were especially at risk of catching AIDS. Dirty needles were an everyday reality in Op 8. Bloody spent works littered the ground and the rooftops pretty much anywhere east of Avenue C. The ones you couldn't see—in pockets, handbags, car seats, or couch cushions—were what worried me. Anyone I tossed potentially could be too scared or too stoned to tell me about a needle they had on them and inadvertently make me their blood brother while searching their pockets, purse, car, or apartment.

Also, there were always project girls (and some guys) looking to get with cops. Some girls never outgrew the dream of being rescued from the D by Prince Charming. Bagging a cop fit that fantasy, somehow. I knew from my first days in uniform that being a cop really attracted some women. They don't call it the "blue magnet" for nothing. And I discovered early on in plainclothes what the rest of the guys in Op 8 already knew—it didn't make any difference whether you were in blue or in soft clothes—there were plenty of girls in the Avenue D projects who loved to flirt with, date, and fuck cops.

There were, to be blunt, two kinds of women I met in and around the buildings. The first kind of girls were fighting the black hole gravity of a no-future life exiled to the edge of Manhattan. They knew that if they gave in they were bound for a high-altitude version of the medieval life cycle of birth, work, kids, heartbreak, and death all within the same five-block radius. These women respected themselves enough to stay in school in spite of growing up broke, and get jobs outside the neighborhood even if it meant going to work for some racist and uncaring creep anglo boss who wouldn't last a minute in the environment these women were looking to get out of.

The other kind were the girls who surrendered to the forces holding them where they were, the ones who were willing to trade something like a good time for something like security whether it was money, drugs, sex, or a higher rung on the Avenue D smack-dealing status ladder. I was single in those days and I met plenty of both. I dated some of the first group and fucked a few in the last group, but the more I became known in the neighborhood, the more careful I needed to be.

There was no cut-and-dried regulation against police rank and file dating anyone who lived in the buildings and neighborhoods they patrolled. A lot of cops in my command, at the Ninth Precinct and the Seventh Precinct on Pitt Street did. We were down there the better part of almost every day, and it was a matter of nature taking its course. Unlike some uniforms and soft clothes guys I knew, I never shacked up with any project broads in one of the apartments in the neighborhood. Regulations did spell out that an officer couldn't live within the precinct he or she patrolled. For a gung-ho Internal Affairs Bureau investigator, spending more downtime in an apartment in your own patrol area than safe at home grilling hotdogs and washing your car could be construed as a rules violation. Strike one.

Strike two was the simple reality that if I was going to sleep and wake up inside the buildings as well as bust the dealers on the outside, I'd need to grow eyes in the back of my head. With our fame within the community growing, Gio and I were becoming better known and more trusted by some, while offering bigger targets to others. Davey Blue Eyes had killed dozens of people. To the best of anyone's knowledge that I talked to on either side of the law, he hadn't killed any cops yet. Scaring the shit out of rookie DEA agents was one thing. Killing or ordering the death of two New York City police officers was, hopefully, another story. But Davey had never before felt pressure like he'd been under since his 1018 Club van hit went south, and Gio and I had devoted five days a week for nearly two years to fucking directly with the Third and D crew and Davey's livelihood. Working the way my partner and I did to achieve the results we had opened me up enough to risk. Taking on a project girlfriend was just too much exposure for me to handle. I flirted a lot and dated a little on the D, but I could never go completely native. It meant my job and arguably my life, and not just via a bullet from a dealer. I know of at least one PSA 4 uniform that found out the local girl he was banging had caught the bug and probably given it to him. I have no idea how he brought that up to his wife.

The police department wasn't quite sure what to do or to say about AIDS any more than the government was. With no guidelines coming out of One Police Plaza, I fell back on common sense. For starters, I tried not to touch blood with my hands or any other part of me. You couldn't work the way we worked in Op 8 without breaking that self-imposed rule, but I was as careful as I could be in scuffles and takedowns. And if I did fuck around with girls in the projects I made sure I wore a condom. As far as needles went, that became the perp's responsibility. Every search, toss, or collar I made included a brief conversation on the topic.

"You got anything sharp on you, a needle, anything that might stick me?" I'd say as I patted a collar down before going into their pockets. "No? Good. Okay, here's the deal: if you're wrong about that and I get stuck with something, whatever it is that sticks me goes right into your eye after. Understand?" Everyone understood, especially when I pointed an index finger within a half-inch of the eye under discussion. If they had a needle, they'd dig it out and follow my instructions to cap it with a cigarette butt and set it down. After they were cuffed up I would voucher it and put it in one of the plastic tubes that had been issued for needle evidence since the seventies.

"Yo, Rambo, what's up?" Gio and I were walking through a hallway at Bellevue on the way to interview a guy Big Arthur Washington had shot in the face. As usual there were patients on gurneys lining most of the wall space between rooms. I went over to the one that called out to me and searched her sunken cheeks and glazed eyes for any idea who she was. Her voice was a phlegmy rattle and from that and the sores on her arms it was clear that whoever she was she had full-blown AIDS.

"Hey," I said, stalling for time. The girl was in such sorry shape that I had no idea who she could be. It was impossible to even guess her age. We bullshitted for a while about the neighborhood and just as I was about to make my good-byes I remembered her. Tessy. She'd dated a couple of the corner dealers and had been a regular informant. Tessy was little and wiry to begin with, but she must have lost fifty pounds since the last time I'd seen her, along with most of her teeth. "Get yourself up and well, Tessy, okay?" I told her.

"Okay, baby," Tessy replied with an inadvertently ghoul-ish smile that seemed to peel her face in two. "You stay safe, Rambo, hear?" She was always nice. Within a week she was dead.

Boo was a girl who'd helped us out with some informa-tion from time to time and always liked to laugh and flirt a little on her way to and from the avenue bodegas. She only bought lottery tickets for the big prize drawings and I used to kid her that the odds of winning were probably nearly the same if she played or didn't. But one Saturday night she proved me wrong and won. Big. After she hit the lottery for $1.5 million I didn't see her around anymore. We thought she was off somewhere living it up but it turned out that she was wasting away from AIDS. The first thing she did when she won LOTTO was buy her boyfriend, a small-time corner dealer named Bass, a Ducati crotch rocket. After she told Bass she had AIDS, he got on it one last time and rode it up the ramp onto the Williamsburg Bridge in a pouring rain storm. Bass wasn't able to find a spot to ride off the bridge like he wanted to, so he settled for doing a one-eighty into oncoming traffic. He died instantly. Boo took eighteen months to join him.

The buildings themselves were built with the "up and out" idea in mind. The plan was that you live there for a few years, save money, and move onto the next part of the Amer-ican dream. But the overwhelming majority of the people I encountered in PSA 4 couldn't manage it. The gravity of poverty and drugs, bad education, and AIDS kept them down and crossed them out. "Getting out." Everyone wanted to do it, but for some reason only the women talked about it. It was a macho thing for guys. They were supposed to endure it. The TV flashed images of the rich and famous but omitted instructions on how to get there from this side of the screen. There had to be a way to get out of this place. People tried everything. Getting out was the reason behind almost every dope sale, lottery ticket purchase, and flirtation. Still, the house odds of getting a break and getting out always remained stacked against them.

Raphael was born prematurely and got too much oxygen in the incubator at the hospital. He was a nice kid but slow and unable to learn much in school or on the street. His mom stepped up, curbed her dope habit and raised him as best she could with what she had on hand, what she made when she worked, and what the government paid out when she didn't. Eventually she wrote down the number of a lawyer from a bilingual subway ad and, after a half decade of legal wrangling, the hospital settled with her for over a million dollars. Raphael was twenty by then and even though he was slow, the settlement, minus the lawyer's percentage, was technically his. When the first money finally came through, he withdrew the full amount in cash, laid the bundles of bills out on his bedroom floor and played with them like they were toy soldiers. After a while he scooped up a few and took them outside to show his friends. When he flashed his cash and giggled at us, we gently but firmly led him back to his apartment and asked him to repeat back to us over and over that he wouldn't show anyone else his money, he'd stay inside with the door locked, and not come out until his mom got home from wherever she had gone.

We were off duty an hour when someone he knew convinced Raphael to open the door, shot him twice in the chest and took every bill.

"That tall guy there, they call him Law. He's a stickup guy. He's got a dope habit from here to Japan. Either he's too smart or doesn't have the *cojones* to stick up dealers and he mostly feeds off of Jersey junkies and college kids. Over there with the dreads, that's White Boy Ronnie, he helps us out here. A lot, sometimes, and we try not to collar him if we don't have to."

Sergeant Andrews, Jerry and Tony were all slated to be cycled out of Op 8. Now me and Gio were the vets and it was our turn to show the new guys the ropes. We were cruising down the avenue in the company car with Bob Angelo, our new sergeant, pointing out some of the local characters he'd soon be getting to know on his own. Sergeant Angelo was young for his rank and seemed like a nice guy. He was also inexperienced and our guided tour had his full attention. He admitted months later that he thought we were making all this stuff up until he learned otherwise. I drove, with Angelo in the shotgun seat and Gio in the back. Gio pointed over Angelo's shoulder.

"Over there that guy in the brown suede, his name is Mace," Gio said. "He's got a couple of drug spots out here. He's a bad dude who's done a few bodies. The big dark guy there, that's Animal. He hustles a few drug spots, too, mostly in Riis Houses further down the D." Sergeant Angelo's head moved from side to side like he was at the U.S. Open.

"The two girls crossing the street that just waved to us?

They work in a whorehouse over on Delancey Street," Gio continued. "They help us out, too, whenever we need something." Angelo's eyes met Gio's in the rearview.

"Help with what?"

"They give us head whenever we need it."

The three of us were silent for a beat. I smiled. "It's a joke, Sarge. Information, Sarge that's all they give us." He didn't look so sure. We parked at Third and D and outlined how the spot we were across the street from worked and reeled off yet more names.

A couple of days later Gio and I were walking the avenue when I saw a blue-gray car parked across the street that set off a bell.

"Ain't that Little Loco's BMW?"

"It sure is." Gio pointed with two fingers to a trio of punks laughing together farther up the street. "And ain't that Little Loco talking shit with Cisco and Q about middle of the block?" Agent Ruiz and Little Loco's status had come up in conversation the day before over Gio's meatloaf and my egg whites at Lillie's. "I guess that answers that question, eh? How you want to play this?"

Our new Op 8 topkick had just dropped us off and Gio and I decided that the best plan of attack was to get him to come back with the car and grab Loco when he got in his BMW.

"Central, can you raise Op Eight sergeant and have him respond?"

"Op Eight sergeant on the air, K."

"Sarge, respond to Fourth and D where you just left us, please."

"Ten-four."

Gio and I withdrew to a building entrance and waited. Loco and his buddies had drifted to the corner but were still talking a blue streak. When the sergeant arrived we got in the car, explained about Ruiz and Loco, and told him to cross the street when Loco made a move toward his own car. Loco said his goodbyes and pulled his keys out. Sarge roared across the avenue and neatly cut off Loco's car. The three of us piled out guns drawn just as Loco shut the driver side door behind him.

"Police! Don't move!" Loco scowled and put both his hands on his head. I opened his door, pulled him out and cuffed him.

"What I do, Rambo?"

"Dunno. I guess the sweet life just caught up to you." An RMP pulled up and we shoved Loco in the backseat."

"Mind taking him back to the Command for us?" Gio asked the uniforms inside.

"You guys coming back to the house, right?" Sarge had clearly enjoyed punching the gas, pulling his weapon, and getting his feet a little wet but the rest of our shift was likely to be a lot of phone calls and paperwork while gift-wrapping Loco for DEA.

"Yeah. Someone has to take this nice shiny blue BMW back, though." The boss smiled.

"Don't be too long," he said and got back into 9864. Gio jumped in the passenger seat of the Beamer and I took the wheel. We cruised up and down the avenue for about fifteen minutes, slowing down and making sure all the bad guys knew it was us driving Loco's prize eighty thousand-dollar ride before returning to the command and turning it and its owner over to DEA.

Agent Ruiz was relieved to have Loco in custody and made sure to thank us and the sarge for making his week. The joy ride in Little Loco's Beamer got me thinking. The Uniform Crime Control Act of 1984, part of the slew of new legislation and policy that inaugurated Reagan's War on Drugs and made money available to start and maintain programs like Operation 8 gave Feds new powers over "asset forfeiture" and the seizing of property assumed and/or proven to have been acquired via illegal means or used in crimes. I didn't know much about it at the time as no one had ever briefed me or anyone at Op 8 about using asset forfeiture since we weren't federal cops. I called Ruiz and asked him right out what the deal was with seizures like the one we'd sent his way with Little Loco. He explained that based on the experience he'd had with us so far, if we came across cash and property we thought was drug related, he'd be only too happy to come downtown, confiscate it, issue a receipt for it to the perp we'd tossed to find it, and let whoever it was try and get it back through the courts. All I had to do was establish that the car or cash or whatever it was in question was owned by someone with no legitimate source of income.

There are a lot of cases reported in the papers of asset forfeiture gone awry—guys losing their houses over ounces of pot, some rogue cops in the LAPD narcotics squad singling out innocent people for forfeiture because they wanted to grab the cars they drove, that kind of thing. But with Ruiz's help I used property seizure as a way to tighten the vise on the Third and D crew and on Davey Blue Eyes. It was a brand-new way to break balls in the most intimate way possible. Most of these guys were in the game for the toys. They loved the cars, the cash, and the stuff it bought. And the money we confiscated or made from auction sales of seized property was split fifty-fifty between DEA and the Housing PD to use as buy money, and go toward operating expenses, equipment, and overtime. It was called "equitable sharing" and both Ruiz's bosses and my bosses loved it.

One afternoon I saw a wiseass Third Street dealer washing a beautiful copper-colored Firebird Trans Am in a cul-de-sac in the Wald Houses with a couple of neighborhood girls oohing and ahing over it.

"Nice car," I say. "Where'd you get it?"

"Oh, you know," he replies with a smirk. The guy had the fucking nerve to open up a new spot not far from where we spoke and I was dead set on making his life as difficult as I could.

"No, no I don't, actually. For real, where'd you get this nice expensive car here. And where did you get the money to buy this nice expensive car?"

"What, I gotta tell *you*, Rambo? You know where I got it." He was still acting the wiseass. Daylight and an audience did that to some people.

"How you paid for it, I mean," I say. "As in, where you got the money to buy it? It wasn't in a card game or on the *Price Is Right,* was it?"

"You know, man."

"Well, I know you're a low-life fucking drug dealer who kisses Davey Colas's shoes. That how you got it? By selling Davey Blue Eyes's smack on my fucking avenue?"

"You know the way it is, Rambo." His too cool act was backfiring badly and he knew it.

I walked to the corner and called Agent Ruiz. "I have a

guy here and based on what he just told me, I suspect that the car he's washing was acquired using drug profits," I told him.

"Hold him," Ruiz said. "I'll be right down." I could hear him smile on the other end. A half hour later the Trans Am was impounded and wiseass was standing on the sidewalk with a carbon copy of a government receipt in his pocket where his car keys used to be.

Eventually Davey's bigger dealers began to wise up and started leasing cars so that we couldn't seize them. But the cash kept getting split fifty-fifty. No job, no pay stub, no checking account and yet you have twelve thousand bucks in twenties in your car? Speak to Agent Ruiz. Any squawk and the perp got a discon and an arrest and warrant check for his troubles, too. There was always something worth checking out on guys that lived to have flashy stuff on them. Once I finished questioning Jimmy Rivera's brother Dean about two bundles of smack I'd arrested him with on a tip from a snitch, I began asking him about the huge gold dookie rope chain with a St. Lazarus medallion that he wore around his neck.

"Looks expensive," I said. He was jammed up as it was—possession and sale for sure—and he immediately got defensive.

"This isn't what you think, Rambo, it's a gift, yo," he said.

"If it's a gift, who gave it to you?" I asked.

"I don't know, no, wait look, it's not even like drug-related, you know? Don't fucking take it, Rambo, I'm already fucked. Come on, yo."

I didn't take it, but Ruiz did. Dean got a receipt and instructions as to how to file a claim if he felt the property had been seized in error. Like everyone else I introduced to Agent Ruiz and his government printing office receipts, Dean never filed a claim. It took a lawyer, which took money, and these guys would just spend their cash replacing what Uncle Sam took away on my cue rather than go downtown and fight it out with a judge.

Fourteen

It was a Friday, Gio was off, and instead of working the four in the afternoon to twelve at night tour with one of the other Operation 8 guys, I had an early call at 111 Center Street. The trial itself, a low-level dealer named Martinez we'd watched exchange a full package of dope for a manila envelope of cash and toss in back of the Wald Houses, was just starting. In all likelihood we'd go a few rounds of jury selection until lunch, the judge would recess until Monday, and I'd have the rest of the day off to get a head start on the weekend. I spent most of the morning in a Special Narcotics assistant district attorney's office preparing my testimony with the ADA when his phone rang.

"Martinez took the plea deal," he told me after hanging up. "He's getting one and a half for the sale."

"Good." I shook my head and stood up. The ADA extended a hand.

"Thanks, for coming down. We'll see each other real soon."

"My pleasure," I told him and headed out his door. I'd been flirting like crazy with Tara, a civilian employee supervisor with an office on the next floor and I vaulted the steps two at a time to drop in and surprise her. Tara was tall, pretty, and straitlaced looking with her hair always pulled back and big black glasses. That was in contrast with a body that no matter how dowdily she dressed looked like a horny teenage kid's notebook margin doodle. Tara had a lot of admirers from precincts all over the city. Unlike the rest of the visiting cops that talked her up then gave up when she wouldn't agree to go out with them, Tara and I had become friends. She was funny and smart. She'd been promoted three times since I'd known her. Most of all, though, Tara was fucking hot.

"Hey sexy," she half whispered as I walked into her office. She was placing pictures in a cardboard file box. There were half-empty boxes everywhere.

"Hey yourself, cutie. What're you doing?"

"Moving. They gave me a bigger office down the hall. I got promoted again." She put another picture frame in the cardboard box, came over, and kissed me on the cheek. She was sucking on a mint.

"I know, I hear you're a big shot now."

"Oh, is that what you hear? Well, I hear some things about you, too, Mr. C, or should I call you Rambo?" I smiled not knowing how to take "Rambo" at first. No one off the D used it much.

"What are you hearing?" I asked, leaning against her desk. Tara smiled wickedly. She had never been this forward before and I was really, really curious where it was going.

"Well, Mike, you know it seems like every cop that has a collar comes through here. So they say things and I hear things. I keep hearing about you; that you're kind of running wild and you like things dangerous. I hear you're dirty, too."

I shook my head. She meant it as some kind of compliment or come-on but I was sick of hearing that bullshit, no matter how it was meant. "I ain't dirty. I never took money from anyone, never. It's like you say, I just like the action."

"I know, baby, I'm just telling you what's going around." Tara stood in front of me now. She really was something to behold. "As long as you're careful, bad boy." She caressed my face. I'd known her about two years, and until this moment I never would've thought she'd initiate something this direct or be as good at it as she was.

"I will, yeah. I'm just doing a job," I told her. I could've said anything. She closed her eyes and kissed me passionately. The mint went into my mouth, she grabbed my belt with one hand and slammed her office door shut with the other. "Don't apologize," she said, breaking the kiss. "I like bad boys." We kissed again and my hands moved across her sides to her ass. I flashed on the door and saw there was no lock on it. "Let me put something against the door," I murmured into her neck.

"No way, baby," she hissed, "you're not afraid of getting caught, are you? I thought you liked the action."

I grabbed her waist and picked her up. She wrapped her legs around my hips and I stepped her back to the edge of her desk. Some necessary fumbling and we were quickly fucking. I leaned in, she grabbed me tighter and we sped up. This wasn't going to be a marathon. She smelled like vanilla for some reason.

The thing she said about other cops talking about me flashed in my mind. Why does everyone assume I'm on the fucking take? Sure I broke the rules, but dirty? That was the last thing I wanted to hear. I pounded into Tara harder and her moans changed note. If I'd wanted to be crook or a scumbag, I thought, I could've just stayed in my old neighborhood, hung out at the Nut every night and gone from shitty heists, to drug deals, to construction shakedowns with Vic Amuso's crew. Then I'd be no better than the assholes on Third and D making Dumpsters of cash for Davey Blue Eyes. But try telling that to some Internal Affairs Bureau dick. I had to break regulations and procedure and quite possibly the law in order to get Davey's guys behind bars and when IAB came calling as they were lately, I then had to lie to them just to keep my job and keep putting bad guys away. Nice system.

Suddenly I realized that even though I was living a moment out of a *Penthouse Forum* letter, I was still thinking about the job, Davey, and Avenue D. What the fuck? It was ridiculous. I couldn't even get laid without my mind going back to the Lower East Side.

Even though she didn't mean it that way, what Tara said about other cops was true. The crooks weren't the only ones that knew our names and talked shit about Rambo and Fastback. And, like everyone else in the Command, our new Op 8 boss Sergeant Angelo had heard rumors and sarcastic cracks suggesting that Gio and I were on the take.

The fucked-up irony was that if you're a cop that actually makes arrests instead of reading the paper and drinking coffee for twenty years, you're guaranteed to have run-ins with the department's Internal Affairs Bureau—the in-house arm of the police department devoted to cops investigating cops, and the Civilian Complaint Investigative Bureau—a similar body that responded exclusively to less harsh allegations brought by members of the public. Under

Mayor Dinkins, civilian complaints became the jurisdiction of the Civilian Complaint Review Board (CCRB)—an autonomous civilian-run organization. During my time on the Lower East Side, civilian gripes were heard by a mix of police employees and appointed members of the public who all ultimately answered to the commissioner, not the mayor. If an alleged offense involved behavior and professional comportment, it was referred to Civilian Complaints. If it involved a problem in procedure or hinted at corruption in any way, it went to IAB.

The funny thing about the whole good guy–bad guy War on Drugs mentality was that effectively policing drug sales always required lies and called for some kind of deception. Big money narcotics investigations and arrests could easily pit the cop that does them against his bosses just as much as against the dealers and users the cop was out to get. Jack warned me—the amount of money involved in heroin sales was so big, and the department's confidence in the rank and file was so shaken by corruption scandals, that Internal Affairs began with the assumption that most narcs were on the take.

It was a shitstorm blowing from two directions. If a cop is able to resist lining his pockets with drug money, did the right thing, and stuck his neck out to bring down dealers, that left him at the mercy of the pissed-off and vengeful bad guys he or she put in cuffs. The bad guys were totally hooked on the money they made and got high on the cars and clothes and toys and stuff that they could buy where and whenever they felt like it. Most of them just couldn't believe we weren't into all that bullshit, too. They'd watch us take their dope and then just assume that we were going to trade enough of it for cash and get ourselves boats and condos in Montauk. Plenty of cops before us had, and plenty have since. Other than the one or two bags here and there kicked back to snitches, I never held on to a grain of smack, and I sure as hell never resold it. But people believe what suits them, especially on the D and that didn't stop the greedy big mouths hanging out in front of the projects from telling stories about my partner and me that remade us in their own scumbag image.

The downside of our local boogeyman status was that everyone who knew our names used them. Drug dealers tend to be fuck-ups, so it also suited the many sloppy and unlucky mopes associated with the Third and D crew to be able to tell Davey Blue Eyes and anyone else they jammed up that Gio and me were the dogs that ate their homework. Where's the dope? "Yo, Fastback and Rambo beat me for it!" Who were the cops who knocked you down? "Rambo and Fastback!" Did you get a look at the driver of the plainclothes car that clipped your Jeep? You guessed it. A teenage girl on the avenue even told her parents that I'd fathered her kid. I'd never even met her.

Gio and my homegrown brand of "community policing" had a lot of lowlifes seeing red. When we fucked with a dealer it was easy enough for any of them who felt like it to turn around and lodge a made-up or petty official complaint with the department in the hopes of slowing us down or getting us off the street and out of their hair. One of my earliest IAB hassles was the result of taking a wiseass dealer kid's sneakers and throwing them off a roof. I'd had to chase the son of a bitch up about ten flights of stairs. When I cornered him on the rooftop, even though he had nearly a package of dope on him, he gave me a lot of lip about his rights and my mother. I'd made him yank off a brand-new pair of Jordan IIs when I'd searched him and found the dope. "You want to live in a free country?" I told him, "Move across the avenue or stop dealing smack." To illustrate my point I picked the shoes up and hurled them out into the air. They were brand new and the height of style and watching them sail to the ground and get snapped up by a homeless guy almost before they touched down actually made this kid cry. Good. He was a fucker. I collared and processed him, and he was out on bail in a day. He knew the system (he'd been through it at least a dozen times) and knew how to dial a phone and within about a week I received notice from the Command captain that IAB was investigating a complaint involving me taking money off a perp and stealing his shoes. Great.

Working IAB is truly the ass end of police work. Cops generally don't shoot other cops. It was a lot easier and less risky to lock up another policeman after a series of behind-the-back interviews with witnesses and some formal hearings with the accused than to run down and cuff a real bad guy. IAB's investigators were either whistle blowers or misfits who, like my academy group sergeant, were ostracized by their brothers at arms, or they were conscripts—cops pressed into the IAB ranks for a mandatory two-year posting that was absolutely irrevocable. Either way the officers that worked IAB were a miserable bunch who didn't and couldn't even trust each other.

One IAB deputy inspector in particular had it in for us. He used to indulge in all kinds of threats and table-slapping grandstanding even though IA interviews were held in a hearing room with only two or three people present. I ran into him a few years later after his IAB tour of duty had gotten him promoted and he acted like we were best friends. I told him to go fuck himself. In essence I said the same thing to the sneaker mope and every IAB and Civilian Complaint investigator I ever faced. Gio and I went up before IAB and Civilian Complaint boards so many times that we used to joke about having our own seats set aside in the hearing rooms where we were questioned with a union rep and a lawyer at our side. In nearly two dozen investigations of complaints or suspicions I was never disciplined once. Not once. Neither me or my partner ever lost even a day of vacation time. We knew how to keep our mouths shut, and we always stuck to our story.

Most importantly at the end of the day, no matter what regulations we violated and policies we ignored, any and all money and drugs we grabbed was used to bring down someone else. We never took anything off anyone for ourselves. Never. There were always terrible things happening on the avenue and we always at least tried to do the right thing, even if we didn't use methods we learned from the *Patrol Guide*. Sometimes the line between right and wrong was just too clear to debate.

That line was probably never clearer than on a day when Gio and I were staring down some dealers from the Op 8 car and a teenage Puerto Rican girl approached us through a light rain. I'd spotted her as she came out the door of 50 Avenue D and headed across the street to where we were. She didn't belong in the crowd we were watching. We'd never seen her before, which meant that she was probably pretty together—still in school, trying to live as right as she could. She'd strode out of the building entrance with an obvious sense of purpose. She walked up to where we were parked and the dealers and scumbags on the sidewalk stared after her instead of yelling dirty shit to her. Her name was Maria. She'd never seen us and we'd never seen her, but she told us she'd heard we were the guys to talk to about a problem she had. Actually it was her friend.

"Your *friend*?" I asked her, assuming she was bull-shitting.

"Yeah, whatever," she said, obviously leery of being fucked with by a non-Puerto Rican cop she'd had to really screw up some nerve to approach. "Look, I need to talk to you guys, but in private. I don't need the whole world to hear me."

"All right, no problem. Meet us on the second-floor stair-way over in nine-oh-five East Sixth Street," I told her. She looked at me suspiciously. For straight-up residents, the stairwells were to be avoided. But for us they were good meeting spots—an easily accessible satellite office closer than the building roofs, and more comfortable in shitty weather.

When Maria met us in the stairway, she didn't look either of us in the eye. "Ana, my friend, she lives in my building down the hall from me," Maria said.

"What apartment?" I asked.

"Five YY. There's a sticker of the baby Jesus on her door. Fifty Avenue D. She lives right down the hall from me."

"What apartment do you live in?"

Maria hesitated.

"Listen, you don't have to be involved in this," Gio said. "We won't come to your home or have anyone ever call you or anything." I also gave her my word that whatever she had to tell us wouldn't come back to her. She relaxed a little and looked straight into my face for the first time. "Okay, now what are we talking about here?" Gio asked. A metal apartment door slamming a few floors above us echoed throughout the stairway.

Maria looked up the steps, waited a few seconds after the echo faded and then whispered, "Ana, we always call her Pretty Ana, she's in a lot of trouble. Her mother died last year and she was having a hard time making the rent, so she took in a black girl from East New York as a roommate. This black girl, she turned out to be really bad. Really bad. She got high all the time and she brought in a bad group of people in the apartment. Now the door is opening and closing all night. I know they're selling drugs in there."

Gio and I looked at each other. We hadn't heard of a spot in a fifth-floor apartment. I wondered if one of our network of rats was holding out on us. Sounded like Brooklyn scumbags without neighborhood connections. I guessed it was small-time and overpriced and they weren't dealing Davey's dope. The buildings were so vast that it was possible to go for weeks without going on the Third and D crew's radar if everyone was new. "They made Ana a prisoner in her own apartment, they turned her into a junkie, they just took over her mother's house." Maria started to cry.

"How did you find out?" I asked. "The door slamming all night . . . ?" Maria sobbed. *"Dios mío,* I hadn't seen Ana in like months but I came home from seeing my aunt and uncle in Bridgeport late last weekend and she was just standing there by the garbage chute like a ghost, holding a bag of garbage. She looked terrible, like she had AIDS. She told me everything. They sold all her mom's furniture, TV, everything, and they use the place to sell dope and get high. I wanted to help her, you know? I tried to get her to come with me, but she said they would kill her. She said they would kill me, too. I told her I would call nine-one-one but she made me swear not to." Her voice got even quieter. "I had to swear to her I wouldn't tell anybody."

I was seeing red. We both were. These scumbags were doing this shit in the Wald Houses right under my nose? How fucking dare they! Didn't they know we'd find out eventually and make them pay? The book said I wasn't the law. My academy instructors, my superiors, even my dad if I ever asked would've reminded me of the same thing. IAB would've been only too happy to take away vacation days or put me up on charges to underscore that point. But hearing Maria's story, I felt like the only law that mattered, and these fuckers had broken it. It was like how I felt about Davey Blue Eyes—they were fucking with me just by existing, just by what they were doing to the people around them. Maria wiped away her tears. "You guys won't let her know I told you, right?" I shook my head no.

"Yo, Pino!" He was the first guy we ran into after hearing Maria's story. Pino stood like he always did in front of 30 Avenue D selling dope. Pino had no fear of being busted. We must have added a page to his arrest jacket ourselves. He also had no fear of talking to us in public. He just didn't care. Pino would give up his own mother with his father standing just out of earshot. He was smart enough to be relatively honest in what he told us, careful enough not to let anyone on the block hear him, and believable enough to persuade anyone that called him out, including his own boss, who in turn worked for Davey, that he was just being polite to Fastback and Rambo, even after telling us where to go and when to be there in order to make a solid drug collar that put Davey's accounts in the red.

"How's business, Pino?" I asked.

"It's okay, Rambo. I'm just helping out a little trying to make a little something before I go to bed."

"Who you working for?" Gio asked.

"I'm just trying to sell a little something for Londie." Pino shrugged.

"What brand dope is it?" I asked.

"It's KTU. Londie's got KTU. You not gonna lock me up, Rambo? I'm almost through."

"Nah, you can work for a while," I said, "but I need something from you in return." Pino smiled and turned away slightly to make sure we had some privacy.

"Okay."

"What do you know about fifty Avenue D, Five-YY?" He studied the faces of the people walking by and then the lightbulb went off.

"Oh shit yeah, over in there on the fifth floor," he said. "There's this new jack nigga all muscled up and shit just outta jail a few months. He's selling dope with this ugly black chick. Yo, if you saw her one damn time you won't forget that face. The bitch could scare a dog. They're fucking nasty, man. They use that place to sell and to shoot up, too. It's a shit hole, always junkies and shit up there. Not cool, Rambo. All ghetto and unprofessional and shit." Pino wasn't done. He gossiped away like a housewife on a picket fence. "You know that guy Black Hank?" We'd heard the name. "Real badass, right? Brooklyn, right?" We'd heard that, too. "He's up there all the time, too. I think they're all cousins or some shit. Black Hank brings the shit in from Brooklyn. Why the fuck would you do that, you know? Like I'm saying, all ghetto and unprofessional. I bet someone puts them down pretty quick. You gonna bust them, Rambo?"

"Maybe so," Gio replied. "So, Pino, you can stay here a little longer but then you have to get going."

"Yeah guys, no problem." Pino nodded as Gio and I walked away.

"Time check K?" Gio barked into the police radio. "The time is now twenty-two forty-five hours, unit," Central replied. It was ten forty-five. Late in our tour but neither of us was going to sleep on it. We were both furious and free to stay that way. Our next stop was a cluster of dealing spots down the avenue. A junkie, a white guy, was wobbling across the avenue and we pounced. I'd never seen him before. He was in his late thirties and clearly hardcore—a tall, thin dude stooped over with track marks deeper than the cracks in most sidewalks. He looked like he died but forgot to lie down.

I pulled the guy's pockets inside out and found three bags marked KTU. "Listen," I said as I continued tossing him, "I just saw you cop this from Pino. He'll swear to it, too. You want to keep this dope, and go on your way, you'll do what I tell you."

"Yeah sure," the guy stammered. "Anything you want, just don't lock me up. I can't do no more time."

A few minutes later, Gio, me, and our new deputy were around the corner from a fifth-floor apartment door. There was a dusting of soot around the door's edge from cook fires and cigarettes. The area around the knob was covered in gummy fingerprints and there was a Jesus sticker in one corner. I pointed to the door.

"Ever been there?" I asked the junkie.

"No." He shook his head. "They selling?"

"Yeah. You've bought out of the buildings, though, right."

"Yeah," he said.

"Of course you have. Well, the three of us are gonna go ahead over there and you're going to knock on the door to make a buy. When someone opens up, though, I want you to take a hike down these same stairs we just came up, and don't look back." The junkie nodded. Sweat poured down his pimpled face. He still hadn't shot up and was coming apart at the seams.

Gio and I assumed positions on either side of the apartment door. I motioned for the junkie to knock.

"Who that?"

"Yo, I'm looking for something." Nice. He didn't even hesitate. This guy really was a natural. The peephole clicked, a door chain clattered, and the lock turned from the inside. Our junkie wasn't the only one sweating. You always hope that everything just sort of comes together when you cowboy into an apartment like this. An advantage to the industrial impersonal design of the PSA 4 projects was that at least we knew how many rooms we were about to crash into and how big they were. That, the gun, the badge, the surprise, and a righteous anger I don't think I ever topped while on the job, were, hopefully, all the advantage we'd need. They were all we had.

The door swung open. The junkie ran back down the stairs. Gio and I pushed our way into the darkened room and shoved the big, muscular black guy at the door inside with us.

"Fuck this," the big guy yelled, "I wanna see a mother-fucking search warrant!" Gio had been winding up since "fuck." He hit the guy so hard it made the floor vibrate. The apartment was bare and pitch dark compared to the hall-way. I could make out the guy falling to the floor. It was a hell of a punch. The impact coupled, I guessed, with crossed brain wiring from freebasing, actually sent the bastard into a quick seizure. Even with him shaking and crying like a baby, as his eyes rolled back down out of the top of his head a trace of that smug untouchable look he'd had when we came in returned to his face. I remembered the story Maria told us and stomped on his head twice. He turned to the side the second time and I caught him on the temple, then I switched to kicking his ribs. He went slack—not passed out, but resigned to the beating. He probably learned that move in prison. Fuck it. He wasn't worth the leather.

We cuffed him and dragged him around with us on the floor for a few feet as we searched the room. The ugly girl-friend was indeed a clock stopper. It didn't help that she had hidden herself under a bug- and stain-dotted mattress against a wall like a slug under a rock. She went slack as we cuffed her, too. The light was so dim and flat that I didn't realize I was looking at a pregnant girl crumpled on the floor against the opposite wall until she sobbed. I walked over to where the girl was. She kept her head down and kept sobbing into her hands. She was tiny and emaciated except for her belly. It was hard to tell because of her physical condi-tion, but I guessed she was about eight months pregnant. Jesus.

"Ana," I said. She nodded yes. "Everything's gonna be all right." Gio had parked the two perps next to each other. He stood over them as I helped Ana up and took her over to a counter alcove that passed for a kitchen. The sink and stovetop were crawling with bugs. I put my hands on Ana's shoulders and held her firmly so she wouldn't have to worry about falling down. She'd probably been crouched like she had been against the wall most of her waking hours. She looked at me. She had dark skin that made her yellowed eyes look huge. I vaguely recognized her. "You know me, Ana?" She nodded.

"You're Rambo the cop, right?"

"Yeah," I said. She wiped her tears and looked at her hand.

"You locked up my cousin once." I half smiled.

"Did he deserve it?"

She nodded. "Yeah, he did."

"Good." She smiled. I smiled back a little harder. As gently as I could I asked her to confirm what Maria had told us. Ana described how the guy and the girl we'd just collared kept her prisoner for several months and forced her to get high first by putting smack in her food, then letting her snort it once the hook was in, then shoot it up into her when she began to really jones for it. She rolled up her filthy sweatshirt and showed me her track marks. She explained how worried she was about the baby, how much she missed her mother, and how afraid she was of what quitting dope was going to do to her. Ana had drawn one of the most fucked-up hands I'd ever seen dealt but she was trying to play it as reasonably as she could with us. The baby was the thing that mattered to her. I fought to keep calm and get as much information from her as possible and not make this experience any worse than it had already been.

She rubbed her stomach finally and described how a guy on the floor and a Brooklyn skell named Black Hank sexually abused her on a regular basis. They'd taken turns, done it together, had contests and pimped her out to the junkies that came and went at all hours for a few extra bucks while they watched. I shook my head.

"The guy in there, right, he's the one who raped you?" Somehow dialing back on the details and the head count, putting the blame where it began helped me to focus. She nodded. I gently took her by the hand and helped her make a positive identification. It was a little bit for her. She'd been in the dark so long I was sure she blamed herself on some level. But mostly it was for me and for what I was about to do. Ana pointed at the guy with her arm straight out and her finger extended taut like some kind of black-and-blue angel in a nightmarish Christmas pageant. I asked again, in a whisper, and pointed at him myself.

"You sure it's him that raped you?"

"Yes. Him and Hank made me," she whispered back.

"Okay, stay here, Ana." I led her toward the back of the apartment and went through a little mental checklist about human anatomy that I'd prefer not to share.

Paying unregistered informants, busting guys on instinct, and creating probable cause later, letting junkies keep a few bags or dealers run dope for a few hours unhassled in payment for information—by this point in my career, I'd rewritten the *Patrol Guide* in order to suit my own needs. I'd lied to bosses, friends, and district attorneys, told IAB to go fuck themselves, and taught people I worked with to do the same. I'd committed my own crimes to ensure that arrests were made and bad guys went to jail. This time, here and now, in this dark, roach-infested apartment turned shooting gallery at eleven thirty at night in 50 Avenue D, I knew what I was doing was wrong. I also knew that it was right. I had gotten too involved but still I didn't care. I looked at Gio.

"Uncuff him," I said, pointing to our scumbag perp. "He raped her. This prick and the other guy raped that girl." Gio shook his head in disgust, bent down, and uncuffed the prick. He knew that he might just as well let me do what I was obviously about to do.

He also knew that I had a thing about hitting cuffed prisoners. It wasn't a distinction most cops made. The chance of being hit back or maybe catch a beating myself, the possibility that the perp could retaliate, maybe even escape, maybe grab my gun, just the danger of it made it fairer somehow. It wasn't really true yet somehow it felt true. A shit-scared degenerate scumbag, still sweating from a seizure that had literally been pounded into his skull a moment before, and I would be even? Uh, no. Fuck it, whatever it was it was. Whatever I did, I did. That was probably a hundred times more thought than this piece of shit gave to fucking up Ana's life.

The perp stood up. He was around six feet tall and muscular—lean, with a long reach and broad, evenly knuckled fingers on big hands. I walked up to him and he backed up against the wall. Keeping my left free, I grabbed around his throat and squeezed him with my right. His carotid artery throbbed then stopped against the base of my index finger. I worked my fingers deep into his taut neck so that I could feel the blood supply cut off to his brain.

"Do something, fuck face!" I growled. "Don't just stand there, do something." His eyes watered and he began to gag. Instinct seemed to be all he had left. He reached for my hand and tried to pull it off but that only made my grip more brutal.

"Do something, fuckin' punk ass!" His eyes drifted upward and I let him take some air into his throat and felt the blood pump back into his head before I clamped down again. We did this a few times—choke, release, breath, choke, release, breath until finally I let him pass out completely and fall to his knees. As he knelt gasping for air and touching his throat where I'd locked on to it, I brought my knee up and hit him in the mouth as hard as I could from a standstill. Blood surged through his teeth. I grabbed him by his collar.

"Get in that bathroom." Before he had a chance to respond I dragged him to the toilet doorway. He began to whimper and plead. I turned away from him, winked at Gio and in as light a voice as I could manage said, "I'm cool."

Gio nodded. "I know."

I flicked the bathroom light switch and was surprised for a second when it actually came on. Roaches scattered and I pulled my snub nose revolver from my waist.

"Kneel there," I said and yanked the perp down next to the toilet. The tiny bathroom was so filthy it looked like it had been tarred with creosote. The seat was long gone. Guys that have been in prison half their lives like this fuck are past caring about those kinds of niceties.

"No man, please, I swear I didn't do anything, I swear," he begged in a scream—shrill and loud like a girl in a horror movie. He was beyond controlling his voice, beyond acting tough, beyond holding a girl down and working her over just for the sake of sensation. I hated guns but I wanted to shoot him so badly. "Please, I'll do anything you want! My shit? You want money? Anything!" I jabbed him in the face with my gun butt then brought it down hard across his head.

"Shut the fuck up, scumbag!" I reached into my back pocket and pulled out a sheet of looseleaf paper and pen I always carried and set them down in front of him. Putting the nose of my revolver against the rapist's head, I took a page from *The Godfather,* cocked the hammer on my gun and said, "Either your confession, or your brains, will be all over that paper in five minutes." Ink and sweat hit the paper in equal quantities as he began to write frantically. "The truth, jerk-off, it better be the truth."

What he wrote was barely legible, but it was readable enough to implicate him, his girlfriend, and Black Hank, wherever the hell he was. There were enough facts to make a case for all three provided no one brought up what motivated this guy to confess. After a complete search of the apartment, Gio and I called for a car to transport Ana to the Command where she would then be taken to the hospital. Gio and I took the two perps ourselves. Passing the case up to the detectives in our Command was the right thing to do jurisdictionally. The whole thing needed some enhancement and fleshing out at a paperwork and evidence level in order to hold up in court, and we weren't the guys to do that. Giving the case over to detectives would also help create a healthy distance between what really happened and how the tip, the arrests, and the confession would be portrayed in court. We were confident that the gold shields we turned the perps over to would be thorough and discrete. They reinterviewed the two scumbags and got the necessary details down like true professionals. I stayed in view of the couple during the interview process just in case one of them had a change of heart or a lapse of memory.

What credit there was would wind up being shared. At this point in our careers, there was no way that we wouldn't get an official nod or citation for breaking this case. It didn't matter. The important thing was that Ana and her baby got looked after and we tracked down Black Hank. Mother and unborn child were in good health considering their dual chemical and physical ordeal. Doctors at Bellevue detoxed them, and the city put them up in an apartment in Queens where they waited out the weeks until they would meet face-to-face.

Fifteen

Ana and her unborn baby recuperated somewhere in Flushing and we hit the snitch switchboard—canvassing the avenue for any leads or sightings of Black Hank. Davey Blue Eyes was going to be public enemy number two until we had Hank in custody or ID'd on a morgue slab. Until we caught Hank, every collar made through Op 8 would have the same Black Hank clause built in. Even a few of Davey's hardcore Third and D crew tried to help out. Word of what had been going down in that apartment traveled fast and created a moral high ground everyone in the neighborhood perched on together.

We kept asking, listening, and looking. Avenue D was too much of a magnet to guys like Hank. It was only a matter of time before he came back, and when he did we would hear about it. It was both a promising and frustrating search. Everyone we talked to said the same thing.

"Yo, Black Hank, man—you *know* him! I don't see him lately but he used to be around all the time, Rambo. You *know* him! Really dark, really ugly motherfucker! Like a really ugly Wesley Snipes!" I heard a different variation on the same tune everywhere we went. All my snitches described him the same way. I personally probably gave back a package of dope to users and informants while looking for the prick, and that's what I heard from every one of them.

"Did you feel that?" I heard something. Gio and I were on a field trip off the D as guests of DEA in Felix Pardo's apartment. The search for Hank continued but life in Operation 8 went on. Felix was the dope dealer with deep Chinese connections that Davey Blue Eyes had kidnapped for a hundred thousand dollars about a year before. After Felix's mother paid Davey, Felix went right back into business and today we were in Felix's apartment in the La Guardia Houses on Madison Street assisting two DEA agents serving Felix an arrest warrant. But what was that sound? Like a faint irregular *tick* . . .

"Hey, what the fuck!" Gio read my mind. He touched the back of his neck and shot me a weird look. As much as IAB was trying to pry us out of Operation 8, DEA was relying on us more and more. Raids, arrests, and searches like this one were becoming a regular part of the Op 8 plainclothes gig. I always felt appreciated and put to good use when I worked with Feds like Ruiz and the DEA agents arresting Felix Pardo today. This one started out pretty routine, but it was now getting a little strange. What the hell was that ticking sound? It was like it was coming from a few places at once.

A few days before, the Feds had called and come down to the Command, told us about who they were after. We arranged a joint operation involving us and them busting down Felix's door so that the Feds could serve their warrant, search for evidence, arrest Felix, and flip him.

The Monday after meeting the two agents, the four of us from Op 8 and two uniforms from the Command met up before dawn at the La Guardia Houses' management office.

At our instruction building maintenance shut off the water line that served Felix's apartment so he couldn't flush anything he didn't want us to find. With the uniforms in position in back of the building watching his windows, the DEA guys dropped Felix's door and we were inside in a heartbeat. Felix was dressed in tiger-stripe briefs throwing what turned out to be his personal coke stash out a window when we came in the bedroom. I looked down and saw the uniforms outside trying to catch a few bags like fly balls, but they were stopped by a garbage-strewn hedge.

In person, Felix turned out to be chill and up close his girlfriend was a knockout. Jerry and Tony made sure the two of them stayed seated on the edge of Felix's waterbed like good boys and girls while the DEA agents tossed the place top to bottom. They came up with wads of cash and a small amount of drugs that was more of Felix and his girl's personal stash.

"Yo, Felix," I called out to the bedroom, "you ever think of maybe getting a maid?" The sink in Felix's kitchen looked like he was running a side business raising roaches. One of the DEA guys found his second and third roll of bills the size of a softball in a coat pocket in the living room. "Fifties," he tells his partner. "Not bad, eh?" Another agent showed me a box of snapshots. I pulled out one of Felix smiling at the camera and toasting with little ceramic glasses at a table full of heavy-looking Chinese dudes on a restaurant deck overlooking Hong Kong harbor a world away from this shit hole.

The more Gio and I looked through the shoebox of photos and the more I saw of Felix's place, the more I began to wonder what his deal was. This guy was jetting around the world and making God knows how many millions a year, but his apartment looked like a kennel. Worse. A standard look inside the oven for drugs and cash let loose such a stampede of bugs that I gagged. Finally, out in the living room, we realized what those little *tick* sounds were. Gio held up what he'd just found on his neck. A roach. I felt a feather light tap on the top of my head and watched two roaches fall and land on a Polaroid of Felix in a Spuds MacKenzie shirt alongside a Chinese guy in the cockpit of a cigarette boat. Gio and I both looked up at the ceiling together. It was alive. Hundreds of roaches crawled across the ceiling, lazily dropped to the floor and made their way back up the walls at will. I had to concentrate not to panic.

"Felix, what the fuck, man?"

"They're hard to get rid of." Felix shrugged. We were all so skeeved that the DEA guys bagged what they'd found, and we escorted Felix and his lady out in record time. Weeks later a snitch told me that we missed over a million dollars in cash inside Felix's stereo speakers. Too bad. None of us could've stood it in there another second.

Within a year Felix was dead. Davey Blue Eyes gave the Navarro brothers from Cherry Street what they'd apparently been asking for for months—the no-blowback greenlight to kill Felix.

One of Rudy Giuliani's successful "quality of life" arrest binges, like his war on squeegee men, was an all-out assault on the millions of dollars of illegal fireworks sales leading up to the Fourth of July that had gone on for decades. It's hard to adequately describe pre-Rudy Independence Day on the Lower East Side. On Third Street the Hells Angels took shopping carts and fifty-gallon oil drums, dumped hundreds of dollars in contraband fireworks into them, doused the whole thing with gasoline and, like it says on the package of Black Cats, would "light fuse, get away."

And they were the responsible ones. The Angels' miniature artillery attack was at least avoidable. Everywhere else in the neighborhood, especially in the projects, it was a random rainstorm of exploding gunpowder, smoldering paper, and car alarms by the hundreds all going off at once. As Felix sat by himself swinging on a chain fence overlooking the East River on the Fourth of July 1988, one of the Navarro brothers walked up behind him and put a .38 round into Felix's head behind his ear. Whatever vendetta the Cherry Street and the Third and D boys shared against Felix ended there. The gun's report was completely lost on families grilling in the park below among the day-long explosions echoing all over Alphaville.

A week after racing the Feds out of Felix's roach motel apartment, Gio and I were driving around solo early in a four-to-twelve tour. We had the windows rolled down and stopped to check things out at Third and D, when we both realized that just about everyone working and hanging out on the avenue wasn't checking us out, they were looking at something or someone at the far end of the block.

Gio tensed. It was part of dealer protocol to make a show of ignoring us and this felt really unnatural and ominous— like we were on a collision course with whatever was down the avenue. Gio pulled the car over. A thirty-something black guy who looked like he'd been sleeping outdoors for a week approached our car. Every pair of bad-guy eyes on the block followed him. He looked like a bum, but he also looked familiar. Like a movie actor who got hit with an ugly stick . . .

"What's up?" I asked. The guy stood and stared with his mouth half open. "What can I do for you?" I said impatiently.

"I heard you guys were looking for me," he finally said. "I'm Hank."

The force of gravity within the Lower East Side projects was an incredible thing to behold. I learned later that before turning himself in, Hank hid out in Brooklyn, Queens, and even Florida. Yet here he was, standing in front of us looking like all our snitches said he would. Jerry and Tony had made detective and were scheduled to get their gold shields before the end of the month. We had organized a going-away celebration after the tour, but it looked like that was going to have to wait. Here was Black Hank, and the detectives handling the case had for sure already signed out for the day. We would have to take Black Hank through the booking process ourselves.

"Never freakin' fails," Gio said. "I dunno why I even bother making plans."

"Well, we have no choice. We may never find this prick again," I sighed. Hank just stood there. We'd both calmed down about the 50 Avenue D case. Ana had sent a note saying that she and her baby, a little girl named Crystal, were doing fine and that she was working and living in Queens. I took it as a good sign that the rookie at the Command who Ana gave the note to and who knew nothing about her ordeal had described the girl that handed him an envelope with our names on it as a hot piece of ass. The world kept going around. Ana was getting on with her life and so were we. Hank would be, too, though outside of a very long prison sentence, his options were pretty limited.

I was mindful of our audience and the need to give the av-

enue a little show and an abject lesson. There also was probably no one on earth that deserved a beating more than Hank
did. Everyone knew about Ana's situation, and what Gio and
I had done to the first creep we caught. I looked at Gio.

"We can't just beat him like this right here. I mean he
gave himself up."

"I know, but . . ." Gio gestured to the people all watching. Hank turned around and looked at them, too. "We gotta
do something." I thought for a moment. Whatever we did
needed to look like we were in control for the block's sake
but not like a violation of Hank's arrest rights for our sake.
IAB was everywhere, it seemed.

"Hank," I finally told him. "You have five seconds to run."

"What do you mean 'run'?" Hank said.

"Count to five and run. Do it or else I'm gonna beat your
ass so bad even your own mother won't recognize you."

"You gonna shoot me?"

"No," Gio said, turning the car ignition off. "But listen to
what the man's telling you."

"I'm telling you one more time," I said calmly. "Start running. Five, four, three."

At three Hank broke at a sharp right angle and took off in
the direction he'd come. He made another hairpin turn into
the projects. We were out and after him in a heartbeat. Gio
caught up with him first. He grabbed Hank by the collar of
his T-shirt, and swung him down to the ground as hard as
he could. Hank fell right at my feet. The supreme boom-
bash that Hank needed began with a series of kicks. In the
two or so minutes we were on him, the two of us didn't fuck
him up anywhere near as much as we had his partner. We
could've put him through a meat grinder and it wouldn't

have made up for what the two of them did to Ana. It must have looked spectacular from the sidelines, though. For the neighborhood, it was the treatment he deserved, and for anyone from the department who saw it or heard about it later, a perp had rabbited on us, and we enthusiastically gave chase and subdued him as we were trained to.

Most Commands assign each officer little cubbyhole mailboxes. Usually, mine was filled with police junk mail—union papers, *Patrol Guide* updates, interdepartmental orders, and other things I rarely read. I'd go days or even weeks sometimes without even looking in my box. Maybe it was the note from Ana but for whatever reason this particular day I took a look in my box and found a handwritten note on what was obviously a page torn from a police notebook. "Mike, call me ASAP—Mark Testa."

Testa was a Brooklyn South major case detective that Gio and I worked with once before. A few months ago Central had radioed his number to us while we were on patrol, so I gave him a call.

"Thanks for returning my call so fast," he'd said after introducing himself and bullshitting a little. "So I hear you and your partner know everyone in Alphabet City." It was a story we heard a lot. Testa was looking for someone who frequented the Avenue D projects, and word was that we were the game wardens there.

"This may be a tough one," Testa said, "but do you know anyone with a green station wagon that visits Avenue D?" He was investigating a fifteen-year-old kid who'd been stabbed to death and sodomized. The kid's body was dumped in Testa's precinct under the boardwalk near my old Coney Island rookie posting. Testa had the kid, lab reports, and a description of a suspect in a green Plymouth Volare station wagon. The car rang a bell. There weren't that many station wagons around our little corner of the world. Gio and I both remembered one that sounded like it could belong to Testa's guy.

"Yeah," I told him. "Don't know what the guy's story is, but I do remember the wagon."

"The perp who drives it supposedly likes young Puerto Rican boys and goes down to the Lower East Side a lot to get high and try to pick up kids. Anybody you can talk to over there that might know him?"

"Maybe, yeah. I'll see what we can do."

This was pretty soon after Sergeant Angelo took over Op 8, and we followed protocol and briefed the sarge before hitting the bricks to see if anyone had a fix on the station wagon and the man who drove it. Sarge was pleased and kind of surprised that a Brooklyn South gold shield had reached out to us in the Housing ghetto. He was new, but he was coming around and no longer assumed we made up the information we shared with him.

"You really think you may know the guy?" Sarge asked.

"We might," Gio answered. We didn't. But our snitches did.

"He's a pervert," a corner dealer told us, "he likes kids and shit. White guy. Likes boys, gets high." We made the rounds, got the same story and a few more details from a few more regulars. Along the way we emptied our wallets of twenties and tens. Each bill went into the hand of someone who knew we were looking to meet this guy and said they'd get ahold of us if they saw him.

A few days later Sergeant Angelo was conducting roll call when someone up front at the Command yelled back into the Op 8 office.

"Mikey C—call coming in for you."

When I picked up the phone, a voice on the other end said, "Rambo, that white guy with the green Plymouth is here looking to buy a bundle." I recognized the voice. It was a guy we'd used as a snitch for months.

"Keep him there," I told the snitch. "Do whatever you have to do, but keep him there."

"Okay, Rambo. We'll be near fifty Avenue D." I hung up the phone and filled in the sergeant and the rest of Op 8 on what was going down. We all piled into 9864 and floored it to Avenue D. A green station wagon was parked right where it was supposed to be. The sergeant, Gio, and I approached the vehicle. My snitch was sitting in the front seat. He held a switchblade against the stomach of a white guy who looked like a chubby Don Knotts. The snitch smiled and rolled down the window.

"He wanted to leave so I told him he couldn't." I was afraid to look at the sergeant. When I did, he looked like he was going to explode.

"Thanks," I told the informant.

He folded up his blade and whispered, "He thinks I'm on the job," and laughed. "Don't forget me, Rambo," he said.

"I won't," I replied, already feeling like I'd sold him out. If the sarge wasn't there, maybe we could've arranged something. But with him standing next to me and looking like he was going to smack my head, it was no use.

"You got to come back with us," I informed the perp who owned the car. "There's some Brooklyn detectives want to talk to you."

"I shouldn't have come down here," he mumbled.

"Yup, you shouldn't have."

The drive back to the Command was quiet. Legally I had to lock up my informant for possession of the switchblade, unlawful imprisonment of the perp, and impersonating a cop. Of course I would never do that.

When we tossed Testa's perp, his pockets contained more dope than the sarge had ever seen, and when Testa and another Brooklyn South detective came in to pick up their guy, the visit went well and attracted the right kind of attention at the Command.

"I owe you for this one," Testa said. He meant it. We'd explained privately how exactly we got his man, and he appreciated the position we were in. It would blow over with the sarge or it wouldn't. Either way, this creep was off the street. The suspect confessed to the killing under questioning later that day.

After they left, the sergeant cornered us. "You guys can't do things like this anymore," he said flatly. "It's dangerous. It's not good." He was half right. We couldn't do things like that anymore when he was around.

Now, months later, I read Testa's note and used the detectives' phone to call him back.

"Hey, Mark, what's up?" I asked. "Everything all right?"

Testa hesitated before answering. "Wait a second," he said, "I should close the door." I listened while Testa asked someone nearby for privacy and a door slammed.

"Mike," he said a moment later, "I have to give you a heads-up about something." We weren't buddies or anything so this had to be serious. "Look, I don't really want to talk on the phone, you working a four-to-twelve today?"

"Yeah, I just got on."

"Good," Testa answered. "Where can we meet to talk in private?"

"There's a little joint over on Avenue A and Third, Lillie's Restaurant. How's that sound?"

"It sounds good. I'll be there around seven," he said, then hung up the phone.

"What the fuck you think this is about?" Gio asked. We sat at a back table in Lillie's, waiting for Testa to show.

"I got no idea. It can't be good. He's coming all the way from Brooklyn just because he didn't want to talk over the phone." Gio nodded. He was slipping into silent mode, which I hated.

"Maybe it's the whole knife thing our stoolie did to his perp," I offered. "I always had a bad feeling about that thing." Gio said nothing. Bells on the restaurant's door jingled.

Mark Testa walked in wiping the rain off his trench coat. He was a sharp dresser and looked like a beefier version of Pat Riley from the Lakers. His coat and his suit were expensive, and he had salt-and-pepper hair slicked flawlessly back even with the rain. With a slight smile, he shook our hands and sat down.

"What can I get you?" I asked.

"Just coffee," he answered. I motioned for the waitress and asked her to bring him a cup.

"So what's up?"

It took a minute, but finally he started talking in a voice so low that Gio and I had to lean in to hear him. His face hardly moved as he spoke.

"Okay, look guys, here it is. There was this bank robbery up in the Nineteenth, so there's a bunch of Feds and other units involved, but anyway, the perp there might be the same perp from a homicide I have in Brooklyn." I nodded. He kept talking. "See, when we were debriefing this informant about these two cases, the informant goes off on some rambling tangent and blurts out how he heard that there are two cops, Fastback and Rambo, on the Lower East Side and they're shaking down drug dealers, and how the dealers all got together and put out a fifty-thousand-dollar hit on the two cops."

Gio and I sat there stunned. "That's fucking bullshit," I finally said.

Testa nodded, "Listen guys, I only know you guys for being stand-up and helping me out, so I'm just letting you know what happened and what I heard." He sipped his coffee. "Like I said, there's all these other units and Feds sitting in on the interview when this jerk-off stoolie goes off about you two guys. Finally this boss from uptown and this Fed get up and call Internal Affairs and the special prosecutor's office so they can hear this douche bag CI's story."

"What the fuck?" Gio finally spits out. "Now what?"

"Well," Testa continued, "IA comes down and leaves with our informant. Now I don't know what's gonna happen, but I want you two guys to be careful and watch yourselves. You know I've been around a long freakin' time, and I've seen good cops get set up by these IAB dickheads. And we all know how easy an informant can be manipulated to say and swear to almost anything. Especially if the Feds are involved." I shook my head. "If it helps, the CI's name is Rudy Morales."

"Doesn't ring a bell, but I'll have to check my records," I said.

Detective Testa sipped his coffee and stood up. "I felt I owed it to tell you guys what happened. I hope you both just watch your asses out there." He put his coat on and pushed his hair back with both hands. "Shit like this only happens to guys that work and you guys are out there working. I respect that and if I hear anything else, I'll get in touch."

"We do too fucking much," Gio said.

I nodded to Testa then stuck out my hand. "Mark, thanks for coming all the way down here. No one will ever know we spoke about this."

"No problem. Fuck them motherfucker Internal Affairs. Like I said, I've had them in my shit, too, and it was total bullshit. Just remember, you may love this job, but this job don't love you."

Gio and I sat quietly as I drove through the Lower East Side. I think we were both running an inventory of all the fucked-up things we'd done and every time we tossed the book.

"For what?" Gio spat out suddenly. "What the fuck did we get ourselves into here? For a good collar, to put some jerk-off behind bars, for a medal or a commendation, for what? I know it wasn't the money, I never took a dime and neither did you, so why the fuck did we ever bother?"

"Because we're not jerk-offs, and we give a fuck." It was a fact. It wasn't much comfort but it was easy to say. "That's why we were out here hustling collars, kicking ass, and takin' names. That's why, 'cause we're not jerk-off do-nothings."

Gio nodded. "Yeah, well now what?"

"Now, we'll be cool. Take it easy a little, do things by the book, cross our Ts and dot our Is, like the boss always says.

That's all. We'll be all right. And as far as the hit, fuck them, too."

Neither of us wanted a permanent transfer out of Op 8 and PSA 4 so we let IAB come to us when and if they thought they had a case and didn't start making inquiries up the chain of command. Job one was to check with our informants and see if the price on our heads was for real. We saw Lydia, a girl from Baruch Houses who snorted dope and dated dealers. She'd fucked a lot of them and there were always about four or five bad guys using her apartment to hang out in. To her talking about the dope scene was just gossip. She was the one who had given me one of my only actual sightings of Davey Blue Eyes. Lydia grew up in the same building as Davey and pointed out a nondescript guy across the street one day when I was fishing for tips from her. She thought he didn't see her and it was her way of acting tough. "Davey? You mean him," she'd said. I looked, and the guy she pointed out turned his head to her and jerked his chin. She looked like she was going to shit. I looked back and he was already gone.

Gio and I found her quick. "Lydia," I asked her, "have you ever heard of these guys putting a hit on us?"

"Oh yeah," she said completely casually. "A couple of weeks ago I was in Macatumba's car when they were talking about it. They said it was a big money thing. They were bitching that they were having a hard time getting anyone to do it. Everyone was scared because you're cops and whoever does it might get caught, and you guys might kill them first and shit."

Jesus fucking Christ. If she knew about it, every bad guy in the neighborhood must know about it. I wanted to ask her why she hadn't mentioned it when I was bullshitting with her the week before.

"Who? Who was talking about it? Who was in the car?" Gio asked.

"Oh shit, everyone's putting up some cash, Fastback," she said. She was clearly stoned and it wasn't making anything easier.

"Lydia," I asked again, "who was in the car?"

"You know," she said dreamily, "like Macatumba, Davey, Jimmy Rivera . . ."

"What did Davey say?" I asked.

"It wasn't him saying shit so much," Lydia replied, "more like the others were bitching about you guys and all the busts and taking their cash and their shit. Finally Davey goes like he'll put up half the dead presidents for the hit, if they put together the other half. He was real all business, like always, but yo, Rambo, you're really pissing off his boys. I'm just sayin' . . ."

The Third and D crew had had their fill of us, went to Davey Blue Eyes with their beef, and not only did Davey give them the go-ahead to kill us, he offered to put up half the money to hire someone from out of town to do it. Twenty-five thousand dollars against fifty thousand to see us dead and buried with the mayor in attendance. I knew what we were doing was working, but apparently it was really working. The biggest problem for the Third and D crew was that because of our blitz of arrests, seizures, and everything else we could think of and get away with, they were having to curtail sales on the D, particularly during our shifts. Davey could still make quantity sales elsewhere but the Third Street crew were his best sellers and, since he was in essence fronting them dope they paid him for out of their street sales, his best customers. The fact that they would risk murdering two New York City cops to get back their market share was a standing ovation. That didn't make either of us any more comfortable about being out on the street that night.

We busted a junkie kid that was getting sick on Second Street, spent the rest of the shift processing the arrest, Gio took the subway home for the first time in a year, and I left my car at the Command and took a cab to a hotel room I booked in Midtown under an assumed name.

The next day I made two trips. The first was to a police store down by the old headquarters building on Lafayette. I bought a small, slim .380 automatic and switched my two-inch .38 to the ankle holster I sometimes used for discretion. Forewarned is forearmed.

The second was to headquarters in Harlem. Gio and I were summoned to Housing PD headquarters by Chief Cummings. Both the Feds and IAB had been compelled by regulations to let our headquarters know about the alleged contract, and word reached the chief the same day it reached us. We didn't talk about any other IAB investigation. The chief loved us for our stats and was a go-getter himself with a wall of commendations from his uniform and plainclothes days to prove it. Without hesitation he handed us the keys to a new Plymouth.

"I'm gonna give you one of my vehicles to use as your own and transfer you guys to Harlem, PSA Five for a few weeks until we get this hit business settled," he said. "I want you guys out of harm's way. I don't want you guys doing anything in PSA Five. Not anything, got me? And I want you working the tours you normally work, but I want you answering to me only. I'll arrange it."

As Gio and I started to leave, the chief sat down behind his desk. "I don't want you guys getting involved with anything. Lay low, you got it?"

Gio and I nodded. "We got it, Chief."

We were in Harlem for a few weeks, but got so bored doing nothing that we started tossing perps just like back on the avenue. One night we tossed two scumbags and came up with a kilo of coke. We'd promised the chief we'd lay low, so we gave the collar to the plainclothes guys in the uptown Command. But Davey's guys could find us anywhere. We even ran into one of his top dealers on 102nd and First Avenue a few days after checking in at the PSA 5 Command. Anyone can kill a cop, but very few people can get away with it. The shield and the repercussions of a contract kill on someone wearing one may have been beyond anyone on Davey's payroll. Issuing a contract on us was just making him more visible and more vulnerable. And IAB? Bring them on. Compared to getting shot stepping off a curb by some coked-out hired gun from Camden, IAB would be child's play.

Finally, after a couple months uptown, we returned to Op 8 and played things as calmly and coolly as we could. If we made too much noise now, we'd be transferred out to another Command and never get a chance to show Davey and the Third and D crew how much they meant to us. We were careful and we were focused—not praying for a miracle, just hoping that a solid opportunity to drop Davey and his guys would come our way. After a few weeks, it did.

Sixteen

"So, what's up? What did he want?" I'd just hung up a pay-phone on the corner of Seventh Street and Avenue C. A uniform at the Command had handed me a "while you were out" phone call memo with "Tom Benton—DEA" and a phone number written on it earlier in the week. We'd been playing phone tag until a few moments ago.

"He wants to meet with us," I told Gio as I got in the car.

"Now?" Even after all the joint operations we'd done with DEA, Gio still didn't think they were on our side somehow.

"I told him now was good, yeah," I said. Gio was driving and it was still early in our shift. With all the anxiety and hassle that accompanied the hit and the IAB scare, it seemed like a good idea to take a break and have lunch on the Feds. Gio couldn't argue with that. I thumbed the radio mike.

"Central, be advised nine-eight six-four is out to five five five West Fifty-seventh Street, DEA headquarters."

I didn't think we'd be out of the neighborhood for more than a couple hours. Instead we spent the rest of the day in conference with Benton, his supervisor Oscar Roland, and a handful of other agents it turned out we had something in common with. We were all looking to take down the Third and D crew and strangle the Avenue D heroin trade.

Prior to Prohibition, enforcing federal drug laws was primarily up to the IRS. Narcotics traffic was still fairly small in those days and there were still only a handful of federal criminal statutes of any kind (most involving interstate theft) on the books. Most European countries had national police forces to complement their municipal and regional cops. But nineteenth century American lawmakers were leery of giving the federal government criminal arrest and prosecution powers beyond those granted to the Treasury. The new century brought new anxieties about crime and federal criminal offenses grew in number. A national policing bureaucracy charged with enforcing those laws grew at about the same rate. The fledgling FBI, created under Teddy Roosevelt, got a major shot in the arm doing domestic spying and counterespionage in the run up to World War I and Prohibition was, of course, a federal law-enforcement gold rush.

The Volstead Act called for the creation of a Bureau of Prohibition within the Treasury. The Harrison Narcotics Tax Act (named for the New York State congressman who sponsored it in 1914) and the surge in illegal heroin and cocaine use and sales that spawned it eventually gave birth to the Federal Bureau of Narcotics under Lucky Luciano's nemesis, Harry Anslinger. The Bureau of Prohibition was absorbed back into the Treasury after repeal, but the FBN kept going. Like his counterpart, J. Edgar Hoover who'd risen through the ranks to head the FBI, Anslinger ran FBN as a personal fiefdom. Both men ardently romanced the press and didn't sweat their own accountability. Neither was above using their agencies to explore the borderlands at the

intersection of law enforcement, personal vendetta, and political ambition.

FBN was so much Anslinger's baby that it only survived a
few more years after he retired in 1962. The paranoia cocktail created by the Cold War and the Kennedy assassination
was a potent one. The fact that here at home drug sales and
abuse were on the rise and that much of the drugs being
sold and taken originated outside the country added to a
national siege mentality. In the mid-sixties FBN merged with
a short-lived FDA spinoff called the Bureau of Drug Abuse
Control into a single agency within the Justice Department
called the Bureau of Narcotics and Dangerous Drugs.

Federal drug law enforcement had become such a hot
topic that Elvis Presley made an after-hours visit to the
White House (by most accounts zonked out of his mind) to
trade Nixon a commemorative Colt pistol for a Bureau of
Narcotics and Dangerous Drugs badge and the title of "Special Agent at Large." *Life* magazine began alternating cover
shots of syringes with pictures of Raquel Welch. The Rolling
Stones charted a top-ten hit with a song about suburban
housewives overdosing on pills. Sergeant Friday talked L.A.
teens on LSD off ledges and debated with dealers every
week on *Dragnet*. Every lawmaker began to preach to their
state electorate about driving the scourge of illegal narcotics from the land of the free and nearly every government
agency and department was getting into the act.

New York's drug problem had long since become America's drug problem, and America's drug problem was being
fed from all over the globe. Organized criminal activity
overseas was generating billions in untaxable blood money
at home. First Lyndon Johnson and then Nixon sought to

consolidate federal law enforcement manpower to create a legal reach that stretched from Washington across the country and beyond U.S. borders to address the globalization of drug cultivation, manufacture, and export. The Feds' drug bust administrative apparatus began to bulge at the bureaucratic seams. Even before the escalation of combat in Vietnam and Watergate, the president and Congress found little to agree on. Nixon's call for the creation of a single, sovereign antidrug law enforcement agency with field offices all over the national and international map was something nearly everyone could get behind. In 1973, the Drug Enforcement Agency (DEA) became the government agency responsible for an "all-out global war on the drug menace" the president declared when he signed the agency into existence nearly unopposed on Capitol Hill.

DEA was still a pretty young agency and relatively free of the lifers, dinosaurs, and old-school emphasis on seniority and status quo that made the NYPD an easy place to step on toes. DEA agents had their own paperwork burden, but they maintained a pretty tight ship manned by mostly young, eager agents who drove nice cars and holstered fancy guns. Benton wasn't much older than we were. Even though he only had a few years of experience on the job, he was sharp and Gio and I both liked him right away.

"You know these guys?" Benton asked as he dropped a pair of mug shot blowups on the table in front of us.

"Sure," I said. "I saw this mope in the *cuchifritos* place on D last night. Joco. He's a droopy pants scumbag trying to deal his way upstairs in Davey Blue Eyes's bunch. All he ever talks about is money."

"I hate that motherfucker," Gio said, pointing at the

photos. "Both of them. Both of these guys are fucking scumbags."

Benton explained that his task force had just walked away from an eight-week investigation of Joco and the other creep, a dealer named Roberto Campos. These guys were dirty and their dirt trail led back to Davey. We knew it and DEA knew it. Alone, these two were responsible for close to a million dollars' worth of dope sales in the last eight months and had been suspected of arranging, witnessing, and possibly actually doing a couple of nasty homicides when they got burned on material they fronted to some guys from uptown.

The U.S. attorney had intended to use one of the two against the other and start climbing up the scumbag ladder in Davey Blue Eyes's organization. But DEA had pulled the trigger on a buy-and-bust collar a little too soon and the gap between what was known and what could be proved in court got too wide to close. With the help of their lawyer, Lynne Stewart, the two perps stuck together, beat the rap, and walked.

Benton and his guys were out months of work, the taxpayers were out thousands in overtime and overhead costs, and the two guys whose faces we were looking at were back out on the sidewalk in Alphabet City drinking beers and watching their spots as we spoke.

"If at first you don't succeed . . . ," Benton sighed with a shrug. "You guys know all the names and faces down there. Feel like helping us win the next round?"

We were glad to help then and even more eager now. We really did hate the two guys the DEA had just lost and hated the idea that they'd squirmed out of jail time. Making life hard for Davey and the Third and D dealers who'd put a price on our heads was exactly what we wanted from life at that point and we told Benton as much.

"What do you have?" I asked him.

What Benton had was a civilian informant. Like everyone else busting drug dealers, DEA relied heavily on snitches. The NYPD was such an enormous sprawling ocean of manpower and a cluster fuck of paperwork and bookkeeping that Albany tended to rubber-stamp budget increases as long as there was money enough in the state kitty to cover them. DEA was small but growing and had the budget needs to prove it. The agency was fully accountable to the lawmakers that approved their annual operating stake. Gio and I were basically making a career out of not being accountable to anyone but our own consciences. DEA agents didn't have that luxury and their snitches had to have their papers in order.

The agency was new enough that there was a streak of administrative realism guiding what they did and how they did it. DEA standard operating procedure made the post-Knapp rules and guidelines that hamstrung NYPD drug busts seem old fashioned by comparison. According to the rules, we could only offer registered informants a pile of forms to fill out and the promise of some reward money down the line. On the q.t., of course Gio and I offered our secret legion of helpful ears and eyes twenty dollar bills from our own pockets and the occasional opportunity to sell a little longer after we left or keep a few of the bags we found on them provided the info they shared was worth it.

DEA cut straight to the chase with their informants. They recruited their CIs not from the street but from where people were most willing to work out a deal—the courthouse. Most DEA CIs were collared perps and accessories looking to cut or eliminate jail time by helping Uncle Sam take out bigger fish. Also, DEA offered their rats money—real money based on performance—and they delivered. Civilian informants working for DEA were paid a bounty—a commission percentage based on the quantity and value of material and cash seized over the course of a successful investigation.

The upside for the Feds was that a good reliable CI could help them fast-forward through months of footwork and surveillance. A guy who had been in the game for long enough to get jammed up by the Feds could bring even the greenest agent closer to taking down a dealer just by shaking a hand and making a buy. Using someone from outside also reduced potential physical risk to the agents. The downside of DEA's CI outreach was that, as I'd learned on Avenue D, "reliable" and "civilian informant" were often mutually exclusive terms. People like Lydia who I had talked to every week and to whom I had personally funneled my own cash in trade for info couldn't even bother to tell me that there was a hit out on me and my partner until we asked face-to-face.

A few years later when I started doing undercover work with DEA, I also discovered that legitimately papered CIs and the accountability that comes with them force a lot of supervisory daylight into an ongoing investigation and can stifle an agent's resourcefulness and creativity. I didn't like being watched and resented answering to anybody when I did undercovers. Those operations were stressful enough without having to justify every move to someone in an office. When I was my own undercover, posing as a wiseguy, I could say or do anything I wanted.

It turned out that the guy Agent Benton had on hand, identified in the mountain of legal documents to come as CS-1, was good. He was from Jersey and had tripped up on a federal narcotics rap. Rather than do time for the guys who had stood to make the most money before their deal soured, CS-1 helped the government strengthen its case and ensure a conviction. When DEA offered him a chance to actually get paid to do the same thing for complete strangers, he jumped. CS-1 hung around drug dealers all the time anyway, so what the hell? It beat working and he liked the money. By the time we met him, CS-1 had already lent a paid hand to nearly a half dozen other drug cases that had all concluded in convictions or solid pleas.

DEA's civilian informant knew how to walk the walk and talk the talk. He would need to keep walking, talking and dealing with the Third and D crew until he hit somebody heavy enough to deserve a wiretap. DEA wanted to use CS-1 to establish ties with guys who had so much going on that they could catch them with drugs, cash, and guns and slap them with multiple count drug indictments. They were going to do what they did best, perform a long, slow, careful investigation and fill a steamer trunk full of corroborative evidence from three basic sources—testimony from their CI, surveillance via covert observation and wiretap, and solid, by-the-book arrests of everyone involved so far reaching and well supported that once they were in custody the bad guys would either cop pleas and rat on each other or they would go far, far away for a long, long time. Gio and I offered to get the ball rolling by figuring out who in the Third and D crew Benton's rat should talk to first. It was our job to point out a dealer CS-1 could use as a boost to get to someone farther up the ladder in Davey Blue Eyes's organization than Joco and Campos.

The special agent in charge of the New York Drug Enforcement Administration field office made a few calls first to Washington, then to our chief, and within a few days, Gio and I were deputized, assigned to Group 34 of the NYDEA field division, given two "G rides" (our own cars—mine was a brand-new Camaro), beepers, federal ID, some papers to sign and send to NYPD human resources and to our union, and more free rein to put the Lower East Side scumbags away than we ever could have dreamed of. It was like Christmas. We had a task force bullpen set up in a room at DEA headquarters with desks, phones, and a bulletin board covering one wall. I took a three-by-five index card, wrote "Davey Colas" on it and pinned it to the top of the board.

Once officially signed on, we began a series of trips up and down the avenue and through the projects in an unmarked van with black tinted windows that DEA kept in a lot on the West Side Highway. The van was a conversion job that looked like a fuck-truck party mobile, with a captain's chair and a bench seat that turned into a bed in back. But, like Davey's armored Chinatown special it also had special shocks, a periscope that peeked out from a nondescript moon roof, and the quietest air-conditioning system I'd ever heard. It also had a bank of still and video cameras, which we trained on the Alphaville dealers as CS-1 sat in the big chair, sipped on a Sprite, and paid careful attention to the bad guys we pointed out. Back on Fifty-seventh Street we reviewed the tapes and stills like game films, compared notes, and prepared a list of who's who in the Avenue D dope racket.

We decided that a good place to start would be with Jimmy Rivera. Jimmy was a Third and D regular, one of the hit squad who put Big Arthur Washington down, and one of the whiners that bitched to Davey about going halvsies on having Gio and me killed. I'd heard that he was mostly making volume sales to out-of-the-neighborhood guys since we'd made the D a hard place for him to run dealing spots himself. Jimmy was good with material and guns and bad with money and had gone to nearly everyone around who could hook him up with quantity. On our advice, CS-1 introduced himself to Eggie—a punk in Jimmy's circle who started out doing hand-to-hands for Jimmy back when it was easier to sell on the LES. CS-1 told Eggie that he wanted to score quantity, and let it become clear that he was hoping to make a solid connection for Chinese smack to sell in Newark, Patterson, and Trenton. Today he just wanted a few packages. Down the line, well . . . Our guy was smooth. He looked and sounded the part because he had lived it and Eggie took him to see Jimmy himself. CS-1 exchanged about three grand in cash for three hundred bags of dope with Jimmy, who was impressed enough with how our man carried himself and how green his money was that he gave CS-1 his beeper number and told him to beep him directly when he wanted more material.

A few deals later, Benton, another agent, Gio, and I sat in the van and watched CS-1 cross Avenue D with Eggie and Jimmy and shake hands with a guy that we knew all too well. Animal knew us, too. He was a big, mean, dark-skinned guy who loved guns, cars, money, and hip-hop and was too smart to ever visit the avenue with anything we could nail him for. He'd been on the scene almost as long as

Davey himself and had made Davey millions in street corner and bulk dope sales. If Animal had any inkling that we
were on the other side of the tinted glass in a government
vehicle along with two DEA guys, one of whom was snapping pictures, and that the guy he was shaking hands with
was also on the DEA payroll, we would've known it. CS-1
would be dead and we would be in pursuit. Animal reassured Jimmy's new best friend that he could hook him up
with unit-sized weight of Chinese heroin and the four of
them, CS-1, Animal, Eggie, and Jimmy smiled together like
they were posing for the pictures Benton's man took.

A week or so later, CS-1 sat opposite Animal at a table in
a White Castle on Queens Boulevard below a sign reading
BURGERS FOR BREAKFAST, WHY NOT? Our guy had a main
mission—to make a quantity buy from Animal smoothly
enough that Animal gave him his phone or beeper number,
but not so smoothly that the seller got nervous. CS-1 was a
natural. Whatever bounty he stood to collect at the end of
the road was going to be worth it. Inside the White Castle
our guy and Animal went around about price and quality.
"That your car?" Animal asked in a lull, pointing out to a
white Maxima in the parking lot.

"Yeah," our informant replied.

"That's a fresh ride," Animal observed.

"Brand new, yo," CS-1 said. A new car, especially a
tricked-out Maxima like the one CS-1 drove, reeked of le-
gitimacy, and CS-1 had mentioned he was in the market for
one at their previous meeting. He'd actually already owned
it for a month before our investigation even began, but as
far as Animal was concerned he'd bought it since their last
meeting. Smart.

Compared to how most civilians behave in their personal and professional lives, on a social and business level, drug dealers tend to be assholes. They'll threaten, whine, show up late, and routinely shortchange each other. A common mistake that cops make when they do undercover buys is simply being too together. Cops don't haggle, have all their money carefully counted out and ready, and agree to whatever time and place the seller suggests for a meet. Crooks, well, they're just fuck-ups mostly, and doing business their way was like pulling teeth about 90 percent of the time.

CS-1 fidgeted in his plastic banquette seat, looked away, and fiddled with a waxy onion ring in the cardboard container in front of him.

"What's the matter?" Animal asked him.

"This place makes me nervous, that's all. I don't like talking business with all this fucking glass everywhere."

Animal smiled. "We got a place near here. It's more private. You'll like it. It's your style."

Future lawbreakers take note—all it takes is five, maybe ten minutes to do an effective countersurveillance. Next time you go to a meet to sell a felony quantity of smack—use some common sense. Get to the meeting place early and have a look around. Even if you live around the corner from where you're doing business, go home via a highway and pull over to the shoulder at some point along the way. Change your rendezvous location at the last minute. Be unpredictable.

If Animal or one of his guys had arrived a few hours early, cruised through the White Castle parking lot, done a little due diligence and made a note of the cars in it and parked across the street they would've seen two rides that were worth discussing. One was a tinted-window conversion van that had been on Avenue D a lot lately. The other was an unmarked DEA Impala. Animal and CS-1 got in their cars and Animal took the lead out onto Queens Boulevard. The DEA car followed but the van stayed put. It wasn't a long trip. Just a few blocks away. Animal led our guy to a garage building labeled Tony's Custom Speed Shop.

Animal made the most of thug life, he was tall and muscular, looked great in gangster threads and gold jewelry, talked about money, pussy, drugs, and guns constantly, and worked overtime to remind the world that he was a badass—which, in all honesty, he was. We were positive he'd done nearly a half-dozen shootings. His partner, Guerro, who Animal introduced to CS-1 inside the shop, dressed like he went to work in an office. He was slightly built, no more than five foot five and was soft-spoken no matter what the topic.

Guerro and the co-owner of the speed shop shook hands with our "guy from Jersey who buys ounces," as Animal called him. Told that their guest was into cars, the co-owner, who we also knew from the Avenue, gave CS-1 a tour, pointing out a cobalt-blue 1980 Porsche Turbo Carrera ("Does zero to infinity in like ten seconds flat!"), another new Porsche in red, and a recent model Mercedes with tricked-out bumpers and fenders, a spoiler, and a lighting rig that made it glow purple from underneath at night. The co-owner estimated the net value of the three cars to be about $350,000 and explained that while Animal supplied Chinese heroin to Manhattan and the Bronx, he personally dealt the junk that was flooding the projects in Queens. Jersey was wide open as far as he and Animal were concerned. Once the tour was concluded, the four men went into the garage's office to discuss prices.

An ounce would set our man back $5,100. They would knock off the extra one hundred in multi-ounce buys. A brick (a 700 gram unit) would be $90,0000—$89,000 per if he bought three bricks at a time. A new CD stereo with a multidisk changer and huge bass speakers for his Maxima would set him back $150—the nice-guy price. CS-1 left Tony's with the price quotes and Animal's beeper number and the instructions to key "666" into the phone when he called.

Cell phones were still a novelty in the late eighties but, like an increasing number of dealers, Animal had one early on. If there was a number to put up on a wiretap that was it. Since it was a mobile, Animal could use it from anywhere. And like cell users everywhere, he made calls on impulse. If something pissed him off, he was worried, or felt like bragging, he made a call. It was an instant gratification and release that would hopefully make him careless, incline him to slip into incriminating language, and say things he should keep to himself or wait to share until he was face-to-face with his boys.

Dealers like Animal and Guerro were in a constant state of paranoia. It's unreal the assumptions and activities that guys with that much to gain and lose will get into. That craziness poses some risk to an undercover. But our guy was cut from the same cloth. He could distinguish bullshit from fact and a flight of anxiety from concrete reality pretty well. The fact is that between greed, loyalty, and trust issues, their own drug and booze habits, and trying to maintain a kind of hypervigilance that most human beings can't healthily sustain 24-7, these dudes were already in a kind of prison. Through CS-1 we began to rattle that cage.

The next move would be to make a quantity buy. CS-1 beeped Animal, typed in the number of the beast, and got a call back on Animal's cell within minutes. Over the course of a half dozen more calls the two arranged to trade a paper bag with twenty-two grand in it for an eighth ounce of smack at the White Castle on the boulevard. Animal pushed the rendezvous once. When our guy bitched about it, he casually explained that he and Guerro were meeting up with their Chinese connection and putting together a quantity deal of their own. Very interesting.

Animal and Joco met CS-1 in the White Castle parking lot the following evening and went inside together. They left separately after Animal told our guy that he didn't have the dope with him, asked him to front the twenty-two grand and CS-1 told him to go fuck himself. We knew from the exchange of calls that Animal needed to put together cash to make his quantity score. The truth was that we would've been only too happy to front the money, but the government paperwork hadn't come through and Animal changed the script without warning. Government undercovers are usually so leery of letting the money they signed for walk that smart and suspicious dealers will sometimes demand front money as a test.

This wasn't a test, it was mismanagement. Animal really just needed the cash. So, when the agents that followed him from the White Castle discovered a knapsack in the back of a 240SX outside Tony's with $68,000 in it, we decided that keeping it would probably put revealing pressure on Animal and keep him bitching to our guy.

Sure enough the next time they spoke, Animal complained that Feds had taken some of his money (a drop in the bucket compared to the cash he likely had on hand from his dope spots) and that they would do the eighth deal as a straight exchange after all. Due to the hassles he was encountering, Animal made it clear that the price would have to be twenty-four grand, not twenty-two.

That night as we watched across the street from Animal's house in Bayside, our guy handed the dealer a paper bag of cash and received a ziplock with a 106-gram brick of 86 percent pure heroin in it. Animal counted the money right there in the open.

"What the fuck? There's only twenty-two Gs here!"

"I'll get you the rest later," CS-1 told him.

"The fuck you will, nigga! In front of my own motherfucking house you playing with me? Fuck you! I've killed people for less!"

"Don't fucking freak, yo, I'll get you the rest. I'll get it."

"You sure ass will. You fucking even speak to me again without that two large in your hand and I'll fucking shoot you right then and there!"

He didn't have to. Animal got his two grand and CS-1 got the numbers of the three errand boys sent to collect it. The goal was to secure a wiretap of Animal's cell phone. Once we did, these other numbers would join a master list of people we could compile evidence on and eventually collar. The great thing about running a wire is that every phone call is always two-way. If people are doing business they're going to have to talk on the phone. These guys weren't just dealing quantity to people like CS-1; they were also running their own dope spots on the avenue, in Brooklyn, and in Queens. Once we tapped the right line, we would be in essence searching multiple "rooms" with a single warrant. Knocking out Animal and enough of his associates would dam up the flow of retail dope in PSA 4 and paralyze Davey Blue Eyes.

Wiretapping has been around for as long as there have been phones. Before Miranda and the other legal decisions that narrowed the legal definitions of entrapment and legal search and seizure, wiretapping restrictions, like search restrictions, varied state to state and were routinely redefined and overruled in various courtrooms and state houses. The evolution of privacy guarantees associated with the notion that the police or the government can listen in on phone calls has kept pace with the rest of civil liberties law.

Into the sixties J. Edgar Hoover's FBI went ahead and just wiretapped whoever the director wanted, whether he intended to use what they heard in a trial or not. A 1967 Supreme Court decision that disallowed wiretap evidence in a California fraud case led to the inclusion of the Wiretap Act as Title III in the Omnibus Crime Control and Safe Streets Act of 1968. Title III defined what were acceptable reasons for police eavesdropping. Under the new law a cop assembled enough evidence of wrongdoing via witness or informant affidavit, personal observations, photographs, etcetera, and went before a judge to plead a Title III application.

Over the course of three more buys totaling nearly $100,000, we used CS-1 to collect phone numbers, addresses, mentions of other buys and deals, and acquire, test, weigh, and voucher enough smack that a judge would sign the order for a wiretap on Animal's mobile phone. Within a couple of months Benton had enough to go before the judge and one Tuesday morning, he joined the U.S. attorney in federal court to do just that. By lunch we were celebrating a brand-new Title III warrant for Animal's cell at a Thai restaurant in Chinatown.

Seventeen

The wire that went up on Animal's phone was a gold mine. Some days I wondered if his finger ever got numb from dialing. Every deal he did, every bust, every hassle, every good, bad, or indifferent event in the day in the life of this particular bad guy warranted a phone call to someone. And as Animal made calls, we made recordings, took notes, collected numbers, and compiled evidence. When he made a quantity sale, we were there at the designated location taking pictures. When he or any of his boys came to Avenue D to check their spots, Gio and I made sure to pull them over and toss them.

The fact that these guys were occupationally paranoid and prerattled was an enormous asset once the wires went up. Everything we did, the apartment raids, traffic stops, small-time busts in plain sight were coordinated and intended to get Animal dialing and talking. He rarely disappointed. And he was often mad, scared, or wasted enough to forget to filter what he said.

A second wire to Guerro's cell phone was just as fertile. Conversations veered from the changing economics of high-volume dope sales, to cars, girls, and where to get machine guns and grenade launchers. These guys and girls we heard on the two phones all had double lives—running the spots we knew on the avenue and selling, brokering, and middle-manning "weight" to anyone with the equivalent weight in cash off the avenue. The names of those talking—Cheo, Eggie, Ish, Tracy, Louie, Chowsky, Hoi, Tomato, Boobie, and two dozen others each had faces. When they met up for a buy or to discuss a beef we were there taking their pictures. Gio and I knew or recognized most of them from the avenue. As the wiretap continued, they were matched to addresses—apartments in the projects, and elsewhere in Manhattan, private houses in Bayside, Corona, and Brooklyn. DEA's surveillance web grew to include the regular dealing spots on Avenue D, a car service front supposedly owned by Davey's cousins the Alvarez brothers on Attorney Street, and a bodega on Second Avenue with half-empty shelves up front and a back room that hosted dozens of dope and money exchanges.

Just two wires were shedding such a bright light on what was otherwise a shadow world of drugs, cash, and guns that it became an organizational marathon keeping it straight. Between running their dope spots and making additional quantity sales like the ones we initiated through CS-1, Animal's and Guerro's phones were going nonstop. More DEA agents were brought in to cover what was closing in on forty different bad-guy associates in the circle. The wire room at DEA headquarters was like Grand Central station some days. On one side of the room a bulletin board was completely covered in a collage of mug shots and covertly taken pictures of our ever-growing cast of characters, their hangouts, homes, families, and cars. What came in on the wiretaps was logged on index cards and filed. To keep up with the constant phone traffic on both Animal's and Guerro's phones, Benton asked us to reach out to our chief and get four more cops from PSA 4 to share some of the listening and logging work. Gio and I had worked with the guys we asked for in both uniform and plainclothes. They were decent cops. Good with paperwork and reliable. They were also nervous as hell to be part of a federal cloak-and-dagger operation. Procedure required that the DEA group supervisor swear them in (they also had to see the U.S. attorney). When the supervisor fed them the "repeat after me's" I added a few clauses about jumping in place and hopping around on one foot. They went with it until the group supervisor, me, and the other agents present started cracking up. Once all four cops were sworn in, they joined Gio and me with full federal marshal status.

If you've seen the movie *Casino,* then you know how listening in on a wiretap is supposed to work. Having obtained a Title III warrant, a duly sworn law enforcement officer is bound by law to only listen to and record incriminating wiretap evidence. The officer on duty switches on the receiver and recorder from inside the facility set up for listening for about thirty seconds at a time. If in the thirty seconds nothing criminal is discussed, then the officer is obliged to switch off and wait for another interval before switching on, listening in, and trying again.

Our targets were all business. No matter how paranoid they acted, the best most of Animal and Guerro's crew could do was refer to a "K" or a "Z" of "videos" or "cassettes," "big ones," small ones," and order a "limo" for nineteen Gs. Animal's relationship with his girlfriend, Tracy, however, mixed business with pleasure so bizarrely, it was sometimes difficult to decide which was which. One day Tracy explained to Animal that an Italian guy at her job told her he could hook her up with dope.

"Bitch, you ever talk about my business again with that guinea motherfucker, I'll kill you! I'll beat that shit out of you and fuck you in the ass and put a fucking cap in your head, you hear me?"

"I'll talk to whoever I want to! I don't need your fucking say-so to do anything! I ain't afraid of you, your gun, your wrinkly-ass dick, or nothing! Fuck you!"

"Fuck you! I'm coming there and I'm bending you over and fucking you in two! You do and say what I tell you or they'll find you floating in Oyster Bay with a bullet in your brain and cum leaking out your ass! We don't need shit from no guinea motherfuckers! Egg roll shit is the best shit there is! Don't fucking tell me my business!"

"You ain't man enough, *pendejo*! You try that shit with me I cut your fucking balls off and feed them to the dog!"

I could never figure out where Animal and Tracy drew the line. Did all the drug and harsh sex talk turn them on? They say couples need to communicate and compromise, but these two were in a world of their own. Despite the millions rolling in, a regular rotation of cars, clothes, electronic toys, and everything else, the two of them seemed to be having the same foul-mouthed confrontational meltdown every time they spoke to one another. After Animal bought a new house for three hundred thousand cash Tracy complained that the carport was too small. Animal threatened to gag her with his cock if she didn't shut up.

"I went into your house and found dope all over your bed," she screamed at him one night.

"How the fuck did you get into my house, bitch?"

"Through the door which was unlocked, *bitch!*" she screamed back. "You better not be fucking using! Are you fucking using?"

"Yeah, I'm using," Animal said. "Leave me the fuck alone!" She hung up on him. Two minutes later she called him again.

"I found the dog licking dope on the bed!"

"If you don't stop calling me, I'm going to kill you and your family." He was clearly on the street and alternating threatening Tracy and negotiating with someone he was with. "I'm going to cop some dope now. If you don't leave me alone, I'm going to send someone after you!"

Animal didn't make good on his threat. But three months after CS-1 first contacted and bought from Jimmy Rivera, Jimmy's body turned up on the corner of Houston Street and the FDR Drive, the same place Frankie Nieves and I tackled Little Punk a few years earlier. Jimmy had been shot four times by a nine-millimeter handgun. Though we didn't get anyone taking credit on tape, both Animal and Guerro made it clear that Jimmy would still be alive if he had paid his dope bills on time. My snitches on the street said Animal did it himself.

Even though nearly everyone involved knew me on sight, and ID'ing me anywhere outside of the Lower East Side might start them finally asking themselves the right questions, I got a kick out of tailing Animal, Guerro, and the others on their rounds outside the neighborhood. I'd only ever seen these guys when they visited the avenue and I was enjoying observing and logging their other routines. Car surveillance and tailing takes practice. In the movies you see cops cutting off civilians while doing tails all the time. The reality is that another driver honking, swearing, and getting into a beef with you wasn't worth it. If the noise didn't alert your target to the fact that you were on him, you were likely to lose him while dealing with the irate civilian. There were a lot of little tricks—I always had a bunch of different rearview mirror and dashboard ornaments and decorations in my glove compartment so that I could change them up. Most people will remember those things more than the make or model of most cars. It helped that our quarries drove flashy sports cars, high-priced foreign jobs, and tricked-out Jeeps. It was tricky staying with a guy driving a Porsche with an engine the size of a washing machine in it, but thanks to Robert Moses's narrow, pothole-cursed BQE and the constant snarl of New York City traffic, there was only so much the guys with the really hot cars could wind up.

As soon as anyone showed up in Alphabet City I pulled them over and tossed them and their ride. I especially liked hassling Animal. He'd had the mechanics at Tony's install a big spoiler on the Mazda he was driving lately and it made him easy to tail. I'd go from hearing or reading him say something incriminating on the wiretap to listening to him brag that I couldn't touch him in person.

"You got nothing on me, Rambo," he'd say each time. "I'm clean and I'm staying that way. You got nothing." If he knew that I was listening to him bitch about getting undercut by an uptown crew to Guerro an hour before he would've shit.

Working the case was a marathon. Weeks stretched into months and with the listening, observing, harassing, listening routine firmly in place I took a week's worth of vacation days. While I was in Brazil training in jiu jitsu with the Gracie family, Guerro's phone rang. It was Joco.

"You got my money?" Guerro asked him.

"Yo, I was on the corner on my way to see you and fucking Rambo grabbed me! Motherfucker ripped me off, can you believe that shit? Nineteen large, yo!" Three thousand miles away and I'm still the boogeyman for these guys.

Working with DEA was a godsend. I could strategically hassle the guys we heard on the wire down on the D and, as long as I stayed out of sight, do surveillance in Brooklyn and Queens where the growing investigation had spread to. It minimized my exposure in the Lower East Side in the wake of the hit scare while still allowing me to have a useful presence in the neighborhood. Once, after rattling one of Animal's guys by pulling him over exactly where he'd said he'd be on the phone the previous day, I grabbed a perp a Ninth Precinct detective had asked me about a few months before the wire investigation began. When I arrived at the Ninth on Fifth Street, it was a total circus. The detective squad room was packed with everyone from rookies to two-star chiefs from all over the department trying to get a look at a guy the newspapers cast as a real-life Freddy Krueger—Daniel Rakowitz.

Everybody in the neighborhood knew days before it simultaneously made the front page of the *Daily News, Post, Times,* and *Newsday.* Musicians sitting around the guitar store on St. Mark's Place, panhandler kids standing out front of Ray's on Avenue A, dabbler junkies perched on barstools at the window of Vazac's on B waiting for their man to come from Avenue D all heard versions of the same story. "The chicken guy killed his girlfriend!" Every day the story got retold, the scenario got worse. "The rooster guy killed her and he cut her up." Then, "Crazy motherfucker chicken dude killed her, cut her up, and cooked her." By the time it got to "Motherfucking psycho rooster man killed her, cut her up, cooked her, and fucking fed her to the homeless in the park," the chicken guy, Daniel Rakowitz, was in custody.

Investigating homicide detectives learned more of what a lot of the neighborhood already knew. Rakowitz was a screw-loose kid in his late twenties who'd been in and out of psych wards in and around his hometown of Rockport, Texas, a short drive up Highway 35 from Corpus Christi. Heeding a call only he understood, he came to the Lower East Side mid-decade and dealt drugs around Tompkins Square Park. No band, no screenplay, no figure study, no novel like the hundreds of would-be Burroughses and Bukowskis who trickled into the neighborhood from small towns and suburbs. Rakowitz was just a Gulf Coast burnout who walked around with a tame fighting rooster under his arm telling himself and anyone that would listen that he was the numerically proven messiah and that he had pot, hash, and speed for sale.

Rakowitz was a pretty lousy drug dealer—he talked too much and was way too willing to get in anyone's face about anything, especially religion, as long as there were eyes and ears on him. He was just one of those people that was always pushing things too far and confused challenging with irritating. You can't turn every conversation with your customers and your suppliers toward God, the devil, numerology, and smoking your way to heaven without fucking up supply and demand. Unless they're really hard up, most people who saw the rooster guy coming down the street turned the corner early.

There will always be a certain echelon of street creep using drugs, gullibility, a big-eyed stare, a beard, and a bullshit rap about Satan to make a social foothold in an outsider community. Rakowitz's central casting blue-eyed Jesus look, the fact that he usually had good pot on him to smoke, no matter how bad the stuff was that he sold, and that he could cook earned him a pass from a handful of the transplants he harangued while selling dime bags and black beauties. The eighties Lower East Side was full of out-of-town girls and boys intoxicated by an image of a no-rules downtown Manhattan they cobbled together from movies, books, and records. In the pre-Internet days it wasn't easy to find people that felt the way you did or liked the stuff you did, especially if it involved things nice people didn't talk about. A generation of kids used the excuse of school or career to roll in the Lower East Side stink to get the smell of narrow-minded, intolerant, abusive, or privileged upbringings off their hide. Nobody bought Rakowitz as a guru, but he earned some admirers among the crusties, weekend peace punks, and runaways who hung out, got high, and lined up for free meals from the Hare Krishnas in the park.

Monica Beerle was none of the above. She was a dance student from the foothills of the Appenzell Alps in Switzerland who paid her school bills at Martha Graham by shaking her ass at Billy's Topless on Twenty-fourth Street and Sixth. In the eighties titty bars like Billy's were grittier and generally a lot friendlier than the upscale gentlemen's clubs that would replace them over the next few years. Boogying on stage at Billy's for tips from horny cabbies with one eye on her tits and one eye on the racing form fit a restless provincial European kid's idea of vintage tolerably sleazy NYC.

Either Monica was drawn to Rakowitz's blue eyes and lanky frame same as some of the patchouli-and-Mohawk teeny boppers who took the LIRR into Manhattan from Long Island when school was out, or she was attracted to the lease on the two-bedroom apartment Rakowitz rented on East Ninth Street. In any case, she began crashing at his place and covering his rent. The arrangement soured quickly when he turned out to be free with his fists and more interested in smoking dope, watching TV, and hanging out in the park than paying bills or showing up regularly at any of his part-time gigs prepping and cooking in catering hall kitchens around the city. Eight weeks after she moved in, Monica told Rakowitz to move out. Rakowitz refused. She asked him again louder and he refused louder. Monica yelled at him to get out in more harshly worded and strongly accented terms. Rakowitz threatened to beat her up and she threatened to call the cops. He shut her up with a hard punch to the throat then numbly watched her suffocate on her own crushed esophagus.

Rakowitz panicked. Using a kitchen knife, elbow grease, and the skills he picked up short-order-cooking his way from Texas to the Lower East Side, he broke up Monica's limbs at the joints, cut her up, and skinned her. Most of her small frame went out to the sidewalk on garbage day in 3 mil plastic trash bags. The most incriminating parts of her went into a series of pots on the kitchen stove. But disposing of a human body was very different and far more difficult than prepping birds for banquet-size servings of chicken cacciatore. Nothing Rakowitz ever prepared caused him as much trouble as Monica. It turned out that cooking an ex-girlfriend down to unrecognizable bleached bone wasn't as easy as it seems when pictured in your batshit crazy mind's eye. The job took weeks and was only partly successful. Out of desperation, Rakowitz stashed the knife, parts of Monica's teeth he had individually removed, wrapped in tissue, and placed in the fingers of a gardening glove, several large bones, and some deodorizing kitty litter together in a joint compound bucket. He eventually checked the bucket into baggage pickup at the Port Authority Bus Terminal.

Whatever plan Rakowitz had was rendered meaningless by the parade of witnesses in and out of his apartment during the boiling marathon, and by the fact that he couldn't help bragging in the park about reducing his ex-girlfriend to *brodo di carne*. By the time the case broke and reporters came around, the park kids were only too happy to repeat every crazy rumor and claim Rakowitz made while passing a joint—he ate Monica, he fed her to the homeless, he used her as ingredients at his job. At the trial, the Manhattan DA even got some guy who lived in the park to say he saw a finger floating in a bowl of soup Rakowitz ladled out on a breadline.

When detectives from the Ninth arrested Rakowitz he led them to the bucket with Monica's remains. Dazzled by the sudden spotlight he confessed to everything that crossed his pretzeled mind. By the time he went on trial, Rakowitz had decided that wasn't such a great idea and pleaded innocent. No attorney materialized to represent him and Rakowitz defended himself using such unusual legal tactics as threatening to squirt a witness with a water gun loaded with "stagnant urine" (the fresh kind was too good for them, apparently) and offering to smoke a joint with the jury, who eventually found him not guilty by reason of insanity. Rakowitz was bundled off for a to-be-determined number of decades at Kirby Forensic Psychiatric Center on Wards Island, and the presiding judge declared the trial, "a lulu." I'm sure Monica Beerle's friends and family used a different adjective to describe their experience.

The detective whose perp I delivered showed me a Polaroid that Rakowitz had made out to the Ninth. It read: "I'd like to have you all for dinner." Like everybody else, I laughed.

Something I read in the papers the next day stuck in my head and eventually something bad started to stick in my throat. After looking at the calendar, I realized Rakowitz was one of the guys I saw dishing out entrées at the El Caribe catering hall in Mill Basin during a close friend's wedding reception just a few days before the arrest. I didn't have anything but coffee for the rest of the day and didn't order Italian food anywhere for nearly a year.

"Hey Mike, talk to you a minute?" Hamilton, one of the cops brought up from the PSA 4 Command had just finished a shift listening to the wire. I couldn't read what was bugging him.

"Sure, what's up?"

"Hey, you still seeing Mirabel?"

Mirabel was a girl I'd dated for nearly a year. We were together long enough that she'd met some of the guys at the Command. She was a looker and a flirt and men tended to remember her. When I met her she was a decorator doing store windows. I saw her driving down Avenue B in a custom Corvette convertible a few times and finally pulled her over and chatted her up. Mirabel lived on Long Island and had friends in the projects. I got her phone number and one thing led to another. We went out for a while but it never got too serious.

It hadn't helped that when we met, I was still fresh from the Davey Blue Eyes hit scare and didn't know who to trust. For the first couple months I was with her, I couldn't fool around with her unless I was facing the door and had my .38 out of its ankle holster and under a chair by the entrance of any room we were in. The .380 I bought when I heard about the hit was under a pillow, and a four-inch Smith & Wesson on the windowsill stayed hidden under the shades. I liked her a lot, but it took months for me to be sure she wouldn't set me up for the guys from Alphabet City. She never found any of the guns.

In the end she was too much of a party girl for me. Mirabel loved that I could get us into the World on First Street and the other clubs that used to pop up, get bled dry by the mob, and then close a year or two later in those days. I avoided abusing "Mastershield," as Jack Genova called it in my rookie days, but waving my badge every now and then to get seats in the VIP section close to the dance floor didn't bother my conscience much.

Mirabel's friends were all night owls—DJs, bartenders, and bouncers—and she mixed well in the club world. It was never really my scene, but I was a bachelor in those days so I made do. The music was usually too loud for us to talk. Most of the people she knew could barely handle that I didn't drink or get high, and when they found out I was a cop, they really freaked out. Sometimes, particularly at the World, we would run into dealers from the Avenue D crews. Those guys loved checking out and hanging out with the rich and famous who would take limos to a nightclub just a few blocks from the projects. Crooks and celebrities have been drawn to one another for years and in those pre-camera-phone days, it wasn't unusual to see rock stars and movie actors getting high with made guys, dealers, and lowlifes. Johnny Depp drank beer in Avenue A bars at a table full of Third Street Hells Angels for a while. I remember one Sixth and D dealer bragging to me that him and his boys had posed for a picture with Madonna one night in her limo outside the World. When I called bullshit he pulled out a Polaroid of him, her, and two other guys all holding up champagne glasses to the camera.

I hadn't seen Mirabel for months and I told Hamilton so.

"Listen to this," he said and handed me a pair of headphones. Hamilton played back a call that came in on Animal's phone during his watch. I recognized both voices instantly. One was Tracy. She used Animal's cell to make calls every chance she got. The other was Mirabel.

"See I told you it wasn't going to do anything," Tracy said laughing like it was girl talk. "You just leave it in your trunk for a couple days, no big deal."

"You're coming to get it, right? I can't drive around with that thing in my car anymore. I'm having fucking heart failure."

"Yo, *mami,* can you just come by with it? I'll come down, I don't want to have to bring it downtown with me."

As the conversation went on, detouring into whether or not a hairdresser they both went to had AIDS, it became clear that the thing in the trunk was an Uzi that belonged to Animal. Among the ordnance that Davey ran and that some of the Avenue D crew toted around, an Uzi was pretty common. But having one in your car was a twenty-year federal rap in the making for Mirabel.

"Any more like this?" I asked Hamilton. He shook his head and flashed me a blank index card. He came to me first before logging anything officially. I was right, he was a good guy.

"Thanks, Hamilton, I'll take care of it," I said.

"No problem, anything for you Mike." Hamilton dropped the blank index card on the desk and walked away.

The case was building to the point where we were starting to apply for arrest warrants. If everything went off the way it was shaping up, we would be taking down enough dealers to fill a major league baseball roster—DL, farm system, and all. I didn't want Mirabel to go to jail with them. She was a good person, she just had shitty taste in friends, and maybe boyfriends. Her getting jammed up may not have seemed like that high a price to pay for the case to go our way, but it still wasn't right. And if Mirabel did get accidentally caught in the web DEA was spinning, what would happen when it came out that we'd dated?

I was taking a risk already, but I realized I needed to take an even bigger gamble—I had to warn her. Somehow she needed to understand that she was hanging out with people that were going to do her harm. It was going to require tact. I couldn't jeopardize months of hard work by letting her know about the wire. If talking to her helped Tracy or Animal to catch on, our case would be ruined, agents' and cops' lives would be in danger, and I would probably go up on corruption charges. Still, I couldn't live with myself knowing that I hadn't at least tried to steer her clear of the head-on collision with the law that the Feds were scheduling for her friends. I'd done as much for sniffling junkies who had helped me out. Though we weren't together anymore, it was still personal.

"I know you've been hanging around with her." I'd arranged to meet Mirabel in a coffee shop in Long Island away from the eyes and ears of the DEA and the Alphaville crew. Her 'Vette was parked in the lot across from where we sat. I hoped that the Uzi was no longer in the trunk.

"No, I haven't," she said. It was instantly awkward. We hadn't been in touch in weeks and now here I was telling her to behave herself like I was her father. She'd hated being told what to do when we were going out and now she was looking at me like I was nuts. The only thing I could do without jeopardizing the wire and the case was keep it blunt and hope that she got the message. I was banking on the fact that she already knew that I was so up in everyone's business in the buildings and she wouldn't interpret "I heard" literally.

"No. You have."

"Mike, I haven't! Why are you telling me this?"

I stayed as calm as I could without pissing her off even more. "Look," I said, "it's a free country, I'm not your boyfriend, I don't want to fight, but I'm just telling you as a cop and as someone who cares about you, if you're going to hang around lowlifes, you're going to get into something you're not going to be able to get out of. I know you have friends down on the Lower East Side. Hell, that's where I met you, but you have to stay away from the projects, all those scumbags, their girlfriends, and anyone else that's close to the Third and D perps."

I studied Mirabel's face. "I can see you heading for

trouble and if something bad happens, I can't make it all just go away."

"I don't know why you don't listen! I'm not hanging out with anyone from the avenue!" Mirabel's voice was getting less emphatic. I hoped it meant that what I was telling her was sinking in. I sighed and admitted to myself that I had done all I could. We moved on to small talk, wished each other the best, and left together, Mirabel to her 'Vette, me to my government-issued Camaro, and back to the wire room. By the time I got there she had already called Tracy.

"I was just talking to Rambo. It was crazy!"

Tracy and Mirabel quickly moved on to other topics. I could spend the rest of the investigation with my fingers crossed, or I could just move on, too. With so much at stake I had done everything I could, so it was back to work. Mirabel stayed out of jail. Her new boyfriend, a party promoter at Webster Hall and the Palladium, was spooked by Animal and his crew so Mirabel took a break from the Lower East Side and she and Tracy drifted apart on their own.

After about eight months of living, breathing, eating, sleeping, watching, and listening, Benton announced that he'd met with the U.S. attorney working with us and they'd decided it was time to make arrests. I'd spent more than half a year immersed in just how fast word traveled among Animal, Guerro, and their crew. Our case had swelled to involve nearly forty potential felons, yet we still needed to bring them in at the same time or risk losing anyone who heard about one of his associates getting led away in cuffs. These guys all had multiple addresses and the smart ones had money stashes and exit strategies.

After a marathon session of picking over index cards

and photos, typing and retyping, the U.S. attorney took the 120 pages we prepared from the evidence we'd compiled to a federal judge. The judge picked over every conspirator's name, their description, and the descriptions of the crimes they'd committed and the laws they'd broken, the drug sales, where they took place and the dollar amounts they represented, then issued forty arrest warrants and nearly as many search warrants.

Oscar Roland, assistant special agent in charge of Group 34, Benton, his partner, Gio, myself and Robert Stutman, DEA's special agent in charge of the New York office met in Oscar's office to discuss arrest strategy. A Colombian flag with a sign on it saying SO MANY COLOMBIANS, SO LITTLE TIME hung in the hallway outside. Inside we finalized the tactical end of what was going to be a forty-warrant simultaneous bust that would slow the heroin deluge on Avenue D and elsewhere in the city to a trickle. Roland was a soft-spoken, light-skinned black guy from New Orleans with a spare frame and a lilting good ol' boy accent. His desk held a cigar humidor full of expensive Cuban stogies, a wide-brimmed straw hat that he wore to and from work, and framed family pictures including one of his wife and one of their kids with Michael Jordan. His daughter, he explained once, was engaged to Jordan's attorney. There were photos on his wall of Roland fishing, standing with confiscated bricks of coke, and shaking hands with President Reagan.

Roland did most of the talking. We all knew what the next moves were, and this tactical meeting was more a formality than a necessity, but Roland was engaging and upbeat and it felt good to see someone excited about something we'd all been working on day and night for half a year. Some upper-tier cops can get pretty rah-rah over anything, but Roland was a good guy, was genuinely proud of the work we'd done, and was looking forward to the next step.

I felt great about the case except for one thing: the index card I'd written Davey's name on, and which had been joined early in the investigation with a blurry photo of Davey taken outside the Riis Houses by DEA, had been taken off the board months ago. For some reason, Davey had stopped dealing with Animal, Guerro, and the rest of the Third and D crew almost entirely. Mentions of him on the wire had been infrequent, and when they had come up, they were fleeting and dismissive. The best that I could guess, and some of what I heard from snitches confirmed this, was that Davey had beefed with Animal over something and that whatever it was wasn't bad enough for him to go to war over. The Cherry Street crew led by the Navarro brothers, the guys who killed Felix Pardo and shot up Macatumba and Londie on the FDR, were still in a power struggle with Animal and Guerro's guys, but their fight didn't have enough of the definitive, case-closed killings I associated with Davey to make me believe that. Had Davey chosen a side? Was he playing both crews against each other as a smoke screen between him and DEA? Wherever the reason, Davey was laying low—so low that he was off the board.

Roland looked at a wall calendar and opened the floor to suggestions of what date to perform the massive bust and hit all the houses, apartments, and businesses we would need to in order to scoop everyone at once. He looked at the list of forty warrants for a moment and then casually noted that we'd need to ask the Housing PD chief for a hundred additional officers to round up our "forty thieves." The name stuck for the rest of the investigation, the arrests, and the legal maneuvering and trial that followed.

A few days later, between three and four hundred law-enforcement personnel from DEA, Housing, NYPD, IRS, INS, and the FBI sat in cars outside Alvarez's limo office, the grocery on Second Ave, every project building that anyone on our bulletin board lived in or frequented, the house in Oyster Bay Animal had bought with cash, and the attached three-bedroom in Ozone Park that Guerro shared with his sister and his mom, who were both also cited in the complaint and warranted by the judge. The Forty Thieves were about to become history.

Arrest kits with photos and descriptions of each of those charged, lists of aliases, places they frequented, the charges themselves, copies of the warrants and a list of prior arrests and convictions sat on the seat next to every arresting officer. The call came. In Ozone Park, Gio picked up his arrest kit at the same time I grabbed mine in Oyster Bay and hundreds of other cops checked their guns, grabbed their documents, and headed to their designated doorways.

I knocked on Animal's door. He answered himself, wearing a robe and two days of beard. I smiled and thought, "I got you, you bastard, I got you and you are mine!" but before I could even tell him he was under arrest he read my mind. Animal's mouth twisted into a sly grin as he looked at me and at the agents already searching his car in the driveway. He almost looked relieved—like he'd finally pieced together something that had been bothering him for a while.

"Rambo. Fuck. You got me."

Eighteen

We sat together, my old compadre and I, in the public area of a large federal courtroom watching the wheels of justice slowly grinding up a major crime figure I'd been following for a long time. He was a feared boss responsible for dozens of murders, undertaken at his order and, earlier in his career, done with his own hands. But this courtroom wasn't in Manhattan where, until recently Davey Blue Eyes ruled the heroin trade and the DEA wire case against Animal and Guerro had been made. This was in the eastern federal district—Brooklyn.

The guy we were there to see wasn't Davey Blue Eyes, it was the head of the Lucchese family, Vic Amuso. I was working a day tour and had a court appearance of my own to make in an unrelated and uneventful evidence hearing. But I'd been following Vic Amuso's racketeering trial in the papers and with a few hours to kill, I phoned my best friend from the old Canarsie neighborhood, Nicky Cappadora, and suggested he meet me at the courthouse. We both had grown up knowing Vic. Nicky's family was particularly close to the Amusos. It seemed like the right thing to do—come down, show some support and respect and get what was likely to be the last look at Vic we'd ever have that wasn't on A&E.

A half decade earlier back in PSA 1, I'd run into the Flynn boys. We shot the shit in the usual way. They ribbed me about being a cop and working around all the "moulies" living in the projects, and I asked after their dad. I didn't ask what they were doing. The two of them in hardhats was enough to know it was wolf business. Neither of those guys would know which end of a shovel to grab if you tossed them one. Whatever it was, it involved replacement windows apparently. There was a flatbed truck stacked with them parked next to Timmy's Chrysler Cordoba.

It turned out that through Vic and the Luccheses' connections in the iron workers union, the Flynns had moved from plush no-show construction jobs and running numbers and taking bets (what the old-timers called "policy") through a network of mob-owned grocery stores and retail joints to become part of a huge construction bid-fixing ring that thrived for a decade. The "windows" racket became such a cash cow of kickbacks, payoffs, and lucrative contracts that it swelled to feed all five of the New York families. That kind of success went to the Flynns' heads in the worst way. The last time I'd seen them, I'd met Nicky outside the Nut. The Flynns talked a bunch of tough-guy crap about their rivals and kept patting me on the back and telling me how great it was to have "a legal gun" with them in case the bar got attacked and reminding me that I was "allowed" to shoot anyone who came in looking for trouble. I wasn't prepared for how far gone they were and was so repulsed by their coked-out bullshit that I had to leave.

But now the windows racket was sunk and the Flynns were, too. Lenny, one of my two Red Hook burglary buddies had flipped after fucking up an armored car robbery and was living in Minnesota somewhere with a new name. His partner Zee's head washed up on the beach at Sheepshead Bay after he'd gone missing owing money to some Colombian coke dealers. Eddie Lino had been dead for years. He was shot four times inside his Cadillac on the side of the Belt Parkway five minutes from Canarsie. Where else.

The windows thing was too huge and went too long to not go south in a big way and it concluded in one of the longest, costliest, and weirdest federal trials in U.S. history. Vic's trial was a more subdued affair and I'm glad Nick and I went to show our faces. I'd flashed my tin at the courthouse entrance, but Nick went through the ID check and a metal detector and security was so Tupperware tight it took forever to get upstairs. By the time we were seated in the courtroom gallery, the proceedings were under way. Nick and I nodded courteously at a lot of familiar faces on the benches, and looked in wonder at the center of the room where a huge prosecution exhibit bulletin board displayed a flow chart hung with pictures of Vic and other heavies like Gas Pipe Anthony Casso, along with Timmy and Tommy's dad, the Nut, and here and there among the dozens pictured, shots of guys whose charcoal steaks we'd eaten, daughters we'd dated, and lawns we'd run across years before.

Suddenly the big wood doors opened at the side of the courtroom. Everyone turned. It was Vic. He walked in flanked by Feds, winked at me, and gave Nick a big smile. The judge banged out order. We listened for the rest of the day as state's witness Little Al D'Arco explained how he'd killed Bruno Facciolo, the guy with the bat from the pizza parlor sidewalk, on Vic's orders. Apparently Little Al and a kid who sat two desks over from me in high school and played offensive tackle on the football team went to California to do a hit for Vic. My former teammate stole the car they used, and Little Al pulled the trigger. When they got back to Brooklyn, word had already gone around about Al's business trip—a serious breach. Lou Eppolito, the infamous "Mafia Cop," tipped Al that the "little bird" doing the singing was Bruno. A few days before his daughter's wedding, Al shot Bruno in a garage, stabbed out his eyes, stuffed a canary in his mouth, and dumped the body in Marine Park. The prosecutors had the police pictures up on their board, bird and all.

No one except Al and the dirty cop thought Bruno did it at the time, and they all realized the wrong guy died since. Dead birds, mistaken murders, and a city cop who marked wiseguys for death—no wonder my father came home from the job, quietly had a nice meal, watched a little TV, and went to bed every night at peace.

That was the final time I ever saw my dad and uncle's old baseball teammate, Vic Amuso. And that's not likely to change. He's in Supermax in Florida for life.

Of Davey Blue Eyes's Forty Thieves, thirty-nine either copped a plea, informed, or ratted. One of the many reasons to be thankful for a small trial was that the only person we hated more than Davey was his lawyer, Lynne Stewart, who was to represent the accused in our case. The self-described anarchist kids in Tompkins Square may have claimed to be devoted radicals, but Stewart really was one. She was a Ramsey Clark and William Kunstler protégée who took her mentors' skepticism and healthy opposition and turned it into something else entirely. Stewart defended drug dealers and murderers and spoke to the press about being a radical activist attorney rather than the menace to society that in our opinion she was. She publicly advocated, "violence directed at the institutions which perpetuate capitalism, racism, sexism, and at the people who are the appointed guardians of those institutions." She put her practice where her mouth was by unsuccessfully defending a twenty-year-old thug nicknamed Loco Larry Davis who shot six cops in 1986, and the Blind Sheik who conspired to blow up the World Trade Center in 1993. Larry Davis was killed in jail. Years later, Lynne Stewart was sentenced to prison for acting as a go-between for the sheik and his followers.

One of the most satisfying professional compliments I've been paid was seeing how much Lynne Stewart seemed to hate my partner and me. At one hearing Stewart, who is enormous, happened to slam into a chair Gio sat in so hard he was knocked to the floor. As each one of her clients flipped, Lynne Stewart's apparent frustration was a nice consolation.

Stewart began the case at a forty-person arraignment held on a set of bleachers at the U.S. courthouse. Every one of the Forty Thieves sat cuffed together and it took twenty minutes for a court officer to read off their names. Thanks to the U.S. attorneys' relentless maneuvering and the strength of the evidence, within a few months Stewart was only representing one person named in the complaint. Even tough-talking, badass Animal eventually decided to cooperate. Much to my and the U.S. attorney's surprise Guerro, the soft-spoken, innocuous coleader of the crew was the sole holdout. We had him, his drugs, his money, his guns, his mother, his sister, their house, and his partner Animal all stitched up, but Guerro wouldn't budge. The prevailing opinion at the time was that he must have had a money stash somewhere so big that it was worth gambling on parole to keep it safe. Guerro got about twenty-five years.

If life was more like the movies of that era, the story would've climaxed with me and Davey in a guns-drawn foot chase through the warehouse in which Davey was holding my beautiful crime reporter or ADA girlfriend prisoner, a shoot-out in a circus hall of mirrors, or a swordfight on a building rooftop in a lightning storm. But that's not how things work anywhere, especially not in Alphaville.

We never got Davey on the wire and never arrested him. What we learned from the thirty-nine canaries we caged was that just prior to our beginning the case, he had indeed fallen out with Animal and Guerro and decided to lay low for a while. The Navarro brothers' hits on the Third Street crew had something to do with it. My grandfather described once how farmers in Sicily would set fire to fields that had been overcultivated and then plant in the new ground fertilized with the ashes. Maybe that was Davey's rationale—let the Cherry Street and Third Street crews burn each other down and then start over. Whatever his ambitions may have been, the federal and state investigations into the hit he ordered on Gio and me had jammed Davey up really badly and sent him deeper into the shadows than he'd ever been. Now, with thirty-nine known associates suddenly telling all, he would have to lay lower and longer than he expected. He wasn't in cuffs but he was out of the picture. Ironically, if Gio and I hadn't done such a good job of putting the screws to Davey's Third Street crew, he probably would still have been around when we went up on the wire with DEA and been indicted like the rest of his former employees.

A few months after our investigation concluded another DEA unit lucked onto a guy who was Davey's accountant. He was an actual CPA from Great Neck, a user, and was so scared of going to jail that he handed over ledgers that itemized every penny Davey made and every bag of dope he sold to the tune of $140,000 a day. Soon after that Davey was popped for gun possession at a movie theater in Whitestone. He was set to plead on the charge in the hopes of avoiding a double-murder rap, but the case stalled and he cooled his heels in Rikers for what may have been close to a year.

One of the agents in charge showed me parts of the arrest paperwork on Davey's case. On the way home that night I stopped at one of the addresses listed as belonging to him in the documents. It was a modest detached brick house in Midwood less than five miles from where I lived in Canarsie throughout most of my time in Op 8. If it weren't for the extra gates and fences and the seizure and auction announcement on the front door you'd never guess it was owned by a guy who'd fucked up as many lives as Davey Colas had. I'd literally been stuck in traffic in front of it a hundred times on my way home from a shift in Alphaville, completely unaware that it belonged to a guy who'd wanted me whacked so badly, he put a price on my head.

One cool autumn morning in Canarsie, I read in the papers about a big DEA bust-up of a Brooklyn heroin ring that involved turning a major heroin dealer who gave up the rest of his crew. A lightbulb went on. Maybe I was still trying to settle a vendetta like the guys my grandfather knew in his day. I called the agent in charge of handling the cooperating former kingpin. Would his narcotics violator want to rat on one more pusher and murderer? Had he heard of Davey Blue Eyes Colas? Yup he would and hell yes he had. The tape went on, the guy started telling what he knew, and Davey now faced charges from running a continuing criminal enterprise, to using a firearm during a narcotics transaction, to felony possession of narcotics. Faced with multiple life terms, Davey cooperated with the government and became a rat as devastating to the narcotics trade on the Lower East Side as Sammy "the Bull" Gravano was to the Mafia.

Davey testified under oath about the mounds of cash, the guns, the killings, and the rest of what it took to run his now collapsed empire. In 1996, after sitting out more than half a decade cooperating with DEA from federal lockup, Davey was finally sentenced to jail for six more years. He was re-leased from protective custody in 2001 to eight years of supervised probation. Currently, he has vanished off everyone's radar. My guess is that he leveraged witness protection somehow. If that's true he could be living next door to you.

It's funny to think about it now. After all that time in Al-phaville trying to nail Davey he wound up at large somewhere with a government handler, a new name, and an unlisted phone number. Well, the Feds showed their gratitude and to be fair I should acknowledge mine. Davey Blue Eyes formed a purpose and a function in my life that's as important to me as it is hard for me to admit. Gio and I brought the fight to Davey and his crew. It was a fight I had trained for my whole life—in Canarsie, at the academy, in Coney Island, and in Alphaville itself—without knowing it until it was over. It was a fight I refused to lose, through lying down by punching in and waiting out my pension, or by dropping my gloves when the rulebook and the people holding it over my head said to. Davey kept me sharp. He kept me focused. He put a name and a face on the horror that was heroin in Alphabet City in the eighties. The contract he put on Gio and me just kept the fight personal. In a way, I needed Davey the way Muhammad Ali needed Joe Frazier. Ali called Frazier an ugly gorilla and a dozen other things before they faced each other in the ring in the Philippines. But the day after beating Frazier in the Thrilla in Manila, Ali said, "Joe Frazier, I'll tell the world right now, brings out the best in me." Davey brought out the best in me. Whether the ends justified the means is a question some people might debate. Some people, not me.

Most of Alphaville today resembles Epcot center, or one of those streets in southern college towns where kids go to get drunk on weekends, more than the place Gio and I spent years trying to clean up. The projects are still there and the drugs are still there, but there's no longer space for an operation like the one we fought to flourish like it did. Housing, transit, and city cops work under a single chain of command, one that since the Giuliani administration is held accountable from the top down like the Feds are.

People haven't changed. They don't. There will always be those that need to get high, those that want to get paid to make that possible, and those, like me, who genuinely enjoyed hanging out among them even while coming between them and enforcing the law. Much as I can look back on those years and shake my head as I remember what I saw and what I did, I knew where I stood then and I know that it was worthwhile now. How many people can say that at the end of a twenty-year career? Where I came from, who I was, and what I became all lined up on Avenue D. I may not have always behaved myself, but I did the right thing more than the wrong thing. Most of all, though, I didn't get caught. And I had fun.

extracts reading groups

competitions books new

discounts extracts extracts

competitions discounts

books new books

reading groups events reading groups

events books extracts

new extracts books discounts

books new reading groups

titles

interviews

events extracts events

discounts events new books

new books events interviews books

events new events new extracts

discounts extracts discounts

www.panmacmillan.com

extracts events reading groups

competitions books extracts new

books